T0302026

# Business Issues
# in the Arts

*Business Issues in the Arts* is a text designed to address some of the most prescient business issues that nonprofit arts organizations face today. This text is not a how-to but an in-depth dive into fourteen topics and their associated theories to augment learning in arts administration programs.

With contributions from leading academics in arts administration, the book guides readers through an exploration of those topics which have been found by practitioners to be most vital and least explored. Chapters include numerous case examples to illustrate business theory in the artistic and creative environment. The academic contributors themselves each come with both professional backgrounds and research experience, and they are each introduced at the start of their chapters, allowing for a collection of voices to navigate through some oftentimes challenging topics.

This book is designed for an advanced undergraduate course or a stand-alone graduate course on the intersection of business and management and the cultural and creative industries, especially those focusing on business issues in the arts.

**Anthony Rhine** is Professor of Management and Management Science at Pace University's Lubin School of Business in New York City. He previously worked as a theatre executive, running multi-million-dollar and Tony-nominated theatre companies.

**Jay Pension** teaches theatre and arts administration at Florida State University. He has worked as a theatre producer on over 100 productions in Boston and New York City.

## Discovering the Creative Industries

*Series Editor: Ruth Rentschler*

The creative and cultural industries account for a significant share of the global economy. Gaining and maintaining employment and work in this sector is a challenge and chances of success are enhanced by ongoing professional development.

This series provides a range of relatively short, student-centred books which blend industry and educational expertise with cultural sector practice. Books in the series provide applied introductions to the core elements of the creative industries. In sum, the series provides essential reading for those studying to enter the creative industries as well as those seeking to enhance their career via executive education.

**The New Arts Entrepreneur**
Navigating the Arts Ecologies
*Gary Beckman*

**Consumer Behavior and the Arts**
A Marketing Perspective
*François Colbert and Alain d'Astous*

**Business Issues in the Arts**
*Edited by Anthony Rhine and Jay Pension*

For more information about this series, please visit: www.routledge.com/Discovering-the-Creative-Industries/book-series/DCI

"I highly recommend *Business Issues in the Arts* by Jay Pension and Anthony S. Rhine because it's a one-stop shop resource for Arts Administration and Management students, practitioners, educators, researchers, and others. The book speaks to the most important business issues facing nonprofit arts organizations today. It covers all the business issues, from human resources in the arts to unions and start-ups, that one would need to have a full grasp of leading a nonprofit arts organization."

**Amanda Alexander,** *Associate Professor and Assistant Chair, Department of Art and Art History, University of Texas Arlington, USA.*

# Business Issues in the Arts

Edited by
Anthony Rhine and Jay Pension

Routledge
Taylor & Francis Group

LONDON AND NEW YORK

Cover image: 3DSculptor

First published 2023
by Routledge
4 Park Square, Milton Park, Abingdon, Oxon OX14 4RN

and by Routledge
605 Third Avenue, New York, NY 10158

*Routledge is an imprint of the Taylor & Francis Group, an informa business*

*British Library Cataloguing-in-Publication Data*
A catalogue record for this book is available from the British Library

*Library of Congress Cataloging-in-Publication Data*
A catalog record has been requested for this book

ISBN: 978-1-032-07532-7 (hbk)
ISBN: 978-1-032-07084-1 (pbk)
ISBN: 978-1-003-20753-5 (ebk)

DOI: 10.4324/9781003207535

Typeset in Calvert
by codeMantra

# Contents

Contents

# Foreword

The arts, entertainment, and cultural management fields have grown rapidly as an academic pursuit. This academic advance is due, no doubt, to a growing need to professionalize processes within arts and cultural organizations. In addition, a growing body of research and theory has developed in the last few decades, indicating the managerial and leadership processes studied and identified in areas other than arts, entertainment, and cultural management, do not operate as effectively in creative enterprises as they do for our industrialized business cousins. However, arts administration researchers have been narrowing the gap between what works outside of arts management and how it can be adjusted, tweaked, or improved to work in our creative processes. This research is, ultimately, the reason this book exists. Many brilliant people have contributed to this growth and new understanding. We are grateful to all those who developed the foundation upon which all our work now occurs.

No book is put together by just its authors. There are always countless people who provide time, effort, support, or more in the process.

We need to thank our editor Terry Clague at Routledge. Creating a book such as this, with a collection of different topics requiring different approaches and different voices, can be a rather complex process. However, Terry has been so amenable, willing to hear our thoughts and ideas, open to approaches, and supportive when we need a little pat on the back. He and Routledge are the perfect partners!

Our contributors, all of whom participated in our research into the most vital topics we needed to include in this book, have been incredible. They have all worked under a very tight timeframe, incorporated edits and suggestions expeditiously and with a staunchly intellectual eye, and remained positive and encouraging throughout the process. Their contributions in the text are only a part of how they have contributed and helped create this book.

Anthony wants to make three personal notes of thanks. First, Joel has, once again, been a tremendous support, and with that support, the work could be finished. He is an incredible partner. Second, Jeffrey Michael Rebudal and Chris Ramos are two of the faculty in the Arts and Entertainment program in the Lubin School of Business at Pace University in New York, and they are incredible colleagues. The atmosphere at Pace, which sits in the heart of New York's financial district, is one of incredible support and collegiality. The importance of a unique and rigorously academic approach to arts and entertainment management is at the heart of all we do there. Our students earn a degree in business, with an emphasis on arts and entertainment, from a school that values the uniqueness of creative industries like ours. Third, he wants to thank Jay. We have partnered on several projects for the last five years, and it is always a pleasure. Jay is one of the easiest people to work with, and he can handle a far greater workload with aplomb. He deserves a shout-out.

Jay would like to personally thank his family and Charlotte for their consistent support and encouragement through the years and as he developed this book with Anthony. He would also like to thank Anthony for being the best writing partner he could ask for. Anthony is a great colleague and friend, and Jay looks forward to many more fruitful collaborations with him that support the teaching and practice of management in the nonprofit arts. Finally, he would like to thank the PhD Arts Administration and MFA Theatre Management programs at Florida State University.

We must also give a special thank you to Mary Beth Vanko. Mary Beth is a consummate editor. She has a gift in how she can both copy and content edit, and her love for the arts shines in everything she does. She has been by our side through a number of projects, and we have both agreed that we would never want to submit any final product such as this until it has been graced with her insight. Her contributions, though not clearly credited for the reader to see, deserve tremendous thanks.

This book has been a labor of love, and hopefully, the start of continuing publication in the field of issues that sometimes are not addressed with the appropriate focus on arts, entertainment, and culture. We are pleased to contribute and hope that as the field and body of knowledge grow, each of these topics can become entire courses of their own.

# Contributors

## EDITORS

**Jay Pension** has worked over the past 15 years as a theatre producer on over 100 productions in Boston and New York City. During that time, he worked as a producer and artistic director for several nonprofit theatre companies and produced numerous for-profit theatre projects. Since 2017, his focus has shifted to working in higher education and researching best practices for nonprofit arts organizations. Currently, teaches theatre and arts administration at Florida State University. Jay is also a frequent guest speaker, zooming into university classrooms to lead conversations about engagement in the arts. Since 2019, Jay has served as a consultant for nonprofit arts organizations, facilitating board retreats and advising on audience engagement, fundraising, governance, human resources, financial management, organizational structure, mission statement development, access, diversity, equity, and inclusion. He is an author (with Anthony Rhine) of the forthcoming "How to Market the Arts: A Practical Guide for the 21st Century" from Oxford University Press. Jay holds a BFA and an MFA in theatre and is a PhD candidate in Arts Administration at FSU.

**Anthony Rhine** is a professor of Management and Management Science at Pace University's Lubin School of Business in New York City. He holds a PhD in business administration and both bachelor's and master's degrees in arts management. Presently, he serves as Secretary on the board of directors of the international academic society of Social Theory, Politics, and the Arts. In addition, he is the author of the textbooks "Theatre Management: Arts Leadership for the 21st Century," from Palgrave MacMillan, "Marketing the Arts: An Introduction," by Rowman and Littlefield, and the forthcoming "How to Market the Arts: A Practical Guide for the 21st

Century" from Oxford University Press, with Jay Pension. Rhine worked for the first two decades of his career as a theatre executive, running multi-million-dollar and Tony-nominated theatre companies. During that time, he also wrote the librettos for over 20 produced musicals, including several that toured both nationally and internationally, and directed scores of professional productions. For the last two decades, he has been a professor of theatre management, focusing his research on advancing and improving theatre management education and its application in improving nonprofit arts organizational outcomes such as increased ticket sales and unearned income. His myriad research has been published in the top-ranked journals of arts management and marketing, and he is the author of the scholarly monograph *Leading the Creative Mind*. He has also published two novels.

## CONTRIBUTORS

**Dr. Julia Atkins** has professional experience in orchestra management, arts marketing, and music education, as well as performing experience as a clarinetist. She received her Bachelor of Music Degree in Clarinet Performance from the Crane School of Music at SUNY Potsdam in 2011, her Master of Music Degree in Clarinet Performance from Florida State University in 2013, and a Ph.D. in Arts Administration from Florida State University in 2022. She worked as the Director of Artistic Operations and Marketing for the Fayetteville Symphony Orchestra from 2013-2018, and was also the Interim Executive Director of the Fayetteville Symphony Orchestra from 2020-2022 where she re-organized and re-established the organization during and after the COVID-19 pandemic. Julia has also taught in higher education, serving as the Adjunct Professor of Clarinet at Methodist University in Fayetteville, NC from 2014-2018, and as an Adjunct Professor for Florida State University teaching arts administration classes from 2019-2021. In addition to her degrees, Julia has earned a professional certificate in Nonprofit Management from Duke University and a Program Evaluation Certificate from Florida State University in 2020.

**Dr. Jen Budney (BFA, MA, PhD)** is a researcher, writer, and curator. She is currently employed at the Canadian Centre for the Study of Co-operatives, where she develops and leads workshops on board governance and conducts research on the co-operative and credit union sectors. She teaches two courses—Ethical Leadership and Democracy in Public Service, and The Social Economy and Public Policy—for the Johnson Shoyama Graduate School of Public Policy, University of Saskatchewan. Previously, she has worked as a curator at two Canadian art museums, as an artist-run center director, and as a program officer at the Canada Council for the Arts. In the mid-1990s, she was an editor at *Flash Art International* in Milan, Italy, and she worked in Europe for several years as a freelance arts writer and curator. Her writing has appeared in professional journals including *Parkett, World Art, Nka: Journal of Contemporary African Art, Art Asia & Pacific, Siksi,* and *Canadian Art,* and her essays have appeared in catalogs for a wide range of organizations including the Menil Collection (Houston, TX), National Gallery of Canada (Ottawa, ON), Waino Aaltonen Museum (Turku, FI), Padiglione d'arte contemporanea (Milan, IT), and Aboriginal Healing Foundation (Ottawa, ON). She has curated more than 20 exhibitions and special projects, including touring exhibitions by Jayce Salloum (*history of the present*) and Ruth Cuthand (*BACK TALK: works 1983–2009*), and the international conference *Stronger Than Stone: (Re)Inventing the Indigenous Monument* (2014).

**Dr. Antonio C. Cuyler** is the author of *Access, Diversity, Equity, and Inclusion in Cultural Organizations: Insights from the Careers of Executive Opera Managers of Color in the U. S.* and editor of a forthcoming volume, *Arts Management, Cultural Policy, & the African Diaspora.* He serves as the Director of the MA Program & Associate Professor of Arts Administration at Florida State University (FSU) and Visiting Associate Professor at the University of Michigan. He also founded Cuyler Consulting, LLC, a Black-owned arts consultancy, that helps cultural organizations maximize their performance and community relevance through access, diversity, equity, and inclusion (ADEI).

**Hannah Grannemann** is Assistant Professor and Director of the Arts Administration Program at the University of North Carolina at Greensboro (UNCG). Hannah was Executive Director of Children's Theater of Charlotte and Managing Director of PlayMakers Repertory Company. Her presentations include conferences for the Association of Arts Administration Educators, Society of Arts Entrepreneurship Educators, the Association of Theater in Higher Education, and the Beijing Dance Academy Forum. She holds a BFA in Theatre from New York University/Tisch School of the Arts, an MFA in Theater Management from Yale University, School of Drama, and an MBA from Yale University, School of Management. Her research interests are in audience experience and audience engagement in the arts and new organizational structures in the arts. She has been published in the journal *Cultural Management: Science and Education* and Arts Professional (UK). Hannah's public scholarship can be read on ArtsJournal. com where she writes Row X, a blog about arts audiences.

**Dr. Brea M. Heidelberg** is an arts management educator, consultant, and researcher focusing on the intersection of the arts and other fields of study. Her work focuses on helping the cultural sector become more diverse, equitable, and inclusive. She currently serves as Director of the Entertainment & Arts Management program at Drexel University. She is also a Senior Fellow with the Lenfest Center for Cultural Partnerships. In her role as Founder and Principal at ISO Arts Consulting, Dr. Heidelberg helps arts organizations find equity-focused solutions to human resources and organizational development issues. Dr. Heidelberg earned her PhD in Arts Administration, Education and Policy from The Ohio State University. In addition to earning a MA in Arts Policy and Administration from The Ohio State University, she also earned a MS in Human Resource Development from Villanova University.

**Dr. Elise Lael Kieffer** is currently Program Director and Assistant Professor of Nonprofit Leadership Studies at Murray State University. She holds a PhD in Art Education with a focus on Arts Administration, a Masters in Public Administration and graduate certificates in nonprofit management and program evaluation. Her Bachelor of Fine Arts degree is in Musical Theatre performance. Her professional career before academia was circuitous, beginning in the world of live theatre and evolving into a successful career fundraising for an international nonprofit organization based in New York, NY. Elise relocated to a rural community at the foothills of the Appalachian Mountains in Kentucky where she founded Burkesville Academy of Fine Arts (BAFA). Her research is focused on identifying inequities in funding and resources allocation to small arts organizations serving specific populations, and providing technical assistance and training to directors of those organizations. She is published in *American Journal of Arts Management*, *International Journal of Lifelong Learning in Art Education*, and the *International Journal of Social, Political, and Community Agendas in the Arts*. She currently lives in Murray, Kentucky with her husband and two sons who call her "Dr. Mommy."

**Elaine Hendriks Smith** has over 20 years of professional experience in the performing arts working as an arts administrator, teacher, director, stage manager, event manager, production manager, lighting and projection designer, and youth mentor. She served as the first director of The Berman Center for the Performing Arts in West Bloomfield, Michigan, from its opening in 2011 until 2019, where she curated a season of over 170 events each year, including hosting a season of touring events, directing a community theatre program and a summer youth theatre camp, and bringing in such artists as; Marc Cohen, Arlo Guthrie, Patti LuPone, Mandy Patinkin, Stephen Schwartz, and Ben Vereen for special engagements. In addition, she served as the artistic director of The Historic Gem & Century Theatres (2010–2011) and the deputy director of The Matrix Theatre Company (2004–2009) in Detroit, Michigan. Elaine's lighting design credits include: *Say Goodnight Gracie* (St. Luke's Theatre, New York, NY & national tour), Trinity Irish Dancers, *Trinity II* (nationwide), and *Passing the Play* (nationwide). Her stage management credits include *Altar Boyz* (Detroit, MI, and Des Moines, IA), *Plaid Tidings*, and *The Marvelous*

*Wonderettes* (The Gem Theatre, Detroit, MI); she is an alumnus of The Second City, Detroit. Additionally, Elaine served as the production manager for Commotion Entertainment, where she managed music concerts with artists such as Fishbone, De La Soul, LL Cool J, Patty LaBelle, Michael Franks, Grover Washington Jr., and Lou Rawls. Elaine has a BA in Theatre from Wayne State University in Detroit, MI, and a MA in Theatre from Florida State University in Tallahassee, Florida. Currently, Elaine is working toward her PhD in Theatre and Performance Research at Florida State University, where she researches what theatre reflects about the surges in anxiety seen throughout society today.

**Dr. Yifan Xu** holds a PhD degree in Arts Administration, Education, and Policy from the Ohio State University. She obtained her BA in Cultural Industry Management from Tongji University, Shanghai, China. She has abundant experience working with nonprofits such as TEDxOhioStateUniversity, World Peaces, Columbus Marketing Association, and King Arts Complex. Yifan has been actively involved in the scholarly field since 2017. Besides attending the Social Theory, Politics, & the Arts (STPA) annual conferences, she was also the 2018 International Festivals and Events Association's Arts Festival Legacy Scholarship recipient and presented at East Carolina University's Emerging Scholars Symposium in 2020. She published a book chapter in *Place Event Marketing in the Asia Pacific Region: Branding and Promotion in Cities* in 2021. With a background in creative industries, arts marketing, cultural consumption, and cultural policy studies, her research focuses on the dynamics involved in the management of arts organizations and festivals that serve various stakeholders and agendas in a changing social, economic, and political environment. Yifan is currently the Arts Administrator at the Chinese Culture Center of San Francisco to support the organization's daily operation and various arts and community programs.

# Introduction

# How to Use This Book

*Business Issues in the Arts* takes the reader through many business challenges facing arts organizations today, guiding them through best practices, procedures, and solutions to help them thrive. Many arts administration programs in academia require a course focused on a collection of issues rather than conducting individual courses for each topic. Topics clustered in such a course need to be addressed, though focusing on each issue as a separate offering would consume more credits than required for a degree. As a result, we have seen courses with titles like "Business and Legal Issues in the Arts," "Business of the Arts," "Arts and Business Seminar," or even "Human Resources and Finance in the Arts." Such courses seem to be a bit of a catch-all for issues that require attention and discussion among students but cannot in and of themselves make up an entire course.

In 2016, Artsblog conducted a poll of several thousand arts practitioners to ascertain the biggest business challenges facing the arts today. The results are not surprising: The largest share of the respondents (37%) felt funding was the biggest issue facing the arts. After that came relevance/changing tastes (24%), diversity (15%), and leadership (13%), followed by other, far smaller percentages to round out the list.

DOI: 10.4324/9781003207535-1

These are all vital business issues. In most industries, business scientists study the most successful performance categories and develop theories about how those work and why. Others then emulate them until those theories become standards. However, many of those traditional business standards are limited in their relevance to the nonprofit arts, as the nonprofit arts operate with a mission-driven bottom line as opposed to a profit-driven one. In addition, standard arts administration survey text, focusing heavily on marketing and fundraising, are scant resources for delving into topics too narrow for an entire course, but too broad for a cursory "how-to" from a survey text.

In 2020, we conducted a survey of professors who teach arts administration, arts management, arts leadership, and more. According to the results, topics often missed when deemed "too small for a class, but vital nonetheless" included: access, diversity, equity, and inclusion, human resources in the arts, regional arts organization issues, governance, unions, mandates, intellectual property issues, start-ups, negotiations, occupational safety, agencies, collaborations, and engagement. Many of these issues are typically covered in "catch-all" classes under the umbrella of broadly named courses that include management or administration.

Because most academic programs in arts administration have such a course, we examined how those topics are currently taught. We discovered that, in most classes, there are many resources required in order to participate. For example, it is not unheard of to see five, six, or more books and several additional readings required. Nevertheless, of those books, often only a couple of chapters are used from each. Likewise, many of these resources focus on for-profit businesses, and instructors and students are left to determine how to apply the material to nonprofit arts organizations. We realized that the challenges we struggled with in our courses were the same as our colleagues: there was no single source for these major issues we needed to teach.

*Business Issues in the Arts* is a text designed to address some of the most prescient business issues that nonprofit arts organizations face today. Lack of understanding of these basic issues could lead to numerous legal disputes and conflicts about inequities, so there is immense value in knowing and having a resource for these challenging and unique business issues. This text is not a how-to but an in-depth dive into 14 topics and their associated theories to augment learning in arts administration programs. It is designed for an advanced undergraduate course or a standalone graduate course in business issues in the arts. Though most of these concepts have legal ramifications, this is not a book on arts law but addresses vital legislation applicable to the management of nonprofit arts organizations.

From the perspective of nonprofit arts enterprises, the text covers topics such as Access, Equity, Diversity, and Inclusion in the Arts, Finance for the Arts Administrator, Challenges Facing Small Regional and Rural Arts Organizations, Human Resource Law, Occupational Safety and Health Act (OSHA), Family Medical Leave Act (FMLA), Americans with Disabilities Act (ADA), Contracts, Negotiations, Governance, and Engagement. These topics were developed from our survey of top arts administration instructors and cover the issues deemed most imperative for students considering careers in arts administration. These subjects require attention but cannot consume an entire course separately without causing a degree to become unwieldy in terms of requirements. Each topic is covered in-depth, but not as deeply as if it were a major field of study in and of itself. Each topic is considered self-contained, borrowing from other fields in a transdisciplinary manner, applying theories to the arts, and teaching through an arts management lens.

This book can be used in conjunction with books on legal issues in the arts or as a standalone text. With undergraduate programs growing rapidly, *Business Issues in the Arts* fulfills the substantial need for an advanced text. The chapters are punctuated by discussion questions that students can answer prior to a discussion that exposes even deeper information regarding the topic at hand. Though the layout is designed to work sequentially, chapters can be used in any order necessary. In addition, the book can be used as a primary text, following it from beginning to end, or as a secondary text, to fill in for topics not covered in the standard survey text.

Each chapter begins with an introduction that briefly states the core concepts in the chapter, followed by a series of objectives for the reader. We have also incorporated various text boxes that provide examples, cases, and deeper exploration. Pedagogical features include the text boxes, objectives, discussion topics, and brief case studies in many chapters.

After we had a solid understanding of what was required of the field for a text on business issues, we sought assistance in putting it together. Though we have some expertise in certain areas of arts administration, we reached out to a handful of others to make chapter contributions. We wanted to be certain that the reader was hearing from someone with a thorough understanding of each topic. Below Foreword, you can read biographies of us (Jay and Anthony) and contributors to the text.

# Understanding Nonprofit Organizations

Jen Budney

# Chapter 1

## INTRODUCTION

In order to discuss business issues in the arts, we had to take a hard look at what the arts are, how they are taught, and what source material might be useful in a compendium of business issues. We recognized that though the arts, entertainment, and culture include a dizzying array of organizational functions, we were most interested in focusing on those arts organizations within the United States, Canada, and other industrialized democracies operating in an environment designed to nurture the arts through tax incentives. We use the term "nonprofit" arts to focus the scope of the discussion and to define those arts organizations functioning as "mission-driven" as opposed to "profit-driven." Nonprofit is in and of itself a somewhat misleading term. In the United States, it refers directly to organizations with specific tax code designations, though the term "nonprofit" never appears in the code. That is not surprising, as it is a term used to describe what an arts organization is not, as opposed to what it is.

So, what are nonprofit arts organizations? Because they are the book's centerpiece, we felt it mandatory to open the first

DOI: 10.4324/9781003207535-2

chapter expounding on their singular characteristics. This framework can then inform the rest of the discussion in this book.

For the first chapter, we turned to colleague Jen Budney, who holds a Ph.D. in Public Policy, has worked in research and academia, particularly in public policy for the arts, and has a venerable career in the arts as a public servant, nonprofit director, and curator. She uses her substantial knowledge of public policy to serve several organizations and has worked on many publications that have helped shape our understanding of where the nonprofit arts have been, where they are, and where public policy can lead them.

This chapter examines the evolving understanding of accountability and common points of "accountability gaps" in arts and cultural organizations by exploring the purpose of nonprofit incorporation and reviewing the history of nonprofit development in the United States and other jurisdictions. Finally, the chapter looks at the difference between opaque and clear transparency, soft and hard accountability, and the ways in which a new generation of stakeholders are demanding hard accountability from arts and cultural nonprofits in areas related to informal mandates, such as equity in staffing and repertoire, the integrity of funding sources, and the composition of boards.

## UNDERSTANDING NONPROFIT ORGANIZATIONS

*A Contribution by Jen Budney*

In the arts sectors of the United States, Canada, and other advanced industrial democracies, nonprofit organizations are ubiquitous, yet they are often poorly understood by policymakers, board members, donors, the public, and even some arts administrators.[1] The purpose of this chapter is, therefore, to introduce students to the central histories, theories, and problems of nonprofit museums, performing arts organizations, and other cultural nonprofits, to lay out the key differences between nonprofits in the arts and other types of associations, and to explain why these differences matter. This chapter pays particular attention to the crucial issue of public trust and accountability.

Jen Budney

## WHAT IS A NONPROFIT?

The arts sector includes the widest possible array of nonprofit enterprises, from tiny, niche-market production houses to philanthropic foundations that exist to give money to artists and other nonprofit arts organizations to some of the world's biggest and richest collectors and presenters of cultural heritage. What unites organizations in this extremely diverse field is something referred to by economists as the *non-distribution constraint*,[2] a legality applying to all nonprofits which simply means that the organization's residual earnings (profits) cannot be distributed to individuals who exert influence over the organization—for example, board members or senior management. Instead, financial surpluses are either retained as endowments, reserves, or temporarily restricted funds; reinvested in capacity-building or charitable services; or given to individuals or other nonprofits as grants.

On the surface, non-distribution is a simple rule, yet it carries several complex implications for arts organizations, related to the idea of public trust. These include their governance or oversight by a board of directors or trustees, their leaders' responsibilities to interpret and deliver on the organizations' missions, and their need to be accountable to an often broad and evolving range of stakeholders. This chapter addresses these challenges as a means of introducing students to the nonprofit model in the arts sector. It begins with a brief historical overview of the sector's development in the United States, which lays out some key theories of nonprofits and demonstrates features of arts organizations that are unique in the sector.

## NONPROFITS IN THE ARTS: HISTORIES AND THEORIES

Nonprofit organizations are now the dominant organizational form for the production and distribution of the arts in the United States and other advanced industrial "Anglo" nations.[3] There are more than 100,000 registered nonprofit arts organizations in the United States,[4] dispersed across approximately 1,200 counties. In Canada, there are roughly 13,700 arts nonprofits, which together account for 9% of the nation's entire nonprofit and voluntary sector organizations,[5] and the United Kingdom is home to upwards of 15,000 charities devoted to the arts.[6] Meanwhile, the Australia Council provides grants to more than 500 arts nonprofits annually,[7] and Creative New Zealand invests in close to 100[8]—for these countries, the numbers reflect only a fraction of their arts nonprofits, as far from all organizations receive federal funding. As these figures suggest, data on arts nonprofits are not collected in the same way from nation to nation, nor are they collected consistently from year to year.

The foundations for the United States' enormous nonprofit arts sector were established in the so-called Gilded Age—an era of rapid economic growth that spanned from approximately 1870 to the first years of the twentieth century. During this period, the development of railroads, factories, mining, and finance led to extremes in inequality. A handful of entrepreneurs became tremendously wealthy, while many workers and new immigrants experienced abject poverty. Prior to this period, artistic productions were exclusively for-profit, and the relationship between "highbrow" and "lowbrow" culture was fluid. Theatre performances, for example, were designed to appeal to a very broad audience, mixing Shakespeare with acrobatics, singing, dancing, and comedy. As inequality grew, audiences began to self-segregate according to economics and social classes. Wealthier, educated citizens drifted toward more staid art productions, while the working classes patronized freewheeling cultural venues such as concert saloons, variety halls, and the burgeoning Vaudeville productions.

Jen Budney

The arts remained dominated by commercial enterprises until some of the newly affluent industrialists sought to put the United States "on the map" by planning, funding, constructing, and maintaining major building projects for the public benefit. These included museums and performing arts venues, along with libraries, hospitals, public parks, and universities. In many ways, this was not unlike the Renaissance, when powerful families such as the Medicis funded the construction of great works of architecture and commissioned paintings and sculptures from the era's most famous artists. However, nineteenth-century American benefactors also sought to contribute to the strengthening of democracy—or so they claimed. To this end, they argued that "high culture"—unlike the "low culture" enjoyed by the working classes—was beneficial for the masses. Because of this, they argued that their projects deserved public investment, and many local governments were convinced to assist the entrepreneurs in achieving their cultural visions, for instance, by donating building sites, providing zoning assistance, and approving cash infusions to be used at the outset of construction.

Beginning in the late nineteenth century, innovations in the United States federal tax code made it possible for donors to obtain generous tax breaks by contributing to charitable, educational, and cultural institutions. Early tax-exemption regulations developed around three major principles: first, organizations that operated for charitable purposes were granted exemption from federal income tax; second, charitable organizations were required to operate according to the non-distribution constraint; and third, charitable giving would be encouraged through the offering of income tax deduction for contributions.[9] These changes led to a great expansion of the nonprofit landscape. Museums, orchestras, and operas were established across the country, in Boston, New York, Cleveland, Denver, and other cities. Historian Carol Duncan (1985) has eloquently illuminated the colonizing, "civilizing" missions of these early arts organizations, whose elitist impulses have now in some ways become structural features of the most established arts institutions.[10]

Legislation regarding tax-exempt organizations continued to be revised throughout the twentieth century, with sweeping changes in the Tax Reform Act of 1969, which established 501(c)

(3) status as we know it today. Despite repeated reforms, the direct and indirect public subsidy of art forms and organizations that continue to be dominated by privileged (wealthier and better educated) audiences is an ongoing point of tension in the sector.

## CASE STUDY: THE METROPOLITAN MUSEUM

In her ground-breaking book, *Civilizing Rituals: Inside Public Art Museums* (Routledge, 1995), Carol Duncan explored the function of art museums as ritual settings and as politically charged, classist, and gendered repositories of the values of elite high culture. One of her case studies is New York's Metropolitan Museum of Art ("The Met"), the largest art museum in the United States.

The Met was founded in 1870 by a group of wealthy politicians and industrialists. They initially charged an entry fee that was off-limits to the working class and closed the museum on Sundays, the only day that workers were free. It was in this sense a private organization for elites, which "democratized" only gradually (and only partially), thanks to the efforts of a younger group of trustees. Duncan explained that the Met's elaborate period rooms enforce an ideology of otherness and impose a class hierarchy that excludes many viewers. Her book is particularly insightful in its exploration of hierarchies within the museum itself, with the educational function consistently subsumed by the curatorial (and collecting) impulse.

Students of museums may also be informed and amused, and perhaps outraged, by the memoir of former Met Director, Thomas Hoving. *Making the Mummies Dance: Inside the Metropolitan Museum of Art*[11] detailed Hoving's activities and dilemmas during his decade-long tenure at the helm of the Met, where he presided over some very expensive and controversial acquisitions, expansions, and exhibitions. His exceedingly honest book makes clear that pressures to serve private interests over public interests are not incidental to nonprofit arts organizations but are persistent, recurring dilemmas for their leaders.

Jen Budney

In the nearly 130 years that have passed since the first tax code changes were enacted, and since 1969 when the 501(c)(3) was last updated, the nonprofit arts sector in the United States has expanded and diversified in ways that the early founders could never have foreseen. No longer restricted to well-capitalized museums and traditional performing arts venues, the field today is dominated by thousands upon thousands of small organizations, such as children's theatres, folk dance companies, chamber music organizations, choral groups, and artist-run centers. At the same time, the largest nonprofit arts organizations have become gargantuan, particularly following the cultural building boom of 1994–2006, when approximately $25 billion was spent on cultural facility projects in the United States.[12] For example, in 2019 the Metropolitan Museum was the nation's 36th largest nonprofit in any sector, with a revenue of $574,798,843 and total assets of $4.36 billion, while the Metropolitan Opera, at #68, had a revenue of $313,444,484, and total assets of $486,124,721.[13] This period of growth also witnessed an exceptional rise in inequality, signaling to many observers a return to "gilded" times.[14]

Sociologist Paul DiMaggio (2006)[15] categorizes arts associations as belonging to one of three types: (1) freestanding tax-exempt organizations; (2) arts programs embedded in non-arts organizations (such as schools, churches, and community action organizations); and (3) "minimalist" artists programs, comprising informal associations, unincorporated artists' collectives, sole proprietorships with mixed commercial and non-commercial aims, arts networks, and more. Most of the time, however, when people talk about nonprofit arts organizations, they are referring to tax-exempt freestanding organizations, which have their own articles of incorporation or letters patent, along with a board of directors or trustees.

Why are so many corporations that produce art nonprofits? And why are some predictably for profit (for example, circuses, Hollywood films, and many Broadway productions)? Scholars use three main theories to answer these questions.

First, the *theory of market failure*[16] proposes that the best art costs more to produce or to present than people are willing to pay, and therefore must be delivered through organizations that are nonprofit and subsidized by governments. This theory depends on the idea that the arts are "merit goods"—goods that, when consumed, provide external benefits, and which therefore warrant public subsidy. Though this tends to make sense to people working in the arts, it does not always persuade those who think the subsidized arts are elitist or irrelevant. According to some proponents of market failure theory, democratic governments subsidize the costs of arts nonprofits up to the ticket price that the "median voter" would be willing to pay. (In this case, the median voter refers to the person whose ideal ticket price falls squarely in the middle of the ranked preferences of all citizens.) Those who would be willing to pay more for the experience will be inclined to subsidize the arts through donations, while those who would pay less will be excluded in the absence of a targeted strategy.

Next, *industrial-organization theory*[17] holds that nonprofits dominate the arts because they are more trustworthy than for-profit firms: due to the non-distribution constraint, nonprofit arts organizations have no incentive to cut costs and shirk quality to create higher profits. This is important because governments are typically unwilling to fully fund the arts, due to the discrepancies of opinion among voters, and their subsidies, combined with tickets or fees set to the preferences of the median voter, are insufficient to produce the quality of art to which the organizations aspire. Most arts organizations, therefore, need to cater to two different markets: one of the median voter (someone who will pay the base ticket price but no more) and one comprising patrons who are willing to pay more, and who can therefore be convinced to donate. Arts organizations that depend on this second market must adopt the nonprofit form to assure patrons that they will use their contributed funds for program and capacity-building purposes, rather than the personal enrichment of the organization's leaders.

Another version of industrial-organization theory proposes that in most cases it is a relatively small number of committed stakeholders who provide most of the income and labor in the founding of arts organizations. The reason these individuals come together is to meet a demand for quality levels or artistic forms for which a large market does not exist. For this reason, their vision is best carried out through a nonprofit that has a clear and specific mission and a board whose job is to make sure that this mission will constrain business decisions and create a durable structure for inducing ongoing contributions of resources.

### CASE STUDY: TRIBE, INC.

Tribe: A Centre for the Evolving Aboriginal Media, Visual, and Performing Arts (Tribe) was an interdisciplinary artist-run center founded by and for Indigenous artists in Saskatoon, Saskatchewan (Canada) in 1995. For most of its 20-year existence, Tribe was led by Cree/Saultaux/Métis artist Lori Blondeau. Tribe's unique proposition was to be a "nomadic" gallery, a concept that drew from the culture of the Indigenous nations of the prairies or great plains, but which was also aimed at generating a broader (not only Indigenous) audience for the work of Indigenous artists.

According to Blondeau, when Tribe was founded in 1994, there was an obvious lack of Indigenous visual arts programming by organizations in Saskatoon and across Canada—in other words, a market failure. "There was some programming going on by non-Indigenous groups," she explained, "But it was what we like to call 'the quota show.'"[18] Tribe collaborated with larger, more mainstream organizations in Saskatoon and across Canada to produce exhibitions and performances in these spaces, knowing that in mainstream venues more people would see their shows. Some of their more notable exhibitions include Dana Claxton's *Buffalo Bone China* (1997), The High Tech Storyteller's Festival (2000), and repeated presentations of the work of Anishinaabekwe/Canadian artist Rebecca Belmore as well as Payómkawichum/Ipi/Mexican-American performance artist, photographer, and multimedia installation artist, James Luna.

In line with industrial-organization theory, Tribe's board of directors was composed of Indigenous artists and curators who kept the organization focused on its singular mission, and it received annual funding and support from provincial and federal granting agencies, alongside other sources. As one of the first and most prominent Indigenous artist-run centers in Canada, Tribe deserves a great deal of credit for the development of the large and dynamic Indigenous contemporary art scene in that country, one that is now widely recognized and supported by museums and galleries across Canada.

Finally, *historical and political perspectives*[19] explain how the terrain of nonprofit arts organizations has been molded by the capacities of historical elites to mobilize resources in this area. *Elites* refers to members of society who have both economic and social privilege as well as some degree of political influence. These perspectives show us how the sector as a whole has been shaped by powerful social groups and individuals whose preferences and actions have established the "rules of the game."

For the early founders of art museums and orchestras, participation in "high" art institutions was part of an aspirational lifestyle that included elite universities, private libraries, and exclusive clubs. Much as Duncan described, the nonprofit organization provided a stable framework for their own class's tastes to be upheld as more worthy of state subsidy than other forms of culture. However, the trustee-governed arts organizations that began proliferating in the early years of the twentieth century were not the only games in town. For instance, many new immigrant groups established their own voluntary organizations for communal cultural practices, and other charities, such as women's clubs, also hosted regular arts events—none of these, however, received state subsidy. Notably, artists themselves—and especially artists of color—were mostly absent from the ranks of formal institutional entrepreneurs, as they tended to lack necessary financial and social capital. Inequalities established a century ago in the formation and funding of many arts organizations—across geographies (urban vs. rural) and across cultural groups — persist to the present day.

In the United States during the 1960s and 1970s, the landscape of existing "high culture" nonprofits was reinforced by a massive infusion of capacity-building grants by the Ford Foundation's rather conservative art program. It was quickly reshaped by the National Endowment for the Arts (NEA, created in 1965), which provided incentives and opportunities for adoption of the nonprofit form by arts and cultural groups that until then had been excluded. Indeed, the NEA sought to level the playing field for the arts, particularly in rural and African American communities, whose art forms and artistic groups were often considered "too grassroots" to be funded by corporate or private philanthropy. In other Anglo nations, federal and regional arts councils were doing work similar to the NEA, sometimes much earlier (e.g., Arts Council of Great Britain, now Arts Council England, est. 1946; Saskatchewan Arts Board, est. 1948). The post-War period also saw a major expansion of higher education, which both increased the audiences for the subsidized arts and created a surplus of artists, many of whom went on to invent and administer an expanded field of more risk-taking nonprofit arts organizations. During this period, a network of state and local arts agencies developed with the encouragement of the NEA.

Different mixes of social, economic, and political forces have continued to shift the terrain of the nonprofit arts sector since the 1980s and will persist in doing so into the future. A few trends remain stable—for example, since the 1980s, 70%–75% of all American arts organizations for which census data are collected have remained nonprofit, or a mix of nonprofit and public, but this status is not distributed evenly across all genres.[20] Commercial enterprises remain the dominant form for organizations engaged in mechanical or, more recently, digital distribution (such as Hollywood productions), and for live performances appealing to large and heterogenous audiences (e.g., dance schools, Broadway theatres, circuses).

Largely as a result of the United States' unique tax policies, the American arts sector, outside the Smithsonian and a few other government-sponsored organizations, relies more heavily on private financial resources than other advanced industrialized nations. Some municipalities and counties provide significant support for arts organizations in the form of cash, operational support, facilities, and/or personnel, but at the federal level, support for the arts is low. In Europe, by contrast, cultural facilities have tended to be clustered in political capitals, where they are owned and operated by the state. The nonprofit arts sectors developed differently in Canada, Australia, and New Zealand, emerging more out of the British charitable tradition, and today, to varying degrees, they are still more reliant on government funding than is typical in the United States. Yet, for better or for worse, American nonprofits in the arts—especially the largest establishments—remain models for the sector globally, and everywhere private philanthropy is an increasingly essential source of revenue.

## LEGITIMACY AND THE PUBLIC INTEREST

No matter what kind of work they do, nonprofits in the arts are granted a license to operate based on the premise that their work serves the public interest. However, as the theories of nonprofits tell us—and as many people working in the arts have experienced—defining "public interest" is never simple. In fact, within broader society, the arts are typically viewed and often function as a *special interest group*, that is, a group of people and organizations who share the same political or business aims and who try to influence governments to help them with those aims. The arts sector as a whole is also far from homogeneous and contains its own special interest groups. Most notably in recent years, these include groups of individuals and organizations advocating and struggling for social justice, which requires the fair and equitable treatment of artists, arts workers, and audiences.[21] There have also been protests over art organizations accepting "tainted money" from corporations or trustees.[22] How arts organizations will attempt to resolve these issues remains to be seen, but it is clear that this new era of heightened calls for accountability requires organizations to prepare and respond. As communities and social norms transform and evolve, so do the demographics and perspectives of stakeholder groups, and new challenges will inevitably arise. Leaders in the sector should understand that nonprofit status is never in and of itself evidence of an organization's legitimacy.

What does legitimacy mean in the context of the nonprofit arts sector? In a nutshell, legitimacy is achieved when stakeholders share a clear sense that an organization is providing for all the stakeholders' needs fairly and adequately. Legitimacy is therefore marked by high levels of trust and strong *norms*, or

Jen Budney

unwritten rules of behavior—in other words, it exists within strong relationships and mutual commitments. For nonprofit arts organizations to function effectively, their boards, employees, audiences, and artists, along with funders and other members of their community must view the organization as legitimate. This will ensure they continue to contribute as funders, volunteers, visitors and members, patrons, advocates, and so on.

The first step toward legitimacy is mission fulfillment. Missions are initially established by the organizations' founders and describe the unique purposes of the organization: why it exists, who it serves, and—in broad strokes—how it serves them. A mission, therefore, functions as an organization's guide or compass for how to go about its business of contributing to the public interest—it is "both a charter and constraint"[23] in that it serves to stimulate and also to delimit action. Most arts nonprofits cater to specialized, distinctive, passionate, or sometimes even controversial niches, rather than to mass cultural preferences, and it is precisely in these areas where stakeholders such as board members, employees, and target audiences feel their strongest allegiances and need for dependable service.

### CASE STUDY: PORTLAND SYMPHONY ORCHESTRA

The Portland Symphony Orchestra (PSO) was founded in 1923 in Portland, Maine, in northern New England. It was formally incorporated as a nonprofit in 1932, and its founding bylaws lay out the organization's mandate:

> The objects and purposes of this corporation shall be to advance and encourage the appreciation and study of music and musical literature, to demonstrate to, and educate the members of the corporation and citizens generally in the advantages and value of good music in the community; to give public concerts; to engage in and encourage association of the members of the corporation and citizens of the community for social purposes through the common enjoyment, performance and study

of music, and to otherwise fulfill the purpose usually devolving upon and fulfilled by such an orchestral body conducted without monetary profit to its members.

Today the PSO is the largest arts organization in the state of Maine and is widely regarded as one of the top symphony orchestras of its size in the United States. Its mission—the organization's "clarion call," which serves to inspire and invite artists, audiences, and volunteers—is much bolder and direct than its mandate:

"Our mission is to serve our community by enriching lives through music."

The PSO's statement is an excellent example of how missions serve as both charter and constraint, because it states clearly why it exists (to enrich lives), who it serves (our community), and—in broad strokes—how it serves them (through music).

Before a mission can be fulfilled, however, it must be interpreted. To do so, the organization's leaders (board/trustees and CEO/Executive Director) need to agree on a vision of the future, or what the organization and its environment might look like five or ten years down the road. Organizations will be able to do this most successfully when they have a diverse range of knowledge and perspectives around the table: too homogeneous a group and their ideas are more likely to be compromised by cognitive biases such as overconfidence, group think, or confirmation bias.[24] Diversity among leadership is especially important in dynamic and rapidly changing environments, where the future is highly uncertain. In such contexts, leaders need to consider the widest range of possibilities and push to consider prospects outside of their comfort zones. This is challenging work, but if organizations do not develop a "right" view of the future, they cannot devise successful strategies for meeting it.

In fulfilling their missions, organizations must be accountable to stakeholders for both their strategic decisions and their day-to-day management practices. Most arts nonprofits, however, operate in complex, evolving environments, and their ability to carry out their missions will constantly be impacted by limitations and opportunities arising from outside and inside the organization. Many nonprofit arts organizations adopt more cautious or conservative interpretations of their mission over time as a way of dealing with increasing competition for resources and legitimacy, and because there are always strong pressures toward conformity with other organizations.

DiMaggio and Powell (1983) describe three forces that cause organizations to become more like each other over time, a process they refer to as *institutional isomorphism. Normative* isomorphic change is driven by pressures brought about by professionalization and the adoption of professional norms. These emerge through education and training as well as people's circulation in professional networks. *Mimetic* isomorphism refers to the inclination of an organization to imitate another's structure because of the perception that the other organization does things better or is more legitimate. *Coercive* isomorphism results from formal pressures on an organization from government or funding bodies, as well as from the informal pressures stemming from a society's strongly held cultural expectations.[25]

Opportunities can also affect an organization's adherence to its mission. For example, access to new pools of funding might inspire a shift in programming, or a donor may offer a large gift with strings attached, which stretches the mission or causes it to drift away from its central purpose. Of growing concern to many arts organizations is the question of public engagement and responsibility to diverse communities in the organizations' immediate locales. In particular, most large, established organizations have been stuck in Eurocentric models of art production, education, and participation, which are unwelcoming to many individuals from non-western cultural groups and racialized communities, as well as to many individuals not possessing higher education. Initially, this issue became a concern to a handful of larger organizations when they realized they were losing funding, relevance, participation, and support—all signs of legitimacy.[26] However, as social movements such as Black Lives Matter continue to put pressure on nonprofits to live up to their public purposes, the idea that arts nonprofits must operate differently to serve a more truly public (rather than elite) interest is becoming more prevalent.

## CASE STUDY: OF/BY/FOR ALL

OF/BY/FOR ALL is a unique nonprofit organization and global network dedicated to helping arts and cultural organizations become more inclusive of their local communities. Founded in 2018/19 by Nina Simon, former director of the Santa Cruz Museum of Art and History, OF/BY/FOR ALL employs a team of diverse executives and staff who consult and conduct workshops and bootcamps for organizations wishing to make a change. OF/BY/FOR ALL describes its primary tactic as "community-centric partnerships" driven by a cross-functional team of staff and trustees who aim to help organizations make changes to projects, institutional policies, and processes. The primary means for organizations to benefit from OF/BY/FOR ALL's work is to join the OF/BY/FOR ALL Change Network, a 12-month, fee-based, online program for civic and cultural organizations, which offers a "dashboard of tools, progress reports, and coaching check-ins," along with ongoing interaction with other members of the network. While OF/BY/FOR ALL was one of the earliest consulting groups to enter the territory of public engagement and change management for arts organizations, it is not alone. There are a growing number of private consultants also offering services related to outreach and diversity, equity, and inclusion initiatives in the arts.

It is vitally important for those working in the nonprofit arts sector to recognize that their field does not represent "culture" as a whole. Great works of art are made in commercial settings, and most culture continues to be produced and transmitted outside of formal organizations altogether. Those working in larger arts nonprofits are now being called upon to put their creativity and resources toward devising new means of recognizing and collaborating with the diverse cultural manifestations that exist beyond their walls, including those produced by smaller nonprofits as well as informal, community-based organizations. Because new resources may not be forthcoming to fund such endeavors, organizations will need to reconsider their prevailing metrics of evaluation, shifting from the standard count of admissions/visions and the bottom line to incorporate more complex measures, such as active co-productions and partnerships, consultation with and participation of communities in programming planning, and innovation in programs and services.[27]

## BEYOND THE MISSION: LEGITIMACY AND ACCOUNTABILITY IN FUNDRAISING AND HR MANAGEMENT

For many people employed in the arts, especially those with creative backgrounds, *mission fulfillment*, the organization's creative development, programming, and public outreach activities, is the exciting work. Fundraising and human resources (HR) management may seem a tad dull by comparison. But along with missions, nonprofits also have mandates, and with mandates come legal responsibilities. A *mandate* is a legal term that captures the organization's relationship with the government; it spells out what the organization is legally required to do by virtue of its incorporation, funding arrangements, and other contracts. For most organizations, it is a statement in their articles of incorporation or letters patent, and it is much drier and more general than the mission. Mandate fulfillment is another essential requirement of legitimacy, and it warrants sharp attention.

As noted above, in recent years many arts nonprofits have been criticized for accepting what some refer to as "tainted money," which includes funding from the fossil fuel sector, arms manufacturers, and so on, and organizations are also being asked to account for the business activities of their trustees. In part, this is because, as historical perspectives show us, participation on the board of a cultural institution boosts an individual's social status and public reputation, and largely sanctions the means by which the individual makes their money. Social justice advocates argue that the arts should not be a way for ultra-wealthy individuals to "scrub their consciences and reputations" or purchase the "immunity needed to profiteer at the expense of the common welfare."[28] They insist that leaders of nonprofits in the arts are not simply stewards of the interests of particular organizations but must consider the broader public interest in philanthropic exchanges.

Beyond meeting state and federal legal requirements, nonprofit organizations can inspire stakeholder confidence by being transparent with their fundraising practices and costs, demonstrating accountability and respect for funders, donors, and taxpayers. This entails the adoption of clear policies that ensure responsible use of funds, as well as open communication with donors and other constituents. Staff, too, should be educated on the organization's fundraising practices and the implications of fundraising on operations. Every nonprofit arts organization should have comprehensive conflict-of-interest policies and procedures for employees and the board, as well as for contract workers such as fundraising and development freelancers. All employees and board members should be made to regularly review these policies.

### CASE STUDY: TWO RIVERS ART GALLERY

Two Rivers Art Gallery, established in 1971, makes its home in northern British Columbia, Canada, in the small city of Prince George (pop: >75,000). Like most northern communities, Prince George is economically reliant on natural resource extraction including forestry and oil. Enbridge, a multinational pipeline company, employs many people in Prince George, and its activities also contribute to the high pollution levels in the region. Funding the small local art gallery, whose annual operating budget is just over CAD $1 million, would be a natural way for the pipeline company to enhance its social license to operate (or demonstrate "corporate social responsibility"), but Two Rivers Art Gallery does not accept Enbridge's money. In a 2016 interview,[29] the gallery's Artistic Director, George Harris, explained that it was important for the gallery to host exhibitions that "push people through painful stuff" and talk about issues such as the human impact on climate change or the effects of oil pipelines. The gallery made the hard decision not to approach Enbridge for sponsorship, so that it could pursue such thematic exhibitions without having to "bite the hand that feeds us." At the same time, it featured some pro-pipeline artworks in its group exhibition *Pipeline: A Land of Division* (2013) and tried to ensure that in discussions with school groups and other visitors that neither pro- nor anti-pipeline perspectives could remain unchallenged.

HR stewardship is another important aspect of legitimacy in the nonprofit arts sector. Unfortunately, many organizations do this poorly. Too often in arts organizations, employees face an "accountability gap" in HR management: only the CEO or Executive Director has access to board members, and the board does not adequately evaluate the CEO's people management practices. In 2020/21, several arts organizations in North America faced highly publicized crises when staff took to social media to complain of workplace abuse,[30] a trend that revealed how commonly boards fail to exercise effective oversight in this area.

Ensuring that the organization is compliant with relevant labor legislation is the absolute minimum standard that organizations must achieve, but this is not by itself enough to create a happy, supportive, and creative work environment. Leaders must be sure that the organization establishes management policies and practices that encourage employees in their current and future work, and which contribute to non-discriminatory and equitable workplaces.[31] Every organization should also establish a whistleblower policy that allows a confidential method for employees to raise concerns about unethical practices with a designated board member or other authority. By doing so, boards provide employees with a legally required mechanism for raising concerns without the fear of reprisal or retaliation.

In keeping with the Eurocentrism of the largest, established organizations in the United States and other advanced industrial Anglo nations, there continues to be a lack of racial diversity among arts sector employees, especially at the highest levels.[32] In 2017, however, New York City's mayor Bill de Blasio announced that municipal funding for museums and arts organizations would be linked to the diversity of their employees and board members. Nonprofit arts organizations everywhere should consider the possibility of similar policies being implemented in their own jurisdictions, as community representativeness among employees and board members is becoming a key feature of legitimacy. Some observers are calling for at least 50% of boards to be filled by BIPOC members,[33] which resonates with academic findings that a critical mass of minorities is needed on corporate boards for their perspectives to have influence.[34]

In the coming years, demands for accountability will likely continue intensifying in the nonprofit arts sector, due in part to ongoing demographic changes as well as the expanding impact and awareness of the inequalities resulting from certain processes of capitalism. In this context, it is essential for the leaders of nonprofits in the arts to understand the functions and implications of transparency and accountability. Far too often organizations practice only "opaque" transparency, that is, they disseminate information but in a way that does not reveal how they make decisions or the results of those decisions.[35] The desire to respect the privacy of donors, concerns about stakeholder responses to decisions over the allocation of resources, or attempts to placate the public when employees or board members are called out for racial discrimination or sexual misconduct have all resulted in communications that are only opaquely transparent.[36] Clear transparency, on the other hand, refers to information-access policies and practices that reveal reliable information about institutional performance, including HR policies and practices, donations, spending, programming, and more. At a minimum, clear transparency produces soft accountability in organizations, wherein leaders justify their decisions. However, many of the protests in recent years are demanding hard accountability from arts organizations: answerability, plus the possibility of sanctions.

Finally, the leaders of nonprofits should regularly scan the business world to understand how developments in the corporate sector may affect them. For instance, the growing global movement of *Certified B Corporations*, businesses that

Jen Budney

are legally required to consider the impact of their decisions on their employees, customers, suppliers, community, and the environment, is building pressure on other companies to improve their ethics. Given the growing concern about climate change, we are likely to see more demands for nonprofits in the arts to reduce their production of waste and greenhouse gases.[37]

## FINAL THOUGHTS

The nonprofit arts sector is emerging as an arena of increasing contestation. Contemporary social justice and environmental activists, along with artists and employees, are calling out organizations for issues such as sponsorship and donations from "tainted" sources and commitments to diversity, equity, and inclusion. Debates over the appropriate roles for arts organizations in supporting grassroots movements and communities have been particularly heated in the art museum sector, but all cultural organizations have an interest in these discussions.

There are fundamental tensions in the nonprofit arts sector arising from the historical and ongoing control of organizations by elites. Although nonprofits are granted a license to operate based on the premise that their work serves the public interest, a variety of isomorphic pressures have often led to arts organizations prioritizing privileged stakeholders. There are signs that this is changing, but it will be a slow process, aided by younger generations of arts administrators who are already working for change, by the growing number of individuals and organizations devoted to change management and diversity, equity, and inclusion strategies for the sector, and by isomorphic pressures from outside the nonprofit sector, such as B Corporations.

The non-distribution constraint, which unites all nonprofits, brings with it several complex implications for arts organizations, including the responsibility for boards and employees to interpret and deliver on their organizations' missions and to devise appropriate evaluation processes beyond simple measures of attendance or the bottom line. Nonprofits must be vigilant to maintain the highest levels of accountability with regard to the funds they receive and spend but, just as importantly, they should strive hard to create and maintain non-discriminatory, equitable, and creative work environments. By doing so, they will be poised to respond to their complex, evolving, and sometimes unpredictable environments in responsible, resilient, and generative ways.

## DISCUSSION QUESTIONS

1. As the examples in this chapter suggest, in North America, the art museum has always been held in the public imagination as more accountable than other arts organizations for promoting the democratization of culture. What factors might account for this?

2. Should nonprofit organizations in the arts be held to higher ethical standards than organizations operating for profit? Why or why not?

3. Some publishing houses are investor-owned, while others are nonprofits. Using the theories of nonprofits outlined in this chapter (market failure, industrial-organization theory, and historical/political perspectives), can you explain why different book publishers might choose to incorporate under different models? How might their choice affect strategic decision-making?

4. For nonprofit performing and visual arts organizations, is attendance the best measure of success? Why or why not? What other measures could be used?

5. Conservative organizations like the Heritage Foundation have argued that the National Endowment for the Arts does not permit underprivileged individuals to gain access to the arts, but merely subsidizes the well-to-do. Is there merit in their argument? Why or why not?

6. In nonprofit organizations, the board directly oversees only the chief executive (CEO or Executive Director). The chief executive is responsible for overseeing the work of all other employees. How might boards gain reasonable assurance that policies and procedures are in place that treat employees well and fairly and offer them a healthy work environment, without interfering with the day-to-day operations of the organization?

Jen Budney

7. Nonprofit arts organizations, including art museums and performing arts organizations, have, in recent years, been asked to "decolonize." What does this mean, and what aspects of the organizations' operations would decolonization affect?

8. "No one in the arts community would complain if support from the government was replaced by support from the audience, and there is no logical reason it couldn't happen" (Charles Gordon, *Maclean's*, March 27, 1995). Do you agree with this statement? Drawing from ideas in this chapter, explain your answer.

9. An intermission is a conventional recess between parts of a performance or production in theatre, concerts, opera, and sometimes film. What are the origins of the intermission and what role does isomorphism play in the convention?

10. What isomorphic effects might funding programs and grant applications have on the programming and methods of evaluation of an arts organization?

11. What are all the issues leaders of a nonprofit in the arts should consider when seeking corporate sponsorship in order to maintain the support of stakeholders?

## FURTHER READING

Jen Budney, Brian McBay, Armando Perla, Devyani Saltzman, and Sharanjit Kaur Sandhra. "The Elephant in the Room: The Leadership Crisis in Canada's Cultural Sector." (Panel Discussion, British Columbia Museums Association, Online.) [https://vimeo.com/553485261]

A recording of a one-hour online panel discussion held in June 2021 to discuss the "leadership crisis" in Canadian arts organizations that should resonate with arts nonprofits in all developed industrial Anglo nations, this video also comes with ASL interpretation. The panel covers toxic leadership and the lack of diversity on boards and senior management.

Paul J. DiMaggio. *Nonprofit Enterprise in the Arts: Studies in Mission and Constraint.* Oxford: Oxford University Press, 1987.

This edited volume assesses the relationship between social purpose in the arts and the significance of the nonprofit model for cultural industries, the ways that nonprofit arts organizations are financed, and the constraints that patterns of funding place on nonprofit missions. Although the book was written more than 20 years ago, it provides an unparalleled foundation for thinking about some of the special tensions that affect nonprofits in the arts.

Elwood Jimmy and Vanessa Andreotti with Sharon Stein. *Towards Braiding.* Toronto: Musagetes Arts Foundation, 2019. [https://decolonialfuturesnet.files. wordpress.com/2019/05/braiding_reader.pdf]

Jimmy and Andreotti, both Indigenous thinkers involved in the arts and education, co-wrote this book as a conversation, asking many questions about "decolonization" in turbulent times, including: What conditions make possible ethical and rigorous engagement across communities in historical dissonance? What are the guidelines and practices for ethical and respectful engagement with Indigenous sense and sensibilities? What kind of socially engaged and community anchored Indigenous-led arts-based program can support the process of healing? Their book (available as a free, downloadable PDF) is essential reading for students interested in decolonizing arts organizations.

**Colin Talbot. "Measuring Public Value: A Competing Values Approach." The Work Foundation, UK. 2008. [http://publiccommons.ca/public/uploads/literature/ measuring_pv_final2.pdf]**

This is an innovative approach to measuring "public value" or contributions to the public good by organizations serving multiple stakeholders whose values are sometimes in competition or conflict with each other's. Although Talbot's paper is directed to public agencies, his approach and proposed metrics for evaluation are highly relevant to nonprofit arts organizations.

## Notes

1  Lester M. Salamon. "The Nonprofit Sector and Government: The American Experience in Theory and Practice". In *The Third Sector: Comparative Studies of Nonprofit Organizations*, eds. Helmut K. Anheier and Wolfgang Seibel, 219–240. Berlin, Boston: De Gruyter, 2013. https://doi.org/10.1515/9783110868401.

2  Henry B. Hansmann. "The Role of Nonprofit Enterprise". *The Yale Law Journal* 89, no. 5 (1980): 835–901. https://doi.org/10.2307/796089.

3  Paul Dimaggio. "Nonprofit Organizations and the Intersectoral Division of Labor in the Arts". In *The Nonprofit Sector*, 432–461. New Haven, CT: Yale University Press, 2006. https://doi.org/10.12987/9780300153439-021

4  Brice McKeever. "Registered Public Charities by Type". *Urban Institute/National Center for Charitable Statistics.* 2018. Source: Internal Revenue Service Business Master Files, Exempt Organizations August 2016. [https://nccs.urban.org/ publication/registered-public-charities-type] Accessed 6 August 2021.

5  Imagine Canada. "Arts and Culture Organizations in Canada". *National Survey of Nonprofit and Voluntary Organizations.* 2006. [https://les-amis.ca/files/PDF/ ImagineCanada_Arts_Culture_Factsheet.pdf] Accessed 6 August 2021.

6  Leung, Raphael and Eliza Easton. "The impact of COVID-19 on Arts and Cultural Charities". Nesta. 2020. [https://www.nesta.org.uk/blog/impact-covid-19-arts-and-cultural-charities/] Accessed 6 August 2021.

7  Australia Council for the Arts. "Annual Report 2019-20". Australia Council for the Arts. 2020. [https://australiacouncil.gov.au/about-us/corporate-documents/annual-reports/annual-report-2019-20/] Accessed 6 August 2021.

8  Creative New Zealand. "Annual Report/Pūrongo ā Tau: For the Year Ended 30 June 2020". Creative New Zealand/Government of New Zealand. 2020. [https://www. creativenz.govt.nz/assets/paperclip/publication_documents/documents/756/ original/annual_report_2020.pdf?1607632468] Accessed 6 August 2021.

9  Paul Arnsberger, Melissa Ludlum, Margaret Riley, and Mark Stanton. *A History of the Tax-Exempt Sector: An SOI Perspective.* Statistics of Income Bulletin, Winter 2008.

10  Carol Duncan. *Civilizing Missions: Inside Public Art Museums.* New York: Routledge, 1995.

11  Thomas Hoving. *Making the Mummies Dance: Inside the Metropolitan Museum of Modern Art.* New York: Simon & Schuster, 1993.

12  Joanna Woronkowicz, D. Carroll Joynes, and Norman M. Bradburn. *Building Better Arts Facilities: Lessons from a U.S. National Study.* New York and London: Routledge, 2015.

13 Mark Hrywna. "NTP Top 100 (2019): An In-depth Study of America's Largest Nonprofits". *The Nonprofit Times*. 2019. [https://www.thenonprofittimes.com/report/npt-top-100-2019-an-in-depth-study-of-americas-largest-nonprofits/] Accessed 6 August 2021.

14 Michael Massing. "How the Superrich Took Over the Museum World". *The New York Times*, December 14, 2019. [https://www.nytimes.com/2019/12/14/opinion/sunday/modern-art-museum.html] Accessed 6 August 2021.

15 Paul DiMaggio. "Nonprofit Organizations and the Intersectoral Division of Labor in the Arts". In *The Nonprofit Sector*, 432–461. New Haven, CT: Yale University Press, 2006. https://doi.org/10.12987/9780300153439-021

16 The tradition premise for the market failure argument is provided by William J. Baumal and William J. Bowen in their well-known study *Performing Arts: An Economic Dilemma*. New York: The Twentieth Century Fund, 1977. See also: Dick Netzer, *The Subsidized Muse*. New York: Cambridge University Press, 1978; Estelle James, "The Nonprofit Sector in Comparative Perspective". In *The Nonprofit Sector: A Research Handbook*, ed. Walter W. Powell, 1st edition, 397–415. New Haven, CT: Yale University Press; and David Throsby, *Economics and Culture*. Cambridge: Cambridge University Press, 2001.

17 See: Henry Hansmann.1981. "Nonprofit Enterprise in the Performing Arts". *Bell Journal of Economics* 12, no. 2: 341–361; and Jennifer Kuan. 2001. "The Phantom Profits of the Opera: Nonprofit Ownership in the Arts as a Make-Buy Decision". *Journal of Law and Economic Organization* 17: 507–520.

18 See the interview with Lori Blondeau in Bryne McLaughlin, 2015. "20 Years of Tribe: Milestones and Future Horizons". *Canadian Art.* [https://canadianart.ca/features/20-years-of-tribe-milestones-and-future-horizons/] Accessed 7 November 2021.

19 See, of course, the writings of Carol Duncan, cited earlier, as well as: Paul DiMaggio. 1992. "Cultural Boundaries and Structural Change: The Extension of the High-Culture Model to Theatre, Opera, and the Dance, 1900–1940". In *Cultivating Differences: Symbolic Boundaries and the Making of Inequality*, eds. Michele Lamont and Marcel Founier, 21–57. Chicago, IL: University of Chicago Press; Tony Bennett. 1995. *The Birth of the Museum: History, Theory, Politics.* New York and London: Routledge; and Peter Dobkin Hall. 2006. "A Historical Overview of Philanthropy, Voluntary Associations, and Nonprofit Organizations in the United States, 1600–2000". In *The Nonprofit Sector: A Research Handbook*, eds. W. Powell and R. Steinberg, 32–65. New Haven, CT and London: Yale University Press.

20 Paul DiMaggio. 2006. "Nonprofit Organizations and Intersectoral Division of Labor in the Arts". In *The Nonprofit Sector: A Research Handbook*, eds. W. Powell and R. Steinberg, 432–461. New Haven, CT and London: Yale University Press.

21 Art museums in particular have, in recent years, been identified as sites of gender and racial inequality, and these concerns have found their way to mainstream media. On gender, see: Julia Jacobs, "Female Artists Made Little Progress in Museums since 2008, Survey Finds". *New York Times*, September 19, 2019. [https://www.nytimes.com/2019/09/19/arts/design/female-art-agency-partners-sothebys-artists-auction.html]. Accessed November 8, 2021. For information on racial inequity in museums, see: Kimberly Drew, "What Should a Museum Look Like in 2020". *Vanity Fair*, August 24, 2020. [https://www.vanityfair.com/culture/2020/08/what-should-a-museum-look-like-in-2020] Accessed 8 November 2021.

   Likewise, several art museums have faced protests by staff over poor pay, abusive management practices, and other labor issues. See, for example, the story on the strike at MoMA: Valentina Di Liscia and Hakim Bishara, "'Strike MoMA' Tour Ends with Confrontation between Museum Security and Protesters". *Hyperallergic*, April 30, 2021. [https://hyperallergic.com/642851/strike-moma-tour-ends-with-fierce-confrontation-between-museum-security-and-protesters/] Accessed 8 November 2021. Workers at the Walters Art Museum (Baltimore) made the news when they attempted to unionize. See: "Walters Art Museum Workers Rally to Unionize". WMAR Baltimore, August 12, 2021. [https://www.wmar2news.com/news/local-news/walters-art-museum-employees-rally-to-unionize] Accessed 8 November 2021.

22 The issue of "tainted money" is arguably the most challenging social justice issue facing arts nonprofits. One of the most visible movements in this arena began in 2018 when the activist group Prescription Addiction Intervention Now staged

protests at museums across the US, to pressure them to reject funding from the Sackler family, whose fortunes were amassed through a pharmaceutical business credited with launching the opioid industry. See: Rose Friedman, "Museums Face Pressure from Activists Over Dubious Financial Ties". NPR, October 22, 2019. [https://www.npr.org/2019/10/22/772170465/museums-face-pressure-from-activists-over-dubious-financial-ties] Accessed 8 November 2021. As many observers have pointed out, however, cultural organizations will be hard-pressed to eliminate all "tainted" or "toxic" donations, given the dominance of private wealth in the funding structures of so many non-profit organizations—particularly the largest and most visible. See: Terry Lynn Helge. "It's Harder than You Might Expect for Charities to Give Back Tainted Money". *The Conversation*, August 3, 2018. [https://theconversation.com/its-harder-than-you-might-expect-for-charities-to-give-back-tainted-money-97526]. Accessed 8 November 2021.

23  Minkoff, Debra C. and Walter W. Powell. "Nonprofit Mission: Constancy, Responsiveness, or Deflection?" In *The Nonprofit Sector: A Research Handbook*, eds. Walter W. Powell and Richard Steinberg, 2nd edition, 591–611. New Haven, CT and London: Yale University Press.

24  See Palazzo, Guido, Franciska Krings, and Ulrich Hoffrage. "Ethical Blindness". *Journal of Business Ethics* 109 (September 2012): 323–338.

25  Paul J. DiMaggio, and Walter W. Powell. "The Iron Cage Revisited: Institutional Isomorphism and Collective Rationality in Organizational Fields". *American Sociological Review* 48, no. 2 (1983): 147–60. https://doi.org/10.2307/2095101.

26  See "It all started here...," the introduction to Nina Simon on the OF/BY/FOR/ALL website [https://www.ofbyforall.org/our-story] and read Simon's book, *The Participatory Museum*, 2010.

27  For more on measures of success or "public value" in complex environments, see Colin Talbot. "Measuring Public Value: A Competing Values Approach". The Work Foundation, UK. 2008. [http://publiccommons.ca/public/uploads/literature/measuring_pv_final2.pdf] Accessed 6 August 2021.

28  Anand Giridharadas. "When Your Money is So Tainted Museums Don't Want It". *New York Times*, May 16, 2019. [https://www.nytimes.com/2019/05/16/opinion/sunday/met-sackler.html] Accessed 6 August 2021.

29  Jen Budney. "The 'Imbecile' Institution and the Limits of Public Engagement: Art Museums and Structural Barriers to Public Value Engagement". HARVEST. 2018. [https://harvest.usask.ca/handle/10388/8547] ORCID 0000-0002-4694-3026.

30  Affected organizations include the Akron Art Museum, in Akron, Ohio; the Guggenheim Museum in New York; and the Brooklyn Museum, among others. See: Zachary Small. "Coronovirus Pandemic Dredges Up Allegations of Racism, Sexism, and Bullying from Akron Art Museum Workers". *ARTnews*, April 30, 2020. [https://www.artnews.com/art-news/news/akron-art-museum-racism-sexism-allegations-1202685387/] Accessed 6 August 2021; Hakim Bishara. "Guggenheim Employees Call for Removal of Three Top Executives". *Hyperallergic*, September 16, 2020. [https://hyperallergic.com/588488/a-better-guggenheim-removal-letter/]; Valentina Di Liscia. "Brooklyn Museum Employees Accuse Administration of Staff Mistreatment". *Hyperallergic*, September 17, 2020. [https://hyperallergic.com/588184/brooklyn-museum-staff-open-letter/] Accessed 6 August 2021.

31  See: Adrienne Campbell. "20 Questions Directors of Not-For-Profit Organizations Should Ask About Human Resources". Ottawa: The Canadian Institute for Chartered Accountants, 2011. [https://ascy.ca/wp-content/uploads/2016/01/20QuestionsDirectorsofNotforProfitOrganizationsShouldAskabout HumanResources.pdf] Accessed 6 August 2021; and Cassandra Carver. "Nonprofit HR: Complete Overview for Small Organizations". Astron Solutions, 2019. [https://astronsolutions.net/nonprofit-hr/] Accessed 6 August 2021.

32  There is no complete data for the nonprofit arts sector as a whole; sometimes data on all nonprofits arts organizations will be collected for a single city, other times data may be collected nationally for a particular genre or type of institution, such as the performing arts or museums. This is true not only in the United States but nearly everywhere. See: Tobie S. Stein. *Racial and Ethnic Diversity in the Performing Arts Workforce*. New York and London: Routledge, 2020. Stein, 2020; and Mariët Westermann, Liam Sweeney, and Roger C. Schonfeld. "Art Museum Staff

Demographic Survey 2018". Ithaka S+R. 2019. [https://sr.ithaka.org/publications/art-museum-staff-demographic-survey-2018/] Accessed 6 August 2021.

33 See comments made by Jen Budney, Brian McBay, Armando Perla, Devyani Saltzman, and Sharanjit Kaur Sandhra in the May 21, 2021 online panel discussion, "The Elephant in the Room: The Leadership Crisis in Canada's Cultural Sector". British Columbia Museums Association. [https://vimeo.com/553485261] Accessed 6 August 2021.

34 See Alison M. Konrad, Vicki Kramer, and Samru Erkut. "Critical Mass: The Impact of Three or More Women on Corporate Boards". *Organizational Dynamics* 37, no. 2 (2008): 145–164. https://doi.org/10.1016/j.orgdyn.2008.02.005.

35 Jonathan Fox. "The Uncertain Relationship between Transparency and Accountability". *Development in Practice* 17, nos. 4 & 5: 663–671.

36 For recommendations on how museums (and by implication other arts nonprofits) can be more transparent and accountable, see Christina Steinbrecher-Pfandt and Serife Wong. "Ethics Recommendations Museums Can Implement Right Now". *Hyperallergic*, February 22, 2021. [https://hyperallergic.com/623310/ethics-recommendations-museums-can-implement-right-now/] Accessed 6 August 2021 Steinbrecher-Pfandt and Wong, 2021.

37 Meow Wolf, for example, is an arts and entertainment group and installation established as an art collective in Santa Fe, New Mexico, in 2008. With two permanent locations (Santa Fe and Las Vegas) and plans for another to open in Denver in late 2021, Meow Wolf is one of the few arts organizations that has obtained B Corp status. Meow Wolf produces a B Corp Impact Report that details their contributions to the public as well as their climate-change mitigation solutions, such as the installation of 240 solar panels which provide 44% of their energy. See: https://meowwolf.com/about [Accessed 6 August 2021]. Meow Wolf is not a nonprofit organization but operates with a dual bottom line for social impact and profit.

# Nonprofit Startups in the Arts

Hannah Grannemann

## Chapter 2

### INTRODUCTION

Perhaps the most frequent question asked in the arts administration classroom is how one goes about starting an arts organization. Of course, that is not a simple question to answer. Even if the litany of guidance required to answer it could be presented in a single chapter, situations, structures, and governance are so unique to the players involved, that there is no one-size-fits-all answer. Instead, a discussion on starting up a nonprofit arts organization is likely to generate as many questions as it does answers. Nevertheless, we felt it vital to build upon the strong introduction to the nonprofit organization provided in Chapter 1 by approaching the concept of starting one of them.

For this task, we turned to Hannah Grannemann. Anthony had the pleasure of meeting Hannah when he did a consultative site visit at the University of North Carolina, Greensboro, where Hannah is the inaugural director of the arts administration program. Because Jay assisted on that consultancy, he became aware of Hannah and the work she was doing working as an academic after a nearly two-decade career in theatre management. We have since had the wonderful opportunity to hear about Hannah's work at arts administration conferences. Because her self-stated, "research interests include audience

DOI: 10.4324/9781003207535-3

engagement and its impact on organizational sustainability, organizational behavior in arts/creative organizations and businesses, and finding solutions to longstanding structural problems in the arts," we felt she was the perfect fit for a chapter on structuring a new nonprofit arts organization.

Chapter 2 explores nonprofit arts startups by considering the commercial and nonprofit distinctions and why they exist. The chapter leads the reader through the primary ways to incorporate in the United States, how fiscal sponsors can aid the process, and how arts organizations can function as sole proprietorships. Next, the chapter winds through the government approval process, attaining tax exemptions, and requirements for maintaining exempt status. The chapter concludes by examining alternative structures that also exist.

## NONPROFIT STARTUPS IN THE ARTS

*A Contribution by Hannah Grannemann*

"Good theater with good people" is the reason that Robin Tynes-Miller started her own theater company, Three Bone Theater in Charlotte, NC with her partner Carmen Bartlett in 2011.[1] After learning about collaborative companies like The Wooster Group and Tectonic Theater, the idea struck that she, too, could start her own company to work in the way she wanted. There was an empowerment that I found that I didn't always get from performance. And that was like, 'oh, you can work with like-minded people and have an impact and have a little more say in what stories are told and how they're told and how you work with artists.' And that was really appealing to me, she said.

Jehra Patrick saw that the path to a coveted curator position in an art museum was narrow, and the ranks of curators were not very diverse, despite pledges and promises from institutions. "I mean, everyone could be doing things differently...but no one's able to take the leap. Big institutions are especially really slow to move, slow to change, or not open for risk. I want to see more of it." She started the Emerging Curators Institute (ECI) to support curators, especially women, people of color and LGBTQIA2S+ people who want to work both in museums and in nontraditional ways and spaces.[2]

Both Tynes-Miller and Patrick understood that running the organization was part of the mission to make art and a positive impact – not separate from it. Though people who start new nonprofit arts organizations are motivated and energized by their artistic and social impact goals, in the startup phase, much time is also spent on legal and financial matters. The more that the people involved with the operations of the nonprofit can see the day-to-day work as part of the mission as an expression of the values of the organization and its people and not separate from the work it undertakes, the happier and more satisfied everyone will feel.

This chapter will focus on the process of starting a new nonprofit, tax-exempt arts organization in the United States. Other countries have different laws, regulations, and procedures to follow, and will not be addressed in this resource. This chapter will focus on forming the most common legal structure for nonprofit arts organizations in the United States, a nonprofit organization that is tax exempt under the IRS Tax Code Section 501(c)3 and state laws. But first, we will walk through the thought process for choosing that legal structure for a new organization. We will also return to some other structural options at the end of the chapter.

Time spent on creating a well-run organization is time saved for the social purpose. Being on the solid financial and legal ground means that more time, resources, and energy are spent on enacting the mission of the organization.

**Company? Organization? Corporation? What's the difference?** "Company" is a general term for any legal business entity. "Organization" is a term more commonly used in reference to nonprofit corporations, probably because it softens the image of the organization. "Corporation" is a specific term that refers to businesses that are formed as either nonprofit or for-profit corporations of some variety.

## CASE STUDY: EMERGING CURATORS INSTITUTE, JEHRA PATRICK, FOUNDER

Jehra Patrick took a "walk before you run" approach to develop her organization, the ECI in Minneapolis, MN. Through her own experience and the experiences of her friends and colleagues, she understood that emerging curators and curators working outside of museum systems lacked support and professional development opportunities. Patrick canvassed the community of emerging curators she wished to serve to ensure she created a program that truly fit their needs. From there, she conceived of ECI's core program, a paid fellowship with educational training, mentorship, and guest speakers, and paired fellows with venues and funds for their own exhibitions.

After starting ECI in 2016 as a program with herself as a sole proprietor, Patrick partnered with the Minnesota-based service organization Springboard for the Arts under their fiscal sponsorship program. In 2019, she started the process of creating ECI as a new nonprofit, tax-exempt organization. "For me, it was less about wanting to start an organization and more about needing this thing [the program for emerging curators] to exist and finding the right format for how," she said.

I think we are ready to make that move to a nonprofit status. It will offer the program more stability and it will enable us to reach out to more funding sources than we're currently able to access. I think that it's also healthy to decouple from me as an individual so that the organization can grow and sustain itself independent from my finances.

Though Patrick decided to establish ECI as a nonprofit, in the initial development phase, she had to consider key questions about organizational structure. Anyone considering founding a nonprofit must explore these factors.

Do you need to create your own, new nonprofit arts organization? It is a big responsibility and only meant for organizations that will last a long time. Other options other than starting a new nonprofit include:

- Doing the work with an existing nonprofit or business as a subcontractor, employee, or partner.
- Operating as a for-profit business. This could take the form of a Limited Liability Corporation (LLC), Partnership, S-Corporation, or a Cooperative.
- Using a fiscal sponsor to be able to have access to a 501(c)3 organization when it is required for grants.
- Operating as a sole proprietor.
- Operating as an unincorporated nonprofit association, which may be tax-exempt.

For Patrick, it became clear that moving to obtain 501(c)(3) status was the best decision for the organization. Based on her experience working in other arts nonprofits, she knew that creating and maintaining a new organization was a significant commitment, so wanted to ensure it was the right option. There were some key moments on the path to ECI becoming a nonprofit [see Figure 2.1].

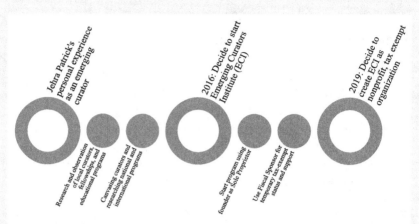

Figure 2.1 Key moments in the creation of the Emerging Curators Institute.

## CHOOSING YOUR LEGAL STRUCTURE

The arts industry includes for-profit companies, nonprofit organizations, government departments, and hybrid combinations of all three. Choosing the legal structure of your new venture is an important decision because it will drive everything in your business model and operations. Your legal structure should be considered a permanent decision; changing it would be difficult and may even require starting over with a new company. Factors to consider when choosing the right legal business structure include legal and financial liability, taxation, sources of revenue and capital, and control.

### Legal and Financial Liability

Creating a company or corporation creates a business entity that has the right and ability to enter into legal agreements, open and use bank accounts, employ people, make payments, get a website and social media accounts, and do all the things needed to do any of the arts activities you wish to do.

A nonprofit corporation operates separately from the individuals who run it. Legal and financial liability for actions taken by the company rests with the company itself. The people who work or volunteer at the nonprofit are not at risk of losing their personal assets (money, real estate, etc.) because of actions taken by the nonprofit. If a person breaks the law, they are liable. If the organization breaks the law, they are liable. But the *personal* assets of the people who work and volunteer for the organization are not at risk under most circumstances. Creating a separate company does not mean that there are no legal and financial *responsibilities* for the people who work and volunteer there, namely, that they must operate within all applicable laws.

The exact terms of liability are different for different types of companies, which is why liability is an important consideration when starting.

## Taxation

If you stopped a random person on the street, one of the things that they may claim to know is true about nonprofits is that they do not pay taxes. That is not true: nonprofits pay payroll taxes, sales taxes (though it is reimbursed in some states), occupancy taxes for hotels, and more. What they *do not* pay is tax on their net profits, like a for-profit business does.

A prudent approach to deciding the legal structure for a new organization is to create different, *realistic* (even pessimistic) financial scenarios (part of your business plan or business model) under different legal structures and see which scenarios show the best result. An important part of those scenarios is your tax liability (the taxes that you will need to pay). Your choice of legal structure AND the activities you undertake will determine your organization's liability. For example, if you plan on having paid staff, you will need to include payroll taxes under all legal structures. When you run the numbers for a LLC, include a line for applicable federal, state, and local taxes on your net revenue (profits). For a nonprofit, you will not need to include taxes on any net revenue earned on mission-related activities. Revenue derived from unrelated activities may be subject to Unrelated Business Income Tax. Experienced lawyers and accountants who work with small businesses and/ or nonprofit organizations can offer valuable advice. Lawyers and accountants often offer reduced fee, flat fee, or even pro bono services for nonprofits, including those just starting. It is important to choose someone who knows the state and local laws, rules, and regulations. Most states have an organization with a name such as "Volunteer Lawyers for the Arts" to help match clients needing pro bono work with volunteer lawyers. Asking for recommendations from others in your arts community better ensures finding someone who understands the situation of startup arts organizations.

### Sources of Revenue

What is your business model? Don't know? Don't start your nonprofit yet.

Founders of any new venture should choose the legal structure that aligns with their mission and a realistic business model, not the other way around. A free after-school arts and tutoring program for children living in homeless shelters is clearly serving a public good rather than creating private benefit. And funders exist currently for such a program, so that is a good candidate for a nonprofit legal structure. But what if you were interested in producing improv comedy, musical theater, teaching dance classes, or selling artwork? There are examples of both for-profit businesses and nonprofit organizations that do these activities.

Many people choose a nonprofit, tax-exempt structure for their new venture because when they run their financial scenarios, the expenses are higher than the revenue. They think, "Well, we'll just incorporate as a nonprofit and get donations to cover the rest!" A revenue shortfall is not a good enough reason to choose a nonprofit corporation as your legal structure. The work of the company must serve the public good and have a reasonably good chance of attracting donations. Many businesses lose money; not all of them could be justified as nonprofit, tax-exempt organizations or attract donations. Consider the factors in this chapter and in the rest of this book when choosing which legal structure is the right choice for your new organization. Talk to people who have founded organizations with both models about the pros and cons.

## Organizations CAN Earn Money as a Nonprofit

There is a common misconception that nonprofits cannot earn money through their activities and need to be entirely

Hannah Grannemann

reliant on contributions. Most arts organizations DO earn money from their own activities through ticket sales, admissions fees, tuition for educational events, etc.

Also – nonprofits are allowed to earn more than they spend. For a for-profit company, this would be called profit. For a nonprofit, income leftover after expenses is called a surplus. A nonprofit can earn and keep a surplus and use it in the future for its work. What makes a nonprofit a nonprofit is the limitation on ownership and distributing profits to owners and/or shareholders. Nonprofits cannot take those actions.

## Sources of Capital

Capital is the money needed for the things you need that will last longer than one year. Capital is usually used for items such as a building or equipment (that is why nonprofit fundraising campaigns to raise money for new buildings are called capital campaigns), but it can also be funds for employees or services that are meant to get the company or a big project started.

A for-profit company finances capital purchases and spending through retained earnings (savings from profit), borrowing money, or selling ownership stakes in the company. In the United States, a nonprofit has these same options, except for selling ownership stakes in the company – they are not allowed to do that. On the other hand, for-profit companies do not ask for donations, since they cannot offer tax deductions to donors and they are not operating primarily for the public good.

Ask yourself: where will you get the funds for your capital needs, like computers and equipment? Will you need offices, studios, a gallery, or a performance space that you fully control? Are you comfortable with fundraising for large amounts of money? Are you comfortable with debt? Let the answers to these questions inform your choice of legal structure. (See Table 2.1 for a chart with information about sources of capital for different types of corporations.)

**Table 2.1** Sources of capital for different types of corporations

| Source of Capital | Available to For-Profit Companies | Available to Nonprofit Companies |
|---|---|---|
| Retained Earnings (savings) | YES | YES |
| Borrowing Money | YES | YES |
| Selling ownership stakes (and later share profits and/or pay dividends) | YES | NO |
| Donations with charitable deductions for donor | NO | YES |

## Control

As a founder or group of founders, consider the level of control you want to have over the organization over the years. It is important for founders to accept that it is the board of directors – not the founders – that is ultimately in charge of any corporation, including a nonprofit corporation. The purpose of having a board of a nonprofit organization is that they are stand-ins for the public at large to ensure that the organization is indeed serving a public good. On a day-to-day level, they bring their skills and expertise to the organization to help it pursue its mission to the best of its ability. A board can be a valuable resource to the founders of an organization as it starts, grows, and sustains itself.

It is entirely possible that the founders' wishes and the board's wishes will diverge in big and small ways over time. Though founders choose the initial slate of board members (which may just be the founders themselves), board members choose new board members during the life of the organization. Therefore, any founder who plans to retain control by influencing the selection of board members will find themselves losing that control as the years go on, the size of the board grows, and board members join and leave.

If you truly want to retain control over the organization over the long term, consider creating a for-profit company, one of the alternative structures described later in this chapter. But if your business model depends on accessing the market of philanthropic dollars from individuals, foundations,

Hannah Grannemann

corporations, and government sources as a 501(c)3 (in the United States system), you might not have much choice than to accept that a board of directors is needed and that control over the organization will be shared with them.

## Nonprofit Incorporation

After deciding that a nonprofit corporation, tax-exempt structure under Section 501(c)3 of the United States Internal Revenue Service (IRS) Tax Code is right for you, the first step is to create your nonprofit corporation. Incorporating as a nonprofit is the first formal step in creating a new organization. A copy of accepted articles of incorporation is required for applying for tax-exempt status, which is the next step.

Though anyone CAN file all the paperwork for incorporation, it is more efficient to use a knowledgeable lawyer who has experience in this area. Using a lawyer will reduce mistakes that will delay the approval of the new corporation. You will need a lawyer that practices in your state. Ask colleagues, your local arts council, or your state service organization for nonprofits for recommendations for someone with experience, who has impeccable ethics and is easy to work with. As stated before, knowing that money at arts nonprofits is always tight, but especially at the start, there are lawyers who help with this kind of work for free (pro bono), at a reduced rate, or for a flat fee.

Nonprofit organizations are incorporated through state governments, not federal or local governments. That means that your primary identity is as a corporation in the state in which you incorporate. Even well-known nonprofits that work across the country, such as the American Heart Association, are incorporated in one state or have different, subsidiary corporations in the states in which they operate. Any organization who wants to work in multiple states should look carefully at the laws and rules in all states it wishes to operate in – your organization might be considered a "foreign" company in another state!

The office in your state that processes new applications for nonprofit corporations is usually called the Secretary of State. (Not to be confused with the Secretary of State in the federal government that leads international diplomacy – that is totally different.) Find the website for the Secretary of State in your state to learn about the specific process. If you are using an experienced lawyer, as recommended, they will already be familiar with the filing process. If you are not using a lawyer, use the resources listed at the end of this chapter throughout the process and ask colleagues for their articles of incorporation (try to get some samples from within the past 5–10 years).

The process of writing your articles of incorporation will focus your planning and force you to make some key decisions, since you will need to write a statement of purpose (mission statement), choose your initial slate of board members, and decide who will be your official representative.

---

## Mission Statements

You will need a statement of purpose (also known as a mission statement) for your articles of incorporation. That is how the state officials will tell if you are undertaking activities appropriate to being a nonprofit.

There is a balance to be struck between being specific enough to have a purpose that people can understand and being too specific that you risk limiting your actions too much. A simple way to think about your mission statement is for it to include (a) what art form you will be primarily creating, (b) what geographic area you will serve, and (c) who your primary audience or beneficiaries will be.

Your mission statement can change its wording over time, but if your company is totally changing its original purpose, then you are risking straying from the rationale under which your organization got its nonprofit status and tax exemption.

---

### Checklist for Articles of Incorporation

Specific requirements vary from state to state, but here are common requirements:

- Name of the corporation that is distinct from the name of other organizations in the same field.

- Statement of purpose that clearly shows that your work is for the public good and not private benefit and will meet the tax exemption requirements. This can also serve as your mission statement.
- List of initial/founding board members and contact information.
- Name of "Incorporator" (the person filing the paperwork, often one of the board members).
- Agent: person or company in the state in which you are incorporating designated to receive official notices for the corporation.
- Filing fee.
- Cover letter.

Filing is most likely done directly on your state's Secretary of State's website, and you will get a confirmation that they have received your submission. After they review your application, you will receive a determination letter stating if your incorporation application has been accepted. States may or may not give you reasons for rejecting your application, but you can reapply after revising your application. If you tried to incorporate on your own without a lawyer and were rejected, try using an experienced lawyer to create your subsequent applications for better success. As Jehra Patrick, founder of the ECI said, "I think I'd get lost if I tried to Google my way into that education process. Outside advice was really helpful."[3]

### CASE STUDY: THREE BONE THEATER

This case study is a compilation of comments from Robin Tynes-Miller, co-founder of Three Bone Theater.[4]

#### On Getting Started

So we actually were super lucky. One of my parents' neighbors had helped a theater in Florida start....And she recommended this organization called SCORE [Service Corps of Retired Executives] and SCORE is [a group of] retired business professionals. And you get assigned a mentor and they walk you through how to start a business and it can be for profit or nonprofit...So we went through that and that's how we developed our first business plan and our first marketing strategy and everything. ...Our mentor still comes to see shows....I think we're we're sort of a success story for him, which is really nice.

We talked with a lot of theatre companies is about their experiences and heard their advice, what their suggestions were. You have to take it all with a grain of salt. And everything works differently for different people, right? But that was really helpful for us.

## On the Benefits of Collaboration

We [Robin and Carmen] brought on Becky Schultz, who's our executive director, within our first season. She was an actress in The Vagina Monologues [one of Three Bone Theater's first productions]. I started talking with her and she had been in finance for her whole career. Carmen and I were keeping books by writing stuff down in a notebook. I was like, "please help us." She became our executive director and this is really why we're still around...You either want to be a theatre company that is putting on shows with your friends for your friends, which is fine and, like, really valid. Or you want to be like a sustainable organization, in which case you need to have business minded people involved. And if that's not you, then you need to go find a Becky.

I think it can be really challenging if you're going into a nonprofit thinking that you're going to get to call the shots. And especially around content, you want to make sure that you're bringing people on [to the board] who are going to support those decisions and maybe add to that. Definitely add to that conversation and ask questions and and challenge, but they are not going to derail...You can argue about the how, but you shouldn't be arguing about the why... That can't be up for debate. How we get there can totally be up for debate and should

Hannah Grannemann

be discussed and evaluated. And, you know, I think that's where we can really benefit from a board that is active, but...we shouldn't be having arguments and challenges about our values or why we exist or why we're doing what we're doing.

## Write Your Bylaws

Bylaws are the rules by which your board will function. They are as much a part of the founding documents as the articles of incorporation and getting tax exemption status. Adopt the bylaws by a vote of the board at the first board meeting. Keep official minutes (notes) of the meeting that are later approved by the board as an official record of the corporation. Submit your bylaws with your application for tax exemption.

Like your mission statement, write your bylaws to be specific enough so that your board members and staff know what to do, but not so narrow and specific in their procedures that the organization cannot function. Write them to allow yourself flexibility and make it easy to meet your self-defined minimum requirements. Find sample bylaws using the resources in the "Further Reading" section later in this chapter, from other organizations you know, or from your lawyer. There are many online resources for creating bylaws; just make sure to use tools and examples from reliable sources. Read several versions so you can get a sense of your options. Plan to review your bylaws every two to three years to make updates.

Bylaws will need some of the same information from the incorporation process, like your mission statement. You will also need to make decisions on items such as:

- **Specific purposes**: In addition to your mission statement, describe your anticipated activities. Define your planned programs broadly, but specific enough that a person reading it will be able to tell what you plan to do.
- **Officer positions, titles, and term limits**: The minimum required number of board members is often either one or three. If it is three, then they usually serve as the chair,

secretary, and treasurer respectively. Decide whether to have term limits for your officers as well as your "regular" board members. Consider how long the board members will serve and if those terms will be renewable and how many times. You will also need to think about the structure of your board: do you want to have a separate president and chairperson? Do you want vice-chairs? Can the secretary and treasurer be the same person? There are no definitive, accepted best practices about board and officer term limits. Some arts nonprofits allow board members to serve for many years, some have short limits (even one year), especially for officers.

- **Required number of board members and qualifications**: This can be described as a minimum or a range and should not contradict the number of members in your articles of incorporation. For qualifications, at least describe the qualifications as the age of legal majority in your state (likely 18 years old). Leave it there for maximum flexibility, but if you want to ensure a certain kind of representation on your board (e.g. voting membership for the founders or staff members reporting to the board), then describe additional membership requirements.

- **Minimum meeting schedule**: It is probably not a good idea to include frequent meetings in your bylaws, as you may fall out of compliance with your own rules (which can cause problems if there are ever legal issues that hinge on board decisions). You can always meet more often than your bylaws require, so consider the schedule in your bylaws as a minimum. Quarterly or every other month might be a good starting schedule.

## FILING FOR TAX EXEMPTION

In the United States, after the nonprofit corporation is established (meaning the articles of incorporation have been accepted by the state government) and bylaws adopted, applying for tax exemption is the next step. The concept behind tax exemption for nonprofit organizations is that our governments (federal, state, and local) and our society have decided to make a tradeoff: the governments (and we as the people) give up tax revenue from these organizations in exchange for having these organizations helping our society. Tax exemption is an indirect subsidy of the arts worth millions of dollars each year[5] and is a major recognition that the arts are valuable to American society. As mentioned earlier, tax-exempt status does not exempt the organization from all taxes, such as payroll taxes. Tax-exempt status means that the organization does not pay any taxes on the profits (annual surplus income) that they have at the end of their fiscal year.

Tax exemption is the route to getting donors to give money. Many grants from foundations, corporations, and government sources are only available to organizations that are tax exempt under the 501(c)3 regulation. Tax-exempt status marks the organization as a charity and makes it possible for donors to get a deduction on their taxes for their donations if they choose. Be careful – not all types of nonprofit organizations allow donors to deduct donations. Donations to nonprofits under the United States IRS tax codes 501(c)4 and 501(c)6 nonprofits are not deductible.

The categories considered eligible for tax exemption under Section 501(c)3 of the federal income tax law are "organized and operated exclusively for religious, charitable, scientific, testing for public safety, literary, educational, or other specified purposes and that meet certain other requirements". The types of organizations that fall under "certain other requirements" are "social welfare organizations, civic leagues, social clubs, labor organizations and business leagues".[6]

You will notice that arts are not explicitly listed as an activity that qualifies for exemption, though there are thousands of arts organizations with tax exemption under this code. During the incorporation process it is common for arts organizations to position themselves in terms of being an educational institution either implicitly or explicitly, even if they do not plan to hold classes or other direct educational activities. The rationale is that the artistic activity by its nature is an educational endeavor. Its presence in a community is educating the community. Your lawyer can advise on wording your application to best position your organization for approval. Reading other organizations' applications can be especially helpful.

Here are the steps to follow for getting tax-exempt status:

A.  Get an Employer Identification Number

    The IRS describes an Employer Identification Number (EIN) as similar to a social security number for a business. Having an EIN is necessary before applying for tax exemption.[7] Applying for an EIN is free[8] and can be done on the IRS website.

B.  Federal Tax Exemption

    Your corporation is created with your state government, but you will start your tax exemption process with the federal government by filing a Form 1023, *Application for Recognition of Exemption Under Section 501(c)(3) of the Internal Revenue Code*.

    Completing your Form 1023 could be the most tedious part of your startup process. The best part may be knowing that you will never need to do it again if you are successful with your first application. Again, it is recommended you use an experienced lawyer and/or an accountant who has filed paperwork for new nonprofit organizations (preferably arts organizations) to help you. They know the pitfalls and potential mistakes and having help will decrease the likelihood of your application being rejected and delaying the start of your formal activities. The Form 1023 is not the place to guess about your answers – use an expert.

    To file for federal tax exemption, complete and file a Form 1023 or Form 1023-EZ with the IRS and pay a filing fee (Form 8718). The EZ form is an option for organizations that have less than $50,000 in annual past or projected gross receipts (revenue). File for tax exemption within 27 months of filing your articles of incorporation. Filing within 15 months will allow your operations to be tax exempt from the point of creating your corporation rather than when your application for tax exemption is approved.[9] It is in your interest to file for tax exemption as soon as you can – it will save you from having to ask for an extension, you will pay less in taxes while you wait, and you will be able to offer your donors a tax deduction sooner.

    When you get confirmation from the IRS that you qualify (a "determination letter"), keep it in a safe place, and make some digital and hard copies. You will need this determination letter in the future for uses such as grant applications (to prove that you are eligible for grants limited to 501(c)3 organizations) and request that you are not charged sales tax by vendors.

C. State Tax Exemption

Once you have exemption from federal taxes you can apply for state tax exemption. Though it is a separate step, states generally give tax exemption to nonprofit corporations that have received federal tax exemption. You will need *all* that same paperwork again: articles of incorporation, bylaws – and your new IRS determination letter stating that the IRS has granted you tax-exempt status. Find the information on how to do this in your state on the Secretary of State or department of revenue or taxation website. It will be <u>much</u> simpler than the federal process.

## Keeping Your Incorporation and Tax-Exempt Status

There are steps nonprofit organizations need to take on a regular basis to stay in compliance with legal policies and procedures. Failure to keep up with these requirements could be detrimental to the ongoing operations of an organization and you could even be stopped from operating. Donors and supporters may lose confidence in the company and withdraw their financial support. It can be a lot of work to maintain a nonprofit organization. For example, The North Carolina Center for Nonprofit Organizations has an 8-page checklist for legal compliance for nonprofits that has 25 items that need to be done annually or every few years.[10] Before you create a new nonprofit, ask yourself: are you ready to keep your organization on the up-and-up legally? Here are a few actions you will need to take:

A. Registering as a charity with your state before raising money

Many states have a registration process before you can legally solicit charitable donations. Again, this is regulated at the state level. To make sure you are complying with this regulation, savvy donors, especially foundations, will ask for your organization's charity registration number as part of a funding application. Many organizations post their charity registration number on the donation section of their website.

B. Follow your bylaws and other corporate rules

You set the rules, now you must follow them. The board of directors needs to meet as often as your bylaws dictate. Minutes (notes) from the meeting must be kept and approved by the board as an accurate reflection of what happened at the meeting. Minutes should include, at minimum, a record of decisions made by the board. Meetings must follow your own rules on having a quorum (the required number of members to take an action), voting, etc. Board seats and officer positions should not be left open for long periods. The organization takes on more legal and financial risk when their own rules are not followed. If you are having a hard time envisioning your group keeping up with these kinds of rules, reconsider your path of creating a formal nonprofit organization and consider operating on a more informal basis.

C. Annual required filings

Recordkeeping is essential to be able to file required paperwork, especially financial records. Any business needs to keep accurate financial records not only to operate smoothly and efficiently but for legal reasons as well, and nonprofits are no different. Also, be aware that some of these documents will be available to anyone who wants to see them. Part of the philosophy of being a nonprofit that is subsidized by donors and relieved of paying many taxes is that the public has more of a right to know about the organization. For this reason, organizations are required to make more information public than private companies do. (Publicly traded companies are also required to make certain information public.) This transparency is rooted in an idea of accountability to the public in exchange for forgoing income taxes from the organization.

## Informational Tax Returns to State and Federal Agencies

The IRS requires that nonprofit organizations file an informational tax return annually. "But we don't pay taxes!", you will say. Right – your organization will be exempt from federal income taxes.

That is why it is called an *informational* tax return, a Form 990. You will likely want an accountant to help you with this form, especially if you are required to file the full Form 990. You will also need digital and perhaps hard copies for grant applications.

Like completing the Form 1023 when first getting tax-exempt status, there are nuances to completing this form that you will want to be aware of. You can see examples of other organizations' Form 990s because they are all made public. The organization Candid (formerly called GuideStar) and the media company ProPublica have made searchable databases of 990s.

## Good News!

If your nonprofit regularly earns less than $50,000 in a year, you are only required to file a "postcard" version of the annual informational tax return. Nonprofits earning less than $200,000 annually AND with assets valued at less than $500,000 can file the "EZ" version, which is also much shorter than the full version. You may go several years without filing heavily involved paperwork. However, that does not mean you should not keep detailed and accurate financial records – you need to do that no matter the size of the organization.

**Annual corporate report.** Most states require a simple annual filing to make sure you are still operating and update contact information. Unlike the informational tax returns, the due dates vary by state and are often related to the date the corporation was founded. Some lucky states (like Ohio) only require this type of report every five years; some unlucky states (like Oklahoma) require nonprofits to file a more extensive financial report.[11]

**Charity registration.** States requiring nonprofits to register as charitable organizations to raise money usually require an annual renewal of their status as an organization to solicit funds. Renew this registration annually or according to your state's schedule. Do not risk shaking the confidence of your donors and potential donors by falling out of compliance and letting your registration lapse.

## ALTERNATIVE STRUCTURES

Though not as common, it is possible to have another legal structure as an arts company. If you are clearly going to focus on making a profit through your endeavors, then a straight-forward for-profit structure like a corporation, an LLC, or partnership would be right for you. If your focus will clearly be on providing public good and your business model is heavily dependent on donations, then the nonprofit, tax-exempt organization is right for you.

But what if you are somewhere in-between? What if your goal is for you and your colleagues and collaborators to make the kind of art you want to make, and share it with people, but "break-even" is OK with you? Or you have an idea for a product or service that has social goals, but you do not anticipate needing very many donations for your business model? What if keeping control over the strategy and activities is important to you? Then you might want to consider one of the less common legal structures, such as:

- L3C, Benefit Corporations and Social Purpose Corporations: For these for-profit companies, profit is not their primary purpose. The purpose of creating a company of this type this category is to notify investors (the people that give you money for capital) that they might earn less profit on their investment compared to typical investment opportunities and to allow foundations to invest using the Program Related Investment (PRI) rules.[12]
- Hybrid organizations: It is possible to create "nesting" for-profit and nonprofit organizations that each have their own way of operating. Being diligent about the activities of each organization is essential so you do not risk the tax exemption of the nonprofit.
- Cooperative, Membership organizations: These are for-profit or nonprofit organizations that are owned and governed by members to ensure accountability. There is still a board, but this structure requires member voting on important issues and would encourage more participation from the people who participate in the work of the company.

Hannah Grannemann

- Unincorporated nonprofit association: If you are comfortable with a higher level of personal liability, you wish to stay with less formal affiliations or only want to have sporadic or infrequent activity, you can get tax exemption if your work is eligible and offer your donors charitable deductions without incorporating.

## CONCLUSION

It's hard to quell the voices of doubt...If you know everything about the process, you might not do it. So I think you want to absorb as much as you can and you go into it, you know, in a smart way and with eyes wide open. But if you want to do it, you also just have to do it.

– Robin Tynes-Miller, co-founder, Three Bone Theater

Though nonprofit corporations that are tax-exempt under the IRS Code 501(c)3 are the most common in the United States, it is important to be thoughtful about what legal structure will best fit the organization's goals. In addition to the areas of consideration outlined in this chapter, consider the competitive environment in which the organization will be entering and whether a new organization will be duplicating or will be perceived as duplicating the work of existing nonprofits, therefore hampering its ability to gather the needed support.

When creating a new nonprofit organization, there is great leeway in governance and staffing practices. Look beyond the historical ways of operating to disrupt the practices that have typically resulted in insular, opaque organizations that can inadvertently perpetuate unequal systems rather than improve our society.

To be sure, it is a lot of work to start a new nonprofit arts organization, and little of it has to do with creating art. But if your greatest satisfaction is collaborating with other people to make something that is more than the sum of its parts, there's nothing like starting your own organization.

## DISCUSSION QUESTIONS

- What did you know about how nonprofit organizations were structured before reading this chapter? What was new to you?

- Jehra Patrick took several years of study and early stages of the Emerging Curators Institute before deciding to create a new nonprofit, tax-exempt corporation. What were the benefits of her "walk before you run" approach?
- How comfortable are you with personal legal and financial liability for your artistic activities? Would you rather have more control and liability or less control and more protection?
- What are your thoughts on tax exemption for nonprofit arts organizations? Which arts organizations do you think should pay taxes: all of them, some of them, or none of them? Support your answer with logic and/or facts.
- Do you think you would want to start your own arts organization? Why or why not?

**FURTHER READING**

**Internal Revenue Service Website, Charities and Nonprofits Section (https://www.irs.gov/charities-and-nonprofits).**

Get the facts about how to get (and keep) your tax-exempt status, right from the source.

**ProPublica Nonprofit Explorer (https://projects.propublica.org/nonprofits/) and Candid (https://candid.org/).**

Find Form 990s from other nonprofits and foundations and other information about nonprofit organizations.

**BoardSource (https://boardsource.org/).**

Solid advice on everything related to boards of nonprofit corporations.

**National Council of Nonprofits (https://www.councilofnonprofits.org/).**

Resources, research, and advocacy for all types of nonprofits.

**Fractured Atlas (https://www.fracturedatlas.org/).**

A fiscal sponsor of artists and arts projects with a long-standing track record. Up to date advice and support for artists to build and sustain their creative careers.

**Notes**

1 Robin Tynes-Miller and Hannah Grannemann, Interview with Hannah Grannemann and Robin Tynes-Miller about the founding of Three Bone Theater, Video Conference, June 23, 2021.
2 Jehra Patrick and Hannah Grannemann, Interview with Hannah Grannemann and Jehra Patrick about the founding of the Emerging Curators Institute, Video Conference, July 19, 2021.
3 Patrick and Grannemann.
4 Tynes-Miller and Grannemann, Interview with Hannah Grannemann and Robin Tynes-Miller about the founding of Three Bone Theater.
5 Tyler Cowen, "How the United States Funds the Arts" (National Endowment for the Arts, October 2004), https://www.americansforthearts.org/sites/default/files/how_0.pdf.

6   Internal Revenue Service, "Exempt Organization Types," Federal Government Informational Website, Exempt Organization Types, June 1, 2021, https://www.irs.gov/charities-non-profits/exempt-organization-types.

7   Internal Revenue Service, *Applying for Tax Exempt Status Overview*, Video, Starting Out, 2021, 2, https://www.stayexempt.irs.gov/home/starting-out/applying-section-501c3-status.

8   Internal Revenue Service, "How to Apply for an EIN," accessed June 24, 2021, https://www.irs.gov/businesses/small-businesses-self-employed/how-to-apply-for-an-ein.

9   Internal Revenue Service, "Publication 557," February 2021.

10  North Carolina Center for Nonprofit Organizations, Inc., "Legal Compliance Checklist" (North Carolina Center for Nonprofit Organizations, Inc., 2018), https://www.ncnonprofits.org/sites/default/files/resource_attachments/2018LegalComplianceChecklist.pdf.

11  Anthony Mancuso, *How to Form a Nonprofit Corporation*, 5th ed. (Berkeley, CA: Nolo, 2002), Appendix A, http://search.ebscohost.com/login.aspx?direct=true&scope=site&db=nlebk&db=nlabk&AN=67338.

12  Peri Pakroo, *Starting & Building a Nonprofit: A Practical Guide*, 9th ed., 1 online resource vols. (Berkeley: Nolo, 2021), http://search.ebscohost.com/login.aspx?direct=true&scope=site&db=nlebk&db=nlabk&AN=2660284.

# Board Governance in the Arts

## Anthony Rhine and Jay Pension

## Chapter 3

### INTRODUCTION

One topic rarely addressed in arts administration training and education is the topic of governance. Students studying arts administration focus primarily on the work of staff members since that is the type of position they will likely have upon completing their degrees. Governance is the primary realm of the board of directors. However, developing clarity around what governance is and how it occurs is vital for arts administrators whether they someday serve on a board or continue working for the arts organization as an employee. Many students learn about the legal structure of organizations, but not how those legal structures operate in practice.

How do relationships work, occur, and interact with one another in the real world? These are the questions students often ask. The reality is that an executive nonprofit arts administrator will be both hired by a board and governance structure and then expected to inform and guide that governance structure while also being evaluated by that structure as an employee. The relationship between administration and governance can be difficult, strained, stressful, and often adversarial.

DOI: 10.4324/9781003207535-4

Understanding why that is and knowing how parties must interact with one another to better an arts organization falls squarely on the administrator. A board for a nonprofit arts organization may have supervisory (and hiring and firing) power over its administrator(s), but rarely do board volunteers understand how they are supposed to guide an organization, and they need help from a seasoned and experienced professional. As a result, arts administrators typically find themselves in a difficult predicament concerning governance. Though governance is the board's responsibility, arts administrators often support or even guide the process of governance.

Chapter 3 takes the reader through the process of governance at the board and executive levels. The examination begins with how executives and the board share duties and operate the organization. Following is a discussion of the documentation developed and used in best practice for recruiting and selecting board members, the relationships between executives and board chairs, and finally concludes with a thorough discussion about strategic planning and its essential value.

## BOARD GOVERNANCE IN THE ARTS

When we think of nonprofit arts organizations, we usually do not think about the governing structure that allows the organization to function with an eye toward the future. Governance is about the high-level planning and organizing needed to move an organization toward its vision. Before we dig too deeply into governance structures, we will review the mission and vision statements in terms of how they relate to governance.

### The Mission

If you Google nonprofit mission statements, you will find myriad examples and guides for crafting the perfect mission statement. You will likely discover that these definitions and examples are slightly different and guide you in slightly different directions. Many nonprofit arts organizations are confused about what a mission statement is really supposed to be and instead write an aspirational statement, which is typically a lengthy paragraph that speaks of "enlightening" the "community." The problem with enlightenment is that it has a different meaning to everyone. Additional terms that speak to how a person may or may not feel likewise do little to help people understand the organization's mission. The term *Community* can also be misleading. Is that a community within a neighborhood? Of a region? City? State? Country? A global community?

When it comes to governing an organization, the mission statement is the guide developed by the board, often with the guidance of the staff, that ultimately defines how decisions are made. The mission statement defines whom the organization serves and how they are served. It has been said that famed business expert Peter Drucker once advised that mission statements should fit on a bumper sticker. The typical bumper sticker is about ten words long, which would seem impossibly short for a single statement that defines whom an organization serves and how—but it can be done.

Consider this statement: "We bring clean, safe drinking water to people in developing countries." The statement is brief (short enough for a bumper sticker), clear on whom the organization serves (people in developing countries), and describes how its mission is fulfilled (bringing safe, clean drinking water). Every decision the organization makes can and should be held against this question: *Will this decision help bring safe, clean drinking water to people in developing countries?*

The big trick to the mission statement for a nonprofit arts organization is figuring out whom you serve. When you say, "the community," or even "citizens of the city of..." you define your market as everyone. Though the arts are certainly designed for everyone, not everyone wants or needs the arts, or at least they have not yet learned that they want and need the arts. Is this organization then serving art lovers, those who have yet to find a love for the arts, artists, or the art itself? It may seem like a simple question, and it is fundamental, but it can be tricky. Remember that the mission statement will guide decision-making. So, if you serve a city's music lovers who want to hear music like a Mozart Requiem, the decision should not be to produce a rock concert to give the artists something exciting to perform. The mission of the organization, in this case, is not to serve artists.

A note about this concept: There is nothing wrong with an arts organization existing to serve its artists. Many do, even if few of them actually say so in their missions. They simply state in their mission that they serve the community but then make decisions that are more focused on serving the artist. However, if the organization is governed most efficiently and effectively, the mission statement will guide decisions and vitally establish whom it serves exactly.

So, the mission statement is a brief, concise, clear statement of a handful of words that guides an organization by stating whom the organization serves and how those people are served. "Symphonies for Sunnyvale" is an excellent example of a mission statement that accomplishes these goals. The organization serves the citizens of Sunnyvale with symphonies. It is then also a directive from the board to the chief executive and the staff. The directive is an unspoken instruction that decision-making in the organization should be driven by this guiding question: *Will this decision help provide symphonies to the citizens of Sunnyvale?*

**The Vision**

Visions are aspirational, but the term "vision," can also mean a mental picture of the future. For the nonprofit arts board, if the mission statement guides the staff on whom to serve and how to serve them, the vision statement tells the staff what direction to head and where they are going. The vision statement explains what the world will look like if the nonprofit arts organization completes its mission. Consider this vision: "No Hunger." It is a statement of what the world will be like when the organization has completed its mission and can now fold up tent or pivot to a new vision. When there is no hunger in the world, that organization will no longer need to exist.

The Sunnyvale Symphony might have a vision like this: "The Sunnyvale Symphony works to be able to ultimately provide ample, self-sustaining symphonies available for free to the public." This vision statement might suggest that long-term, the organization wants to have the financial resources in place to endow the symphony forever. However, a vision statement like this: "We see Sunnyvale as the world's premier location for new symphonic works," would suggest that decision-making must be incredibly different than it would under our first example. What is important for the organization's governance is that the vision is highly unlikely and challenging but not completely impossible. Though you may not be someone who walks around having "visions" that tell you how to run your life or business, the vision statement is an opportunity to have that sort of guidance.

The process of brainstorming and developing these statements can and should be as deliberate and detailed as the statements. If used correctly, they are the guiding principles for the organization, and they should be visible and transparent to the community in which the organization is based. The statements hold the staff accountable to both the board and the constituents.

However, this is not to suggest that missions or visions are immutable. In fact, an active nonprofit regularly reassesses those statements to ensure that the organization is approaching them appropriately and that it has the resources, desire, and some sort of community mandate to execute them. When there is a disconnect from the mission and vision, the organization can either course correct to return focus on those statements or write new guiding principles to allow the organization to better take advantage of its strengths and opportunities.

**LEARNING OBJECTIVES**

After reading this chapter learners should be able to...

- Describe the value of job descriptions for a nonprofit arts organization board and staff.
- Identify the approaches a nonprofit board might take in selecting new board members.
- Outline the responsibilities of a board in governing a nonprofit arts organization.
- Summarize the relationships that exist between boards, executives, and other staff.
- Explain strategic planning and some of the steps many organizations take in creating a strategic plan.

## CASE STUDY: THE COMMUNITY HOUSE

The Community House is a nonprofit organization in Hamilton, Massachusetts, a small town north of Boston. The organization's roots go back to the end of World War I when the Mandell family purchased a plot of land and had a building erected in memory of eight local soldiers (including their son) who lost their lives during the war. The building was the foundation of a service organization that eventually established 501(c)(3) status. They served their community by providing a space for meetings and events. The organization also provided space for community members and other organizations to offer classes on various topics for the community.

In the mid-2010s, The Community House began designing and promoting arts programming offered directly by the organization itself. This expanded undertaking was a significant shift for the organization from serving primarily as a venue to becoming a community arts organization that produced theatre, music, and educational arts offerings. For decades, the organization's mission centered on The Community House's value as a physical space rather than as an organization that produced programming.

Executive Director, Melissa Elmer, recognized the community's changing needs and the shift in how the nonprofit was serving that community. To reflect the ongoing change within the organization, she created a committee composed of staff, board members, and stakeholders from the community to redesign the mission statement. The committee recognized that the mission statement should guide everything the organization does, so careful consideration in creating a new statement was vital. The committee spent several weeks creating multiple options to reflect what the organization was already doing and what they could do to meet the community's needs.

Ultimately, The Community House began operating under a statement that officially shifted its focus to the arts and events, becoming a new community arts organization for the cities and towns north of Boston. The new statement reads: "The Community House is dedicated to enrichment through arts and events that promote togetherness and strengthen the community." Since the transition to the new statement, The Community House has continued to thrive. They have experienced continued growth in the number of programs and productions they offer and the number of community members they serve. Though an organization should not consistently change its mission statement, there are many examples, like The Community House, where, after many years, a nonprofit should consider reviewing its mission statement to ensure it still reflects the organization's practices and the community's needs.

## OPERATIONALIZING A BOARD

As noted in the previous chapters, creating a board of directors in order to incorporate is a requirement for a nonprofit organization in the United States. However, few guidelines mandate what a board must do and how it must do it. Though the board is the oversight body for the nonprofit organization, and their function is to represent the public's best interests in their oversight, boards are rarely initiated with this intention. Typically, the first boards are hand-picked to be accommodating and helpful, but with little instruction on oversight, fiscal or otherwise. Nevertheless, the public has entrusted the board to make effective decisions for the benefit of the public good, which is the essence of the 501(c)(3) tax code. It is designed to allow the organization to exist for the public benefit, and shepherding that notion is the board's function.

The board has essentially three functions: To supervise the fiscal stability of the company, to set a strategic direction and plan for the company, and to hire and evaluate the chief executive.[1] Beyond this, when board members participate in the organization, they typically do so not as a member of the board, but only as a volunteer.[2] Board members can and often do wear many hats for the organization, but when they volunteer, they are working for the executive, and when they are board members the executive works for them. It is a slightly confusing and even more precarious set of relationships than many would care for, but it is how the process works.

## The Executive Staff

The chief executive, often referred to as the executive director in nonprofit arts organizations, is often the one employee hired and supervised by the board of directors. Although responsible for the nonprofit's daily operations, the executive director also serves as an advisor to the board of directors, though typically not a voting member. Though they may attend board meetings in a consulting or advisory capacity, the chief executive is rarely a board member. Most granting agencies for arts organizations would not provide funding to organizations where the executive was also a voting member of the board. This position stands to reason, as the conflict-of-interest is great, and the chance for problems increases when the executive is also a board member, especially due to the executive director's advisory capacity.

As a result, the executive is often the only person responsible directly to the board and is also the person responsible for guiding the board.[3] Again, that strange juxtaposition can make for challenging communication and relationships. However, board members cannot be expected to spend countless hours trying to corral and communicate with all members of the board, so it is incumbent on the executive to work as both executive and assistant to the board chair or the entire board.

## The Board Manual

It has probably been said a million times that boards would be so much easier to work with if they came with a manual. Board members might say the same thing about staff members, though staffs seem to have a great deal more clarity about their functions and roles and how that intersects with the board. The challenge, of course, is not that there is a need for instructions on interacting with others but agreement on how boards and their members will operate. In order to achieve this, a nonprofit may choose to develop a board manual that includes these details and guides board members in their work for the organization.

Anthony Rhine and Jay Pension

## Job Descriptions

One of the primary ways staff members know how each other works, interacts, and intersects is through job descriptions that lay out expectations for the employee. The job description is an agreement that defines the duties and responsibilities of the employee within the organization and the skills required to do the work. Though many people think about staff when they consider job descriptions, for nonprofit boards especially, job descriptions can be particularly useful.[4]

When thinking about job descriptions for a nonprofit arts organization board, the notion seems almost absurd since board members are typically volunteering their time, energy, and resources. Many companies avoid job descriptions for board members as they make the relationship feel like it is a transaction, much like a position of employment, particularly since the job description is a type of contract. However, the job description allows both the company and the board member (or potential board member) a clear understanding of expectations up-front at the beginning of the relationship.

With a volunteer board, subtle nuances are required in drafting board member job descriptions, particularly as the board's function is a fiduciary one with the added obligation of overseeing the long-term stability and development of the organization.[5] The job description will be limited to the work required in the capacity of a board member. That is to say, if board members are expected to volunteer in an additional capacity, ushering, for example, then the job description should indicate there is an expectation that the board member will also serve as volunteer labor for the organization for a certain amount of time. However, the board member job descriptions should not detail the duties and responsibilities of the volunteer labor work.[6] That information belongs in a separate job description for volunteer labor.

Why create two separate job descriptions? Board members hold a unique position in that they are there to look at the long-term stability and growth of the organization and, typically, are responsible for hiring, evaluating, and terminating one chief executive.[7] Beyond this employee, the board does not oversee staff or make daily decisions for the organization. When a board member steps into a volunteer position, they assume work supervised by a staff member. If the roles are not clearly defined in two separate job descriptions, then who is reporting to whom, and more importantly, who answers to whom, can create quite a controversy and lead to innumerable problems. This is not to suggest that there is no need to show deference to a board member when they are wearing their "volunteer labor" hat; it is important to understand the distinction for everyone involved.

## Board Descriptions

What goes into a board member job description? Two vital aspects need to appear in the board member's job description to be as detailed and clear as possible, assuring clear communication. Those two aspects are the skills and abilities required *for* a board member and the duties and responsibilities expected *of* the board member. What is included in each of these is up to the individual board and organization. These aspects also do not have to be separately labeled sections, but the content of those two topics needs to appear in the job description. For example, board job descriptions often begin with expectations about governance and leadership of the organization that details how the board member will participate in strategic planning, monitoring and approving the budget, working collaboratively with the chief executive officer (CEO) and board, evaluating the CEO, serving on board committees, representing the organization in a favorable light to the public, overseeing and evaluating performance metrics, and assisting in recruiting other board members. This list is not exhaustive but suggests the high-level responsibility of the board member.

Another section of the job description may address fundraising, donations, and volunteerism. It may define expectations of fundraising and contribution that indicate what the board member is expected to give (or get) every year, and often, this section also explains that the reason for this requirement is to ensure that outside donors see 100% participation from the board. Often the section continues with an explanation of the volunteer labor requirements that the board member is expected to meet, or this may be rolled into a larger section about additional expectations. In the latter instance, this would be the place to detail how many board meetings, committee meetings, and additional events or meetings the board member would be expected to attend in a given year. If the board member is expected to provide volunteer labor, a clear explanation should be supplied in the board member's job description, along with how much and what degree of labor is expected on a regular basis. For a board member who also volunteers, this second job description becomes an addendum to their board member job description.

Frequently, the board member job description also contains a section that details the structure of the board position as defined in the organization's by-laws. For example, it may detail the length of term, the selection of board officers, the number of scheduled meetings planned in a given year, and other operational issues affecting its members.

Finally, the board member's job description needs a section detailing the qualifications required to be an effective board member. For example, this could include expertise in a specific business area such as finance or marketing. For board officer positions, separate job descriptions need to exist that expand upon the general board position, explaining further responsibilities and expectations for individual officers, such as president, secretary, and treasurer.

### CASE STUDY: PUNCTUATE4

Punctuate4 is a nonprofit theatre company dedicated to developing new pieces of theatre. A small group of artists and administrators formed a board and incorporated it in May 2018. The company serves its community by presenting theatre for audiences and also by working with and supporting playwrights. They assist playwrights with their writing, offer dramaturgical support, and produce readings and full productions of new plays.

Since they founded the company, Puntuate4 has operated with a working board and no year-round staff members. The company has hired temporary employees to support production needs on a production-by-production basis, but board members have stepped beyond their role as board members to manage the operations that staff would traditionally control. Initially, this model worked well for the organization. It allowed the company to be nimble and closely integrate the founding principles into every decision. Over time, however, the function of this working board became strained.

The organization faced a challenge too few arts organizations face in their early years: rapid growth. Punctuate4 quickly found that their community craved their work. The company developed and produced more new plays with greater depth than could be reasonably expected given their short organizational history. As a result, board members began taking on ever-growing responsibilities to keep up with demand. Though met with rapid growth, the founders were not yet able to hire an executive director to take on the administrative load that rested with the board.

The founders conducted a job analysis to streamline their work, clarify what was happening, and prepare to hire the organization's first year-round administrative staff members. Before the job analysis, position descriptions for the board and administrative positions did not exist. The analysis collected the responsibilities of every board member to create a full picture of every administrative component the board was managing—and how much time each component demanded. They then used all the data to create clear position descriptions. They were careful to separate administrative duties from board responsibilities so that board job descriptions and staff job descriptions did not overlap.

The descriptions were not specific to the individual performing the duties. Instead, each board member could opt-in (or out) for different positions and fulfill each position's needs. In addition, the job descriptions provided clear lines between responsibilities as board members and responsibilities of staff (or volunteer) positions. This clarity that resulted from the job descriptions allowed for better decision-making, enhanced communication, and, ultimately, more effective operation within the organization.

Anthony Rhine and Jay Pension

## Mandating Donations

One question that often arises, particularly in relation to board member job descriptions, is how to address a requirement for an annual donation to the organization. Many organizations pride themselves on the fact that every member of their board donates annually to the organization. How much a board member should donate is up to the individual organization to determine. Nevertheless, whatever the requirement is (if it exists) should appear on the job description as an expectation of the board member on an annual basis. Some organizations prefer not to set a minimum amount of required donation but, instead, request a gift commensurate with the board member's ability to give. Many organizations ask that each board member make the organization their top giving priority. In contrast, others may require board members to "give or get" a certain amount of money each year, suggesting that the obligation is to either make a personal donation or find others who will make an equal amount of contribution.

Certainly, many organizations choose to set a minimum contribution required for members of their board, and this is by no means unusual or uncouth. By making it clear on the job description what amount of contribution (if any) is expected of the board member, prospective board members can make an objective decision about whether or not to invest their time, energy, and money into the position. However, arts organizations should work to make board service as accessible as possible to diversify board voices. If a "give or get" policy stands in the way of developing diverse opinions and perspectives on the board, it may be wise to reconsider its use.

## SELECTING BOARD MEMBERS

One question that often arises among nonprofit organizations is how to recruit new board members. A Google search might lead to lots of great advice about how to engage in the board recruiting process, but the advice often seems to be counterintuitive. If an organization works with well-drafted board member job descriptions, the process should become much simpler and more of a true hiring process than a game of darts.

## Determine Needs

Before engaging in board recruitment, it behooves the organization to take stock of their needs in an individual board member. What areas of expertise are required of this person? Does the organization need a financial mind, a community engagement mind, an ADEI (access, diversity, equity, and inclusion) mind, a marketing mind, a well-connected socialite, a lawyer, a businessperson, a civic leader, a Chamber of Commerce leader, or someone with another skill set? The specific expertise may not be a requirement in the job description, but it is important to know what you are planning for this board member to bring to the table.

By not clearly defining what needs must be satisfied by the prospective board member, the organization runs the very real risk of asking someone to join the board who cannot bring the appropriate expertise to the board. For example, suppose an organization needs someone who can eventually step into the role of board chair. In that case, it is an important need to address with a potential board member, who may be capable of the duties but not willing, or vice versa.

## Determine Prospective Member's Rationale and Interest

Once it is clear to the organization the type of person needed for the role of a new board member, it then becomes the job of someone in the organization to determine potential candidates who can satisfy the organization's needs. Within an organization, sometimes there are specific people tasked with identifying potential board prospects. These people can include a committee of, or specific members from the existing board, the board chair, the chief executive, the director of development (particularly if needs have to do with donations), or some other identified member of the organization. For the board recruiting process to work as smoothly as possible, all invested stakeholders involved in the hiring process should have regular meetings to discuss people under consideration to stay abreast of the process.

As potential candidates are identified, it is important to understand their abilities and willingness to serve and get a sense of their rationale for serving. Occasionally, a new board member joins to strengthen their resume or acquire the prestige of appearing on the board, but their desire is not to contribute to, support, or help grow the organization. Inevitably, these become non-working board members whose contributions to the organization can be as much a detriment as they are a benefit.

## Trying the Fit On

One of the smartest ways to incorporate new board members into an organization is to allow them to be "visiting" members for a period of time. This experience allows them to participate (without a vote) in board activities, work with the board chair and CEO, and get a sense of how the operation runs. It also allows all parties involved to ask questions of one another during the visiting period. After several meetings, both the board and the potential member should have a good sense of where each other is and how they might work together. At that point, the time is right to make the relationship official—or not. The visiting period also provides an opportunity to ensure that prospective board members will have the tools necessary to fully participate and be satisfied in their service as a board member.[8]

## RELATIONSHIPS AND OPERATIONS

The CEO and chair relationship is important for a well-functioning nonprofit arts organization.[9] It is symbiotic in the sense that they work in close cooperation with one another to keep both of their roles functioning appropriately. There are several areas where the board chair and the CEO have duties or responsibilities that can sometimes overlap or run perilously close to one another. Therefore, to avoid confusion, it is essential to understand the responsibility of each in the organization.

## Staffing and Salaries

The board chair (and the board as a whole) are responsible for hiring the chief executive. Typically, all other staff hiring, firing, and salary decisions are made by that executive (or their designee). In some nonprofit arts organizations, the board may choose to also hire the artistic director or the main artistic executive within the organization as part of the mandate from the mission. However, boards that hire executives both on the administrative and the artistic sides typically refrain from any staffing decisions beyond those two positions. All other staffing positions are hired, supervised, disciplined, and fired by the executive or the artistic executive.

Salaries for the chief executive and the artistic executive are determined by the board chair or the board as a whole. Additionally, salaries for staff members hired by the executives are determined by those executives, based upon the amount of money allotted for salaries within the board-approved budget. It is important to note and reiterate that the board chair and the board do not hire, fire, set salaries for, supervise, or evaluate any staff members except the executive and perhaps the artistic executive. The executives or their designees make all other staffing decisions.

## Board Meetings and Committees

The needs of the organization determine the size of the board. The number of board members, particularly with large boards, can become quite unwieldy when making specific policy decisions. So, boards often organize themselves by having standing committees that vet ideas and proposals and bring suggestions to the board for final approval. Typically, nonprofit arts organizations have a finance committee responsible for overseeing the budget and audit processes. In addition, a fundraising committee often assists the development director and chief executive in their work, raising funds for the organization. Other committees can be developed, including ad hoc committees, that the chair can create on a case-by-case basis.

At board meetings, the board chair is in charge. However, the chief executive and the staff work with the board chair to develop the meeting agenda to prepare for board meetings. Additionally, the staff may prepare materials for the entire board at its meeting, and the executive typically participates in board meetings without a vote. As noted, many funders are not willing to provide grants and support to organizations where the staff members, including the executive, have a vote on the board. For this reason, many nonprofit arts organizations allow the executive to participate in board meetings without having a vote, as an ex officio board member, a title that is granted due to their status or the position they hold.

## Financial Management and Budgets

The board chair, and often the treasurer, holds responsibility for the financial management of the nonprofit arts organization.[10] The executive typically brings a recommended budget to the board each year, often with income projections and anticipated expenses from the staff. However, it is the board, and ultimately the chair, who approves the budget. The process is usually handled by the board treasurer, who works with the company's financial manager to develop the final budget. That proposal would then be taken to the board's finance committee (often chaired by the board treasurer) for discussion, vetting, and ultimately a recommendation to the full board. The full board then votes on approving (or not) the final budget at the behest of the board chair.

The board is also responsible for overseeing both internal and external audits of the organization. For example, many granting agencies require nonprofits that receive funds to demonstrate their solvency by providing an external audit. Likewise, many states require annual audits based on the size of the organization's revenues.

Though the board holds the ultimate responsibility for the organization's finances, the executive and staff are responsible for managing the day-to-day funds of the organization. They are charged with meeting the budgetary goals and projected income numbers that are detailed in the budget. The budget is often used as one metric for measuring the performance of the staff and, ultimately, the chief executive.

## Evaluations for the Board and CEO

The executive or their designee is responsible for the supervision and evaluation of staff members. The executive lays out duties and responsibilities for each staff member and holds those staff members accountable to those duties and responsibilities. The evaluation records can be tracked over time and used to review a staff member's effectiveness.

The board chair is responsible for coordinating board member evaluations (typically annually) and evaluating the board's overall effectiveness. The executive sometimes facilitates this, but the results are designed for the board chair and the board to be self-evaluating. Occasionally, a board may opt to contract an outside firm to conduct a board evaluation to provide a perspective that reaches beyond self-evaluation.

The board also evaluates the chief executive based on specific goals and benchmarks laid out for their performance. Those goals are often found in a job announcement or description. However, to ensure the most objective evaluation, goals should be stated in SMART ways: specific, measurable, attainable, relevant, and time based.

Associated with evaluations is a plan of succession for both staff and board members. The board is responsible for planning how board members depart as their terms end and filling the departing members' contributions to the board. They also manage succession planning for the chief executive position, ensuring there is an appropriate pipeline of talent being developed should the executive position need to be filled. The executive is responsible for succession planning within the ranks of the staff.

### Policies and Procedures

Though the terms *policy* and *procedure* are often mentioned together, and many organizations have binders or books labeled "policies and procedures" for the staff to follow, the terms belie different concepts. Policies discuss why the organization does something and usually stem directly from the organization's mission, vision, values, and strategic plan. Policies, most specifically, are shaped by and help demonstrate the organization's values. Procedures are guides for how to do something within the organization. Procedures are typically nested within the appropriate policies but explain the steps necessary for accomplishing a task. Board members typically develop organizational policies in line with the nonprofit's mission and visions.[11] The executive or their designees often create organizational procedures to fulfill these policies.

### STRATEGIC PLANNING

Strategic planning is one of the board's primary responsibilities. However, that is not to suggest that every nonprofit arts organization operates on a strategic plan, as many arts organizations confuse annual season planning for strategic planning; but the two are vastly different.[12] Strategic planning is a process whereby the board determines the future pathway for the organization, defines who will do what, how it will be done, and by when. The strategic plan defines the organization's future and how it will operate on its way to that future.

The process of strategic planning requires significant research to provide data that can inform discussion and debate. The first step in any strategic plan requires an accurate evaluation of the starting place from which the organization will build. Creating the most accurate picture of the organization at the plan's start provides a useful baseline. Unfortunately, the greatest amount of time in strategic planning is often spent brainstorming what the future should be, while too little time is spent determining constructive steps to accomplish the goals.

There are many experts who propose disparate approaches to conducting a strategic planning session, and any number of steps that can be involved in the process. Let us take a look at the main functions of strategic planning and what activities experts agree must occur in the process.

### Evaluation of Mission, Vision, and Values

To evaluate mission, vision, and values, organizations first determine and define what they are mandated to do by the government and their community, what the expectations are for the organization, and how it must behave. Then, once mandates are determined, the board, often with participation from the staff, will evaluate and rewrite (if it is determined necessary) the organizational mission, vision, and values. This assessment gives the organization a periodic opportunity to evaluate whether the organization is drifting from its mission, if organizational values are still meeting and exceeding societal expectations, and, most importantly, if the future vision for the organization is coming more closely into view.

### Develop a SWOT

In this process, the board considers the available data about the organization (typically provided by staff) and develops an analysis that looks at the core strengths, weaknesses, opportunities, and threats (SWOT) facing the organization. As you may imagine, with a thoroughly vetted list of all the strengths and weaknesses from inside the organization and opportunities and threats from outside the organization, the board can see more clearly where a path to the future seems the rosiest. One note about SWOT: sometimes, people will say that an issue is both a strength and a weakness. Full houses provide a good example. As a strength, it may mean the organization is reaching many community members. As a weakness, it means there may be no room for growth. However, if the same item appears on more than one list, the item has not been drilled down far enough. In our example, the strength is that the organization can capture a full house for its entire run. The weakness is not that the house is full but that there may not be enough performances to accommodate every potential audience member. Note that these two things are different. The full houses are a strength, but they also cause a limitation, which is the weakness.

## Determine Issues to Be Addressed

This decisive step is at the heart of strategic planning. Up until this point, the board has examined and defined where the organization is at present. By fully understanding the realistic situation, the board can determine, again often with staff assistance, what reasonable goals to reach for throughout the strategic plan, typically about two to three years. The goals could be as simple as increasing sales by 10% or as complex as building a new building. They can be to increase community participation, improve quality, expand staffing, or just about anything. What is important is that the goals move the organization from its present position closer to its vision of the future. It is important to remember that these should be SMART goals: specific, measurable, attainable, relevant, and time based.

## Turn Issues into Duties

Once strategic goals are determined, benchmarks must be set along the timeline of the strategic plan to ensure that work is directed toward the goals. These benchmarks determine how far along the organization should be in achieving each strategic goal. Also, in this process, specific people are assigned specific duties as part of the strategic plan roadmap that describes and details where the organization is headed, and who will take what steps by when to get it there. In this process, various steps will be taken between inception and completion of the plan, and resources allocated for strategic plan execution.

### Share, Review, and Approve the Plan

At this point, the plan is largely complete, but the plan is circulated for feedback to ensure full buy-in from all stakeholders and make certain that no errors or omissions have occurred. Of course, how far and wide the plan is distributed depends upon the individual organization. For a nonprofit arts organization, it would make sense that the plan should also be made available to the community, regular patrons, and donors for comment beyond the full board and staff.

### Establish Evaluation Processes

In this stage, the board determines who will evaluate progress on the plan, how often that progress will be evaluated, and how the board will address deficiencies in the plan. Any deficiencies could mean that the plan must be revisited to assess if it was too ambitious in its goals, or not ambitious enough if the goals are too easy to meet. In addition, evaluation serves to characterize the sincerity with which the board and chair have made it their responsibility and priority to ensure that the plan is being taken seriously, focused on, and put into action. Far too often, organizations spend considerable amounts of time developing a strategic plan, only to skip this determination of how it will be periodically evaluated, and as a result, the plan sits on a shelf gathering dust.

## A Note about the Strategic Planning Process

Though some organizations can conduct and complete the process within a single meeting of an hour or two, the process generally takes significant deliberation to consider all applicable options and possibilities. Often boards will have a weekend retreat, sometimes with the staff, to focus entirely on the strategic plan. Other organizations will dedicate weekly or monthly meetings over the course of several months to the process. However, the strategic planning process occurs—it is important to note that when done correctly, the process usually takes a substantial amount of time.

## When to Do Strategic Planning

Organizations often ask when they should be doing strategic planning or how often it needs to be done. These questions do not have easy answers, and for every organization, they may differ. If done correctly, the strategic plan is a living document that is worked on and constantly evaluated from inception until the strategic goals have been met. At which point, the organization will embark on its next strategic plan. How long does one plan take? That is determined in the planning process; however, it is unusual for a strategic plan to reach further than five years into the future, as accomplishing plans that reach too far into the future becomes more difficult as the world and societies change around the plan. Most organizations devise strategic plans slated to take two to three years to accomplish, at which point, a new strategic planning session occurs, and a new plan is put into place.

## DISCUSSION QUESTIONS

- Why do you think nonprofit boards should hold financial responsibility rather than individual staff members? Should they, or should they not? Why, or why not?
- The chapter noted that strategic plans often focus on a future vision rather than on how to achieve the vision. Why do you think that is a common factor? What could be done to fix this?
- The chapter noted that mission statements can evolve. In what ways do you think a change in mission statement may impact the organization?
- If you were meeting with a prospective board member, what type of questions would you want to ask?
- Boards typically conduct self-evaluations. Do you think this is a positive approach? In what ways do you think a board's self-evaluation helps the organization? In what ways might it hurt?

### Notes

1 Walmsley, Ben, "Arts and Cultural Management," *Entertainment Management: Towards Best Practice*, CABI 2014, 157.
2 Forenza, Brad, "Sustained Community Theater Participation as Civil Society Involvement," *Nonprofit and Voluntary Sector Quarterly* (2016), doi: 10.1177/0899764016660385.

Anthony Rhine and Jay Pension

3  Murray, Kevin, "Theater Production Management Guidebook," *The Arts Management Handbook: New Directions for Students and Practitioners* (2015): 38.

4  Brown, Gerry, *The Independent Director: The Non-Executive Director's Guide to Effective Board Presence,* Springer, 2015.

5  Hiland, Mary, "The Next Level: Understanding Effective Board Development," In *Leading and Managing in the Social Sector,* pp. 139–154. Springer International Publishing, 2017.

6  Murray, "Theater Production Management Guidebook".

7  Walmsley, "Arts and Cultural Management".

8  Hiland, "The Next Level".

9  Brown, Gerry, *The Independent Director: The Non-Executive Director's Guide to Effective Board Presence,* Springer, 2015.

10  Hiland, "The Next Level".

11  Walmsley, "Arts and Cultural Management".

12  Rhine, Anthony. (2015). An Examination of the Perceptions of Stakeholders on Authentic Leadership in Strategic Planning in Nonprofit Arts Organizations. *The Journal of Arts Management, Law, and Society* 45: 3–21. doi:10.1080/10632921.2015.1 013169.

# Access, Diversity, Equity, and Inclusion (ADEI) in Cultural Organizations

## Challenges and Opportunities

Antonio C. Cuyler

# Chapter 4

While working at Florida State University (FSU), Anthony had the fortunate opportunity to work with Dr. Antonio C. Cuyler, a prominent academic with a research focus on diversity and equity issues in arts administration. When Jay began his academic pursuits at FSU, he also met Dr. Cuyler through academic conferences, and later, Dr. Cuyler was one of Jay's professors. Dr. Cuyler is a published author of several works

DOI: 10.4324/9781003207535-5

and is well-regarded internationally for his consistent focus on exploring what is happening with *access, diversity, equity, and inclusion* (ADEI) in the arts and how inequities can be ameliorated. In addition, Dr. Cuyler provides consulting services to arts organizations in the area of ADEI. Because the arts have such a powerful mechanism in place for helping shape the social conscience, Dr. Cuyler's field of research is urgently needed, long overdue, and vitally important. For this reason, he has named the chapter "Access, Diversity, Equity, and Inclusion (ADEI) in Cultural Organizations: Challenges and Opportunities." He sees the negatives and obstacles of the past, present, and a future where the arts can take the lead on re-shaping how we think about societal adversities and how to neutralize them.

One particular aspect that can be troubling for emerging research areas is that working definitions are often loose, changing, and unstructured. Dr. Cuyler addresses this issue by developing a working framework from which he organized this chapter. The reader can distinguish specific effects on ADEI from this framework. Dr. Cuyler also leads the reader on a path, debunking some of the most common myths surrounding issues of ADEI before exploring how ADEI issues affect, and are vitally important to, the arts. Finally, he explores potential ways to solve some of the challenges posed by ADEI issues.

It is particularly important to note that unlike many other topics in this book, the issues of ADEI are unfolding largely in the present, and changes seem to be occurring on a near-daily basis. This chapter provides an essential look into the current state of the arts in relation to ADEI.

## ACCESS, DIVERSITY, EQUITY, & INCLUSION (ADEI) IN CULTURAL ORGANIZATIONS: CHALLENGES AND OPPORTUNITIES

*A Contribution by Dr. Antonio C. Cuyler*

Before COVID-19 ravaged the world with particular impact on communities of the global majority in the United States, and Black Americans faced a remarkable summer of killings at the hands of police; a colleague confessed that he considered ADEI work noise. Others in the cultural sector likely did, too. Nevertheless, George Floyd's hyper-public killing by police galvanized a global racial reckoning that cultural organizations around the world in Australia,[1] France,[2] Germany,[3] and the United Kingdom[4] simply could not ignore. For the first time, many cultural organizations released public statements exclaiming that "Black Lives Matter," when doing so before May 25, 2020 may have cost them critical financial, political, and social capital that they needed to sustain themselves.

Across dance, film, literature, music, theatre, and visual arts, "statements of solidarity" became so pervasive that I had difficulty keeping track of who published a statement versus those who did not. In fact, the Founding Director of Women of Color in the Arts (WOCA), a national grassroots organization dedicated to creating racial equity in the performing arts, penned a letter in the *Medium* about the cultural sector's voluminous solidarity statements stating:

> I've stopped counting (and reading) the endless emails I've received from arts organizations touting how they stand in solidarity with Black people. Statements which proclaim they're shutting down their operations and programming — galas and town halls and education programs are "going black." How cute. Now, all of a sudden, historically and predominantly white arts institutions want to be "in solidarity" with Black folks? I know what solidarity looks like. And it ain't this.

Many people who have experienced systemic marginalization and oppression – ableism, ageism, cisgenderism, classism, heterosexism, racism, and sexism to name a few – in the cultural sector shared Johnson's sentiment. After May of 2020, a series of headlines revealed that the cultural sector, too, had fallen prey to systemic marginalization and oppression. Some of the headlines included: "New York Knows Its Arts Organizations Have a Diversity Problem. Now What?" "Black Theater Workers Call Out Racism on Broadway," "Confidential settlement reached in BSO flutist's gender pay-discrimination suit," and "The Guggenheim's First Black Curator Is Denouncing the Museum's Treatment of Her." Addressing systemic marginalization and oppression in the creative sector remains the most significant issue warranting the sector's undivided attention.

To assist this work, in this chapter, I define ADEI. In addition, I identify myths and misunderstandings that some people in the creative sector hold about ADEI. I also describe how cultural organizations can apply ADEI to their thinking about artists & programming, audiences, boards/volunteers, and staff so that those from historically marginalized and oppressed groups (HMOGs) may fully experience the transformative qualities of culture. In closing this chapter, I examine four key developments that the sector should pay special attention to while institutionalizing ADEI in cultural organizations.

---

**LEARNING OUTCOMES**

After reading this chapter, you will have the ability to

1. Define ADEI.
2. Explain the differences between ADEI.
3. Describe ten myths and misunderstandings about ADEI.
4. Explain why ADEI is vital for effective nonprofit cultural organizations.
5. Evaluate ways in which inequity impacts HMOGs in nonprofit cultural organizations relative to artistic programming, audiences, boards/volunteers, and staff.
6. Propose solutions to enhance the institutionalization of ADEI in nonprofit cultural organizations.

---

## DEFINITIONS OF ADEI

Defining ADEI has challenged the creative sector's efforts and momentum in addressing systemic marginalization and oppression. Many definitions exist of these constructs,[5] undermining the sector's development of a shared language for ADEI. Furthermore, while activating their creativity, too many cultural organizations focus on demonstrating their unique understanding of these constructs rather than on their utility in helping them to achieve their missions to serve their communities.[6] For the purposes of this chapter, I define ADEI as follows:

Antonio C. Cuyler

**Access** – is the removal of all barriers to participation.

**Diversity** – is a qualitative and/or quantitative assessment of human difference and representation.

**Equity** – is fairness in addressing the historic unfairness of HMOGs.

**Inclusion** – is belonging, one of many measures of quality of life.

As shown in Table 4.1, cultural organizations can catalog specific challenges they may experience into the ADEI quadrant to determine the best solution for addressing specific issues.

**Table 4.1** Cultural organizations can catalog specific challenges they may experience into the access, diversity, equity, or inclusion quadrant to determine the best solution for addressing specific issues.

| 1 – ACCESS | 2 – DIVERSITY |
|---|---|
| • A lack of Black, Indigenous, or People of Color (BIPOC)<br>• A lack of LGBTQISA+ people<br>• A lack of people with disabilities<br>• A lack of people from lower socioeconomic status<br>• A lack of women | • How many BIPOC are represented?<br>• How many LGBTQISA+ people are represented?<br>• How many people with disabilities are represented?<br>• How many people from lower socioeconomic status are represented?<br>• How many women are represented? |
| **3 – EQUITY** | **4 – INCLUSION** |
| • What policies or practices will ensure the success of BIPOC?<br>• What policies or practices will ensure the success of LGBTQISA+ people?<br>• What policies or practices will ensure the success of people with disabilities?<br>• What policies or practices will ensure the success of people from lower socioeconomic status?<br>• What policies or practices will ensure the success of women? | • What policies or practices will help BIPOC feel that they belong?<br>• What policies or practices will help LGBTQISA+ people feel that they belong?<br>• What policies or practices well people with disabilities feel that they belong?<br>• What policies or practices will help people from lower socioeconomic status feel that they belong?<br>• What policies or practices will help women feel that they belong? |

Depending on the HMOG, it may help cultural organizations to better understand and plan the best solution to their specific issue more equitably. For example, comparable to their numbers in the general population, LGBTQISA+ people and women are overrepresented quantitatively as arts managers in the United States cultural sector.[7] Because of their overrepresentation in the cultural sector, cultural organizations' work addressing these specific communities will primarily lie within quadrants #3 and #4.

When it comes to people of the global majority (Black, Indigenous, and People of Color), people with disabilities, and people from lower socioeconomic status, cultural organizations have a great deal of work to do to engage these HMOGs. Thus, their work must begin in quadrant #1. Cultural organizations must think carefully about all the ways in which people may interact with them as artists and through programming, audiences, boards/volunteers, and staff. But before more deeply discussing each of these roles with an ADEI lens, I will describe and discuss the ten myths and misunderstandings about ADEI that challenge cultural organizations' work to address enduring discrimination, marginalization, oppression, and subjugation in the creative sector.

## MYTHS AND MISUNDERSTANDINGS ABOUT ADEI

As an ADEI consultant, educator, and researcher, I have observed ten myths and misunderstandings about ADEI that continuously challenge cultural organizations. I will discuss these myths and misunderstandings to help readers look out for them when seeking to practice and institutionalize ADEI. Myth #1 is some version of, "We welcome everyone, and do not need ADEI." A lack of intellectual humility emboldens this myth. It also reads as a defensive response to a need for cultural organizations to deeply self-reflect on the ways in which they have not welcomed everyone. When challenging this myth, advocates for ADEI should point out who is not in the room. For example, if the board has intentionally or unintentionally excluded people with disabilities, acknowledge it, and relentlessly advocate for their inclusion on the board. Gaps in contributed and earned revenue also provide a solid rationale for pushing back against this myth. If everyone felt welcomed no funding gaps in contributed and earned income would exist in the organization's budget.

Myth #2 – "We want to do ADEI, but we do not know where to begin and we do not want to make a mistake." Jones and Okun[8] recognized the perfectionism implicit in this myth as a characteristic of White supremacy culture. When practicing ADEI, cultural organizations should anticipate and accept that they will make mistakes. The key is to make mistakes graciously. This means acknowledging the mistake, apologizing for it when it harms people, and valuing the learning that resulted from making the mistake.

Myth #3 – "We want to do ADEI, but we do not want to change." This myth is the one that I hear the most. Clearly, cultural organizations do not verbalize that they do not want to change. However, it is unspoken in their passive-aggressive resistance to changes that will inevitably shift their organizational culture. For example, the Indianapolis Museum of Art at Newfields faced public backlash for a job posting that stated that it sought a director who would work not only to attract a more diverse audience but maintain its "traditional, core, white art audience."[9] Hopefully, all cultural organizations learned a great deal from this case, but in addition, when addressing this myth, make the case for why the organizational culture needs to shift while highlighting the benefits of the inevitable change.

Myth #4 – "We do not need to budget for ADEI because it is not worth the money." When teaching modules on budgeting, I teach my students that one can discern an organization's priorities by viewing their budget. If cultural organizations do not budget for ADEI, how will they prioritize and complete the work? By budgeting for ADEI, cultural organizations budget for their futures. It is critical that the board and staff insist that the budget include an expense for ADEI. To do so is implicit in the organization's mission to serve its entire community.

Myth #5 – "ADEI and artistic excellence are not complimentary. We would have to lower our standards to pursue ADEI." This myth and misunderstanding comes up a lot as well. Too many in the creative sector miss the point that ADEI are the building blocks of a truly meritocratic organization and sector. When managed well, ADEI ensures fair competition so that the person most qualified wins the opportunity. As I have argued before, the best person for the job is not always abled-bodied, cis-gender male, middle class, heterosexual, and/or White.[10,11]

Myth #6 – "ADEI does not benefit us." A plethora of benefits accrue to cultural organizations that practice ADEI smartly and strategically. These benefits can include deeper audience engagement, community relevance, and financial solvency, among others. However, if cultural organizations practice ADEI with a wavering commitment and impatience before the benefits can fully materialize then it makes sense why some wrongly conclude that ADEI does not benefit them. Cultural organizations must remember that relationship building with HMOGs takes a sincere commitment and time.

Myth #7 – "We cannot use ADEI to diversify our board because we do not know any BIPOC." Cultural organizations should always aspire to build a diverse social network that will not only help them to understand the communities that live within their community, but to also identify leaders in those communities who might partner with them to achieve the organization's mission. The board and/or staff's lack of diverse personal networks does not excuse the organization from seeking to diversify its social network. Again, to do so is implicit in the mission to serve the entire community.

Myth #8 – "ADEI is only about gender and/or race." Gender and race are not the only social identities by which cultural organizations can marginalize and oppress people. In addition to gender and race, cultural organizations should examine the ways in which they have knowingly or unknowingly perpetuated marginalization and oppression based on people's ability, age, class, religion, and sexual orientation. Cultural organizations should also consider political party affiliation as it has become a way that people have divided themselves into tribes even if culture has historically enjoyed bi-partisan support.

Myth #9 – "ADEI is divisive and political." When hearing or reading this myth and misunderstanding, my first reaction is to ask when did treating people with dignity, equity, humanity, and respect become political? At the same time, because of the current political landscape and culture war, I understand that

Antonio C. Cuyler

nothing is apolitical. In fact, "diversity training" has become so politicized that the 45th President of the United States signed an executive order in September of 2020 banning it.[12] Furthermore, in Australia, France, the United Kingdom, and United States, the radical right has conflated discussions of diversity training, race, racism, and whiteness into Critical Race Theory (CRT); when CRT only and accurately purports that humans have built race and racism into the laws and institutions of majority European societies. Nevertheless, when pursuing ADEI cultural organizations should remain aware of this potential challenge and push back by insisting that their mission requires them to serve the public, and the public includes everyone.

Myth # 10 – "I am privileged by my ability, age, class, gender, political party affiliation, race, religion, and/or sexual orientation. When it comes to ADEI, I need to just keep my mouth shut and listen." While listening is an important factor in the equation of successful ADEI work, I hear this myth and misunderstanding too often from those who benefit most from historic marginalization and oppression. Unfortunately, those privileged by their social identities underestimate the harm that unearned privilege poses to them as well. Those privileged by their identities should seek liberation from the system of marginalization and oppression as should those victimized by it. Therefore, cultural organizations should adopt an "all hands on deck" policy so that no one can opt out of participating in its ADEI work. Now that I have identified the ten myths and misunderstandings about ADEI, I will describe ADEI's implications for cultural organizations relative to artists & programming, audiences, boards/volunteers, and staff.

## CASE STUDY – NAVIGATING RESISTANCE TO ADEI

A cultural organization has decided to pursue ADEI work at the urging of the executive director and some board members. In their quest to build consensus they have argued that ADEI will help them to deepen relationships with the community, transform programming, and achieve financial solvency by closing enduring funding gaps in the budget. Most importantly, they argue that practicing ADEI is the right thing to do. However, some board members and staff actively resist ADEI causing a struggle for power over the organization's future. In addition to citing all of the myths and misunderstandings you just read about, the anti-ADEI caucus believes that cultural organizations should not hold or share specific moral or political positions. In this case, which groups' position do you most personally align with, and why? Do you agree that the cultural organization in this case has reasonable motivations for pursuing ADEI? Do you agree that a cultural organization should not hold and/or share a specific moral position? Are there circumstances that exist where it is appropriate for a cultural organization to have a moral or political position and share it with the community they serve? Do the potential gains from engaging in ADEI outweigh the potential losses? What are the implications of the cultural organization in this case not making the right decision about the best way forward?

## ADEI, Artists and Programming

When it comes to ADEI, artists and the programming built around them remain among a cultural organization's most valuable assets. In fact, according to Americans for the Arts,[13] 73% of US citizens agreed that the arts helped them to understand other cultures better, and 72% believed that the arts unify communities regardless of age, ethnicity, and race. People across demographic and economic categories shared this perspective. Nevertheless, the creative sector has consciously and/or unconsciously shut out HMOGs, keeping them from freely and fully enjoying and living a creative and expressive life on their own terms.

For example, a recent study revealed that significant depictions of disability in film and television shows have nearly tripled over the past decade compared with the previous ten years. However, almost all of these titles do not feature disabled actors.[14] In addition, only 11% of all museums' acquisitions over the past decade have been of work by women.[15] Furthermore, at all levels in classical music in the United States people of the global majority continuously face exclusion within opera companies and orchestras only allowing the tokenized few entries and participation into what many consider an elite art form.[16,17] Although I articulate these three examples, the practice of dishonoring, devaluing, and dismissing the artistic and cultural contributions of HMOGs remains pervasive across the creative sector to its detriment. For example, the almost 140-year-old Metropolitan Opera (MET) only produced its first opera by a Black composer this year even though throughout its history several Black composers submitted operas for their consideration.[18] What creative surpluses might humanity gain if Black composers had been able to more freely and fully participate in operatic composition including premiers of their work at the MET? Conversely, what creative deficits have humanity suffered because of anti-Black racism in operatic composition?

Yet, some cultural organizations have expanded access to those with decision-making power about the kinds of arts consumed in interesting ways. For example, the Baltimore Museum of Art engaged security guards as guest curators of the show *Guarding the Art*.[19] This case serves as a remarkable pivot from the "all knowing" curator mentality that can plague museums and undermine their ADEI efforts. I also strongly encourage this practice because it allows museums to employ their human capital in a new and meaningful way. In my personal experience, security guards have been museums' best cultural ambassadors with discerning aesthetic insights and tastes. Whenever visiting museums, I actively seek out the suggestions of security guards. Unsurprisingly, their observations prove astute, informed, and incredibly valuable.

The performing arts, too, offer insights about how ADEI can inform cultural organizations' social impacts through artistic programming. Although the John F. Kennedy Center for the Performing Arts faced criticism for the $25 million it received from the federal government for operations and maintenance at the beginning of the COVID-19 pandemic,[20] its social impact initiatives led by Marc Bamuthi Joseph have proven instructive for the sector about what cultural organizations can do when they program artistically with an ADEI mindset. These areas of work include investment in the local creative economy, arts across America, the cartography project, REACH activations, cultural leadership, and #BlackCultureMatters.[21] I strongly encourage all cultural organizations to grant themselves permission to think outside of the box when applying an ADEI mindset to artistic programming. Most importantly, artistic programming should open as many doors into the organizations for as many different types of people as is possible.

## ADEI AND AUDIENCES

Because audiences deem artistic programming valuable, without it audiences would not exist. Still, several barriers exist to developing audiences reflective of cultural organizations' communities. According to the National Endowment for the Arts,[22] approximately 73% of arts attendees attend to socialize with friends or family, 64% to learn new things, 63% to experience high-quality art, and 51% to support the community. However, when it comes to non-attendees, 47% do not attend because of time, cost precludes 38% from attending, access prohibits the attendance of 37%, and 22% do not attend because they do not have anyone to go with them. Contextualized in ADEI, HMOGs have also faced a history of disenfranchisement. For example, before the Civil Rights Act of 1964 segregationists laws served as a barrier to Black people freely and fully engaging in all aspects of US culture.

Cultural organizations must remain cognizant of this history when seeking to develop audiences from HMOG. For example, while disabled adults composed nearly 12% of the US adult population, they remain under 7% of all adults attending performing arts events or visiting art museums. Disabled adults are just as likely as non-disabled adults to attend an art exhibit or a live performing arts event in a place of worship.[23] Furthermore, as Culture Track[24] showed, a huge racial disparity exists in audiences' composition. Unfortunately, Culture Track's first wave of data only included education, employment, income, generation, geography, LatinX, and race. The second wave of data will include ability and gender, but exclude political party affiliation, religion, and sexual orientation making it difficult

Antonio C. Cuyler

for cultural organizations to make evidence-based decisions about how to best serve people from these groups culturally. Yet, social identity theory suggests that people will more likely consume culture in which they can see themselves.[25,26] Cultural organizations that remember this fact when planning artistic and cultural experiences increase their likelihood of developing audiences from HMOGs.

## ADEI AND BOARDS/VOLUNTEERS

Cultural organizations' boards hold considerable decision-making power. Yet far too many do not represent their communities which compromises their ability to fulfill their missions. Regarding race, 91% of cultural organizations' boards in the United States identify as White.[27,28] Even in Los Angeles, where 9% of the population identified as Black, this HMOG holds only 32 of the 585 board seats at the top cultural organizations.[29] When it comes to gender, women constitute 53% of boards. Relative to age, most board members identified as 51–65 (43%) or 36–50 (32%).[30] Similar to artists and audiences, too often cultural organizations do not collect demographic data on ability, political party, religion, or sexual orientation which makes it difficult to monitor their progress on including board members reflecting these social identities.

Given that White and female identified individuals comprise the demographic profile of the "typical" arts donor, it makes sense that cultural organizations recruit people with these identities and wealth to join their boards.[31] If cultural organizations rely solely on a peer-to-peer strategy for identifying and recruiting board members, then it also makes sense that they would see little demographic shifts on their boards, especially because 75% of White people do not have non-White friends.[32] Though the Alliance of American Museums has begun to address the "diversity issue" through a $4 million initiative funded by the Andrew W. Mellon, Alice L. Walton, and Ford Foundations,[33] how might cultural organizations unbind themselves from this board recruitment practice which inevitably enables stasis? Could cultural organizations ever conceive of a time where they actively pursued board members from a lower socioeconomic status? Or a board member who does not like the arts? Could board members with these backgrounds hold capital valuable enough to inspire cultural organizations to think differently about the possibilities they miss out on by not engaging them?

Thinking with an ADEI mindset, cultural organizations should first revisit their board criterion for implicit bias and make changes that would welcome a diverse slate of candidates. Second, cultural organizations should value potential board members for more than their financial capital. Board members with community, cultural, and social capital bring insights to cultural organizations' operations that could significantly enhance their ability to achieve their mission. Third, when onboarding, cultural organizations should make it a requirement for new board members to identify three to five potential candidates with a demographic profile different from them by the end of their terms.

While cultural organizations have much work to do before their boards reflect their communities, I am heartened by the Black Trustee Alliance for Art Museums which aims to increase the inclusion of Black artists, perspectives, and narratives in US cultural institutions by addressing inequalities in staffing and leadership; combating marginalized communities' lack of presence in exhibitions and programming; and incorporating diversity into the institution's culture.[34] If other HMOGs adopted the Black Trustee Alliance for Art Museums model combined with the three suggestions offered, cultural organizations could see meaningful change and progress on their boards relative to ADEI. I also encourage implementation of these ideas when recruiting volunteers. A pool of volunteers cultivated with an ADEI lens can serve as an additional resource from which cultural organizations can recruit potential board members. In addition, cultural organizations should commit to maintaining lifelong relationships with all volunteers.

## CASE STUDY – WHEN DIVERSIFYING THE BOARD GOES AWRY

After 40 years, a cultural organization has finally decided to diversify its board. Historically, 95% of the board has identified as White, 52% as female, and in most cases affluent as each board member gets or gives $10,000 annually. The Call for Board Nominations specified that the nominating committee sought nominees who would bring age, geographic, ethnic, and other demographic diversity to the board. They also wanted nominees who had previous involvement with the organization through attendance and/ or service to the organization. A current board member nominates their Black male friend because in addition to meeting all of the criteria, the board has never had a Black male member. Another board member nominates her White transgender friend to serve on the board because the board has also never had a transgender person serve as a member. However, the now transgender board member served on the board before their transition. Further complicating this board's pursuit of diversity is that only one seat is available and the by-laws provide no guidance on the pursuit of diversifying board members. Who should receive the board's consideration as the nominee, and why? Which board member most satisfies the criteria articulated in the Call for Nominations? Because the board has never had a Black male or transgender person serve, how would you avoid tokenism in onboarding the new member? If you served on this board, what addition to the by-laws would you suggest to help manage the pursuit of board diversity in the future?

## ADEI AND STAFF

In a 2015 study, I found that arts managers primarily identified as White, cis-female, abled-bodied, straight, ages 25–44, and master's degree holding.[35] Although cis-men represented 23% of the workforce, they held more executive-level positions and earned higher salaries than their female counterparts.[36] Furthermore, in an international study two colleagues and I discovered that arts management graduates, too, primarily identified as of European descent, cis-female, abled-bodied, straight, and millennials.[37] Though diversity fellowships and internships have shown promise for helping cultural organizations to attract people from HMOGs,[38,39] some arts managers privileged by their social identities resist this strategy.[40]

As an example, in 2016, Samantha Niemann (a White woman) sued the Getty Museum for denying her entry into an internship program designed to develop more diverse museum staff. Given that data from 2015 to 2020 continuously showed that White women remain the majority on museums' staff[41] and in the arts management workforce,[42,43] and that researchers have made reports on this data publicly available, on what grounds could Ms. Niemann ethically claim discrimination? This case reveals an ugly truth that cultural organizations should prepare for when pursuing ADEI, specifically as it relates to staff. Though their privilege may blind them, cultural organizations' implementation of ADEI will make some people with privileged identities feel excluded from opportunities intended to correct enduring and historic inequities.

Given my examination of artists, audiences, boards/volunteers, and staff, it appears that the stasis of people who lack diverse social networks re-makes itself throughout all of the ways in which cultural organizations interact with people. But, to what end? To maintain the lie that able-bodied, cisgender men, and middle to upper-class, straight, Christian, White people are the only contributors to humanity's artistic and cultural productivity? For me, the troubling trend of exclusion in the cultural sector raises the question, why should those systematically and systemically excluded from culture, rather intentionally or unintentionally, support the public funding of culture? Cultural organizations must remember that they wield incredible power. Culture helps people to discover the adventure of what it means to exist as a human. All people, no matter their difference, have a right to this discovery compelled by culture. Despite resistance from some artists, audiences, boards/volunteers, and staff, cultural organizations must take every opportunity to use ADEI to provide access to this gift for every human.

**CONCLUSION**

In this chapter, I defined ADEI, identified myths, and misunderstandings that some people in the cultural sector hold about ADEI, and described ways in which cultural organizations can use ADEI to more deeply engage artists & programming, audiences, boards/volunteers, and staff so that HMOGs may freely and fully experience the transformative qualities of arts and culture. I close this chapter by examining four key developments that cultural organizations should pay special attention to while seeking to further institutionalize ADEI.

## Activism to Inform and Impact

I opened this chapter with a brief discussion of the global reckoning with race compelled by COVID-19's impact on people of the global majority and the incessant killing of Black people by police in the United States. As an aside, several human rights experts consider the attacks against Black people in the United States a crime against humanity.[44] Many HMOGs have galvanized their power in an effort to transform the cultural sector so that it looks more like them and, so that the field recognizes their dynamic and unique contributions to culture. As more HMOGs empower themselves, I envision the emergence of more cultural organizations about, by, for, and near them. In addition, I believe that HMOG will develop informal mentoring networks that help to steer talent away from cultural organizations who have reputations for "playing" diversity as Professor Jackson of the University of Alabama stated (L. Jackson, personal communication, August 6, 2021) versus those who have committed to truly practicing and institutionalizing ADEI.

## Chief Diversity Officers

Before George Floyd's killing, the Phillips Collection remained one of a few cultural organizations that institutionalized ADEI through a Chief Diversity Officer.[45] Since the Summer of 2020, large cultural organizations such as the Broadway League, Guggenheim,[46] Metropolitan Museum of Art,[47] Metropolitan Opera,[48] New Jersey Symphony Orchestra, Paris Opera, Philadelphia Museum of Art,[49] Recording Academy, St. Louis Art Museum,[50] Tennessee Performing Arts Center, and the Virginia Museum of Fine Art,[51] among others, have hired Chief Diversity Officers. As cultural organizations continue their efforts to institutionalize ADEI, Chief Diversity Officers will become more ubiquitous across the cultural sector.

But how might arts management educators help the field to develop Chief Diversity Officers when only 86% of them teach about diversity issues in their courses, and the likelihood of their teaching about diversity issues depended on if they identified as BIPOC, LGBTQIAS+, or female?[52] If arts management educators blunder the opportunity to participate in the professional preparation of Chief Diversity Officers in the arts, they will lose a vital opportunity to further advance their relevance to the field.

## Funding

In 2019, Grantmakers in the Arts published my article, *The Role of Foundations in Achieving Creative Justice* in its Reader. In it, I argued for foundations funding only BIPOC cultural organizations for the next ten years or allocating at least 50% of their funding to these organizations for the next ten years. Since that time and likely because of the horrors of the summer of 2020, 16 major donors and foundations committed $156 million to support BIPOC cultural organizations through the *America's Cultural Treasures* program.[53] In addition, the Mellon Foundation created the Black Seed, a national strategic initiative that will provide close to 100 Black theatres $10,000–$150,000 one- or two-year grants.[54] In July, the Wallace Foundation[55] announced a five-year $53 million initiative focused on BIPOC cultural organizations. Although unexpected, the Ford and Andrew W. Mellon Foundations partnered to create the Disability Futures initiative to spotlight and support the work of creatives with disabilities.[56] Although it pleases me to see these initiatives come to fruition, I hope that they continue and inspire a shift in cultural public funding informed by ADEI.

## Research

Lastly, research on BIPOC and other HMOGs will become important in making the case for ADEI and informing cultural organizations' practice of it. For example, Dunn et al.[57] found that the US film and tv industries lose $10 billion annually due to anti-Black racism. How much does the nonprofit creative sector lose annually because of marginalization and oppression? In a capitalist and consumerist world, can a sector so reliant on contributed and earned revenue really afford to exclude anyone? Although Sidford[58] warned the US cultural sector of inequities in cultural funding, it can no longer ignore an inevitable truth that change is coming.

Antonio C. Cuyler

## DISCUSSION QUESTIONS

1. What difference exists between ADEI, and why is each component important?

2. Which of the ten myths and misunderstandings have you heard people use when resisting ADEI? How did you respond? After reading this chapter, would you respond differently or similarly?

3. In what ways do artists & programming, audiences, boards, staff, and volunteers present cultural organizations with an opportunity to practice ADEI?

4. This chapter suggested that budgeting for ADEI remains integral to its institutionalization in cultural organizations? If you managed the budget, how would you determine which percentage of your organization's budget to earmark for ADEI?

5. The cultural organization in which you worked has asked you to serve on the search committee to hire a new Chief Diversity Officer, what characteristics do you believe a Chief Diversity Officer should have to succeed in their position?

### Notes

1 Aileen Huynh, "Diversity in the Arts: Not a Black and White Issue." *The Big Smoke*, August 24, 2020, https://www.thebigsmoke.com.au/2020/08/24/diversity-in-the-arts-not-black-and-white-issue/

2 Alex Marshall, "Paris Opera to Act on Racist Stereotypes in Ballet." *The New York Times*, February 8, 2021, https://www.nytimes.com/2021/02/08/arts/dance/paris-ballet-diversity.html

3 Roslyn Sulcas, "Staatsballett Berlin and Dancer Reach Settlement over Bias Allegations." *The New York Times*, April 22, 2021, https://www.nytimes.com/2021/04/22/arts/dance/staatsballett-berlin-ballet-racism-settlement.html

4 Alex Greenberger, "Controversy of Museums' Black Lives Matter Statements Continues as Critics Pillory British Institutions." *ARTnews*, June 8, 2020, https://www.artnews.com/art-news/news/british-museums-black-lives-matter-statements-controversy-1202690203/

5 "Definitions of Diversity, Equity, Accessibility, and Inclusion." American Alliance of Museums, accessed August 9, 2021, www.aam-us.org/programs/diversity-equity-accessibility-and-inclusion/facing-change-definitions/

6 Antonio C. Cuyler, "Why ADEI?" *Cuyler Consulting, LLC*, accessed May 20, 2021, www.cuylerconsulting.com

7 Antonio C. Cuyler, "Diversity Internships in Arts Management, Do They Work?" *American Journal of Arts Management*, 3(1), (January, 2015): 13.

8 Kenneth Jones and Tema Okun, *Dismantling Racism: A Resource Book* (Western States Center: 2001).

9 Sarah Bahr, "Indianapolis Museum of Art Apologizes for Insensitive Job Posting." *New York Times*, February 13, 2021, https://www.nytimes.com/2021/02/13/arts/design/indianapolis-museum-job-posting.html

10  Antonio C. Cuyler, "Affirmative Action and Diversity: Implications for Arts Management." *The Journal of Arts Management, Law, and Society* 43(2) (2013): 98–105. https://doi.org/10.1080/10632921.2013.786009.

11  Antonio C. Cuyler, "Why ADEI?" *Cuyler Consulting, LLC*, accessed May 20, 2021, www.cuylerconsulting.com

12  Associated Press, "Trump's Diversity Training Ban Faces Lawsuit from NAACP." *Fortune*, October 29, 2020, https://fortune.com/2020/10/29/trump-diversity-training-executive-order-lawsuit-naacp/

13  Randy Cohen, "10 Reasons to Support the Arts." *Americans for the Arts*, March 3, 2020, www.americansforthearts.org/2020/03/23/10-reasons-to-support-the-arts-in-2020

14  "Visibility of Disability: Answering the Call for Disability Inclusion in Media." *The Nielsen Company*, 2021, https://www.nielsen.com/us/en/insights/article/2021/visibility-of-disability-answering-the-call-for-disability-inclusion-in-media/

15  Julia Halperin and Charlotte Burns, "Museums Claim They're Paying More Attention to Female Artists. That's an Illusion." *Artnet News*, September 19, 2019, https://news.artnet.com/womens-place-in-the-art-world/womens-place-art-world-museums-1654714

16  Antonio C. Cuyler, "Why ADEI?" *Cuyler Consulting, LLC*, accessed May 20, 2021, www.cuylerconsulting.com

17  Alex Ross, "Black Scholars Confront White Supremacy in Classical Music." *The New Yorker*, September 14, 2020, www.newyorker.com/magazine/2020/09/21/black-scholars-confront-white-supremacy-in-classical-music

18  Zachary Woolfe, "A Black Composer Finally Arrives at the Metropolitan Opera." *New York Times,* September 23, 2021, www.nytimes.com/2021/09/23/arts/music/terence-blanchard-met-opera.html

19  Gabriella Angeleti, "Security Guards Become Guest Curators at the Baltimore Museum of Art." *The Art Newspaper*, July 12, 2021, www.theartnewspaper.com/news/security-officers-to-guest-curate-exhibition-at-the-baltimore-museum-of-art

20  Elizabeth Blair, "Emergency Relief Package Provides for Tens of Millions in Funds to Help the Arts." *National Public Radio*, March 26, 2020, www.npr.org/sections/coronavirus-live-updates/2020/03/26/822215614/emergency-relief-package-provides-for-tens-of-millions-in-funds-to-help-the-arts

21  "Social Impact Initiatives." *Kennedy Center*, 2020, www.kennedy-center.org/our-story/social-impact/

22  "When Going Gets Tough: Barriers and Motivations Affecting Arts Attendance." *National Endowment for the Arts*, January, 2015, www.arts.gov/sites/default/files/when-going-gets-tough-revised2.pdf

23  National Endowment for the Arts, "A Matter of Choice? Arts Participation Patterns of Americans with Disabilities." *National Endowment for the Arts*, April 15, 2015, http://arts.gov/sites/default/files/Arts-Participation-Among-Adults-with-Disabilities-v3.pdf

24  "Culture + Community in a Time of Crisis." *Culture Track*, July 7, 2020, https://s28475.pcdn.co/wp-content/uploads/2020/09/CCTC-Key-Findings-from-Wave-1_9.29.pdf

25  Naomi Ellemers, "Social Identity Theory." *Britannica*, August 16, 2017, https://www.britannica.com/topic/social-identity-theory

26  Pamela Newkirk, "Diversity, Inc." (*Bold Type Books*: 2019).

27  "Museum Board Leadership 2017: A National Report." *American Alliance of Museums*, January 19, 2018, https://www.aam-us.org/2018/01/19/museum-board-leadership-2017-a-national-report/

28  Francie Ostrower, "Diversity on Cultural Boards: Implications for Organizational Value and Impact." *University of Texas at Austin*, 2014, https://www.arts.gov/sites/default/files/Research-Art-Works-UTX-Austin.pdf

29  Deborah Vankin and Mmakeda Easter, "Black People Hold Just 32 of 585 Board Seats at L. A.'s Top Arts Groups." *Los Angeles Times*, May 25, 2021, www.latimes.com/entertainment-arts/story/2021-05-25/museums-theaters-black-board-of-directors

30 Francie Ostrower, "Diversity on Cultural Boards: Implications for Organizational Value and Impact." *University of Texas at Austin*, 2014, https://www.arts.gov/sites/default/files/Research-Art-Works-UTX-Austin.pdf

31 Ruth Rentschler, *Arts Governance: People, Passion, Performance*. (Routledge: 2015.) https://doi.org/10.4324/9781315818016.

32 Christopher Ingraham. "Three Quarters of Whites Don't Have Any Non-White Friends: Data Show That for Most White Americans, None of Their Best Friends Are Black." *The Washington Post*, August 25, 2014, https://www.washingtonpost.com/news/wonk/wp/2014/08/25/three-quarters-of-whites-dont-have-any-non-white-friends/

33 Antonio C. Cuyler, "Looking beyond What We've Done Before: Minding Potential Blind Spots in Diversifying U. S. Museums." *International Journal of the Inclusive Museum, 13*(4), (2020): 6.

34 Robin Pogrebin, "Black Trustees Join Forces to Make Art Museums More Diverse." *The New York Times*, October 9, 2020, www.nytimes.com/2020/10/09/arts/design/black-trustees-art-museums-diversity.html

35 Antonio C. Cuyler, "Diversity Internships in Arts Management, Do They Work?" *American Journal of Arts Management, 3*(1), (2015): 13.

36 Antonio C. Cuyler, "U. S. Executive Arts Managers: A Descriptive Analysis of Their Demographic Diversity, Salary & Benefits, and Job Satisfaction." *Cultural Management: Science and Education, 1*(2) (2017): 8.

37 Antonio C Cuyler, Victoria Durrer, and Melissa Nisbett, "Steadfastly White, Female, Hetero and Able-Bodied: An International Survey on the Motivations and Experiences of Arts Management Graduates." *International Journal of Arts Management, 22*(3) (2020): 5–16.

38 Antonio C. Cuyler, "Diversity Internships in Arts Management, Do They Work?" *American Journal of Arts Management, 3*(1), (2015): 13.

39 Antonio C. Cuyler, "Looking beyond What We've Done Before: Minding Potential Blind Spots in Diversifying U. S. Museums." *International Journal of the Inclusive Museum, 13*(4) (2020): 6.

40 Brea M. Heidelberg, "Evaluating Equity: Assessing Diversity Efforts through a Social Justice Lens." *Cultural Trends, 28*(5), (2019): 391–403. https://doi.org/10.1080/09548963.2019.1680002.

41 Roger Schonfeld, Mariët Westermann, and Liam Sweeney, "The Andrew W. Mellon Foundation Art Museum Staff Demographic Survey." *The Andrew W. Mellon Foundation*, 2015, https://mellon.org/media/filer_public/ba/99/ba99e53a-48d5-4038-80e1 66f9ba1c020e/awmf_museum_diversity_report_aamd_7-28-15.pdf.

42 Antonio C. Cuyler, "An Exploratory Study of Demographic Diversity in the Arts Management Workforce." *GIA Reader, 26*(3), (2015): 4.

43 Antonio C. Cuyler, Victoria Durrer, and Melissa Nisbett, "Steadfastly White, Female, Hetero and Able-Bodied: An International Survey on the Motivations and Experiences of Arts Management Graduates." *International Journal of Arts Management, 22*(3) (2020): 5–16.

44 Ed Pilkington, "Police Killings of Black Americans Amount to Crimes Against Humanity International Inquiry Finds." *The Guardian*, April 26, 2021, www.theguardian.com/us-news/2021/apr/26/us-police-killings-black-americans-crimes-against-humanity

45 Julia Fiore, "Meet the Chief Diversity Officer Overhauling the Phillips Collection." *Art Market*, October 2, 2019, www.artsy.net/article/artsy-editorial-meet-chief-diversity-officer-overhauling-phillips-collection

46 Helen Holmes, "The Guggenheim Museum Has Hired Its First Chief Culture and Inclusion Officer." *Observer*, July 28, 2021, https://observer.com/2021/07/guggenheim-museum-diversity-ty-woodfolk/

47 Robin Pogrebin, "For Diversity Leaders in the Arts, Getting Hired Is Just the First Step." *New York Times,* January 17, 2021, https://www.nytimes.com/2021/01/17/arts/design/diversity-directors-arts-hiring.html

48 Helen Holmes, "The Metropolitan Opera Has Hired a Chief Diversity Officer to Transform the Company." *Observer*, January 26, 2021, https://observer.com/2021/01/metropolitan-opera-marcia-sells-diversity-officer/

49 Stephan Salisbury. "Philadelphia Museum of Art Names Diversity Officer Following Difficult Year." *The Philadelphia Inquirer*, June 28, 2021, www.inquirer.com/arts/philadelphia-museum-art-names-diversity-officer-following-difficult-year-20210628.html

50 "Saint Louis Art Museum Promotes Renée Brummell Franklin to Chief Diversity Officer." *Saint Louis Art Museum*, December 18, 2020, https://www.slam.org/press/saint-louis-art-museum-promotes-renee-brummell-franklin-to-chief-diversity-officer/

51 Trevor Dickerson, "Patrick Patrong Named VMFS's New Chief Diversity Officer." *RVAHUB*, July 21, 2021, https://rvahub.com/2021/07/21/patrick-patrong-named-vmfas-new-chief-diversity-officer/

52 Cuyler, Antonio C. "A Survey of Arts Management Educators' Teaching on Diversity Issues." *The Journal of Arts Management, Law, and Society 47*(3) (2017): 192–202. https://doi.org/10.1080/10632921.2017.1315352.

53 "Ford Foundation: Sixteen Major Donors and Foundations Commit Unprecedented $156 Million to Support Black, Latinx, Asian and Indigenous Arts Organizations." *Ford Foundation,* https://www.fordfoundation.org/the-latest/news/sixteen-major-donors-and-foundations-commit-unprecedented-156-million-to-support-black-latinx-asian-and-indigenous-arts-organizations/

54 "The Black Seed Unveils Generous Grant Program for Black Theatres." *Andrew W. Mellon Foundation*, January 18, 2021, accessed August 9, 2021, https://mellon.org/news-blog/articles/black-seed-unveils-generous-grant-program-black-theatres/

55 "Wallace Foundation Announces a Five-Year, $53 Million Initiative Focusing on Arts Organizations of Color." *The Wallace Foundation*, July 19, 2021, https://www.wallacefoundation.org/news-and-media/press-releases/pages/wallace-foundation-announces-five-year-$53-million-initiative-focusing-on-arts-orgs-of-color.aspx

56 "Disability Futures Fellows." *Ford Foundation*, 2021, www.fordfoundation.org/work/investing-in-individuals/disability-futures-fellows/

57 Jonathan Dunn, Lyn Sheldon, Nony Onyeador, & Ammanuel Zegeye, "Black Representation in Film and TV: The Challenges and Impact of Increasing Diversity." *McKinsey & Company*, March 11, 2021, https://www.mckinsey.com/Featured-Insights/Diversity-and-Inclusion/Black-representation-in-film-and-TV-The-challenges-and-impact-of-increasing-diversity

58 Holly Sidford, "Fusing Arts, Culture, and Social Change: High Impact Strategies for Philanthropy." *National Committee for Responsive Philanthropy*, October 23, 2011, https://www.ncrp.org/publication/fusing-arts-culture-social-change

Antonio C. Cuyler

# Conversational Budgets and Financial Management in the Arts

Anthony Rhine and
Jay Pension

## Chapter 5

### INTRODUCTION

Finance and budgets are topics vital to address when
considering arts administration. However, we often think
of budgets and finance requiring a degree in accounting or
substantial training in finance. That is certainly the case for
the large budget financial controller, whether at a multinational
corporation or a large nonprofit arts organization. However,
smaller organizations often operate on a cash basis, controlling
their finances as one does their personal financial accounts.
As organizations grow, they may find themselves at a point
where more detailed and documented methods of planning and
recording income and expenses become essential.

The purpose of this chapter is not to prepare for the CPA
exam. Nor will this chapter create fluency in budgets and

DOI: 10.4324/9781003207535-6

finance for the arts organization. Those tasks require a great deal more study than a single chapter in this text. Instead, this chapter is designed to help the arts administrator gain the ability to converse with financial experts who track detailed revenues and expenditure numbers. This chapter will help the arts administrator understand what financial management is and how to understand and interpret how financial numbers translate into the activities of an arts organization.

Though it is unnecessary to be an accounting expert to administer an arts organization, it is crucial to be conversant in finance and budgeting to discuss business effectively. Being conversant also allows the arts administrator to communicate effectively with their financial accountant, a critical capability.

Though finance and budgeting can be dry, it need not be considered boring, as it is more a challenge of communicating the status of a business through numbers. This chapter aims to help readers learn how to participate in that communication. The chapter will expand upon borrowing, credit, the three financial statements, and leasing properties. The chapter also discusses producing and presenting and their financial distinctions.

## CONVERSATIONAL BUDGETS AND FINANCIAL MANAGEMENT IN THE ARTS

Nonprofit arts organizations are often formed by people stepping into an arts administrator role for the first time. Most of these arts administrators have backgrounds, not in business or management, but in the arts.[1] Unfortunately, a perception exists that artists and math do not mix. This perception extends even to arts administration students who complete graduate management degrees and those in the field seeking to hire positions at nonprofit arts organizations. In 2018, a study was conducted to examine the perceptions of decision-makers in theatres in the United States.[2] The study found that these decision-makers believed that students who complete a Master of Fine Arts (MFA) degree in Theatre Management were least prepared to serve in a financial capacity. In addition, decision-makers believed the MFA students were significantly less prepared to work in financial management than in any other area of arts administration. However, with some basic understanding, we believe any arts administrator can manage

Anthony Rhine and Jay Pension

simple budgets and the financial responsibilities of executive roles in nonprofit arts organizations. This chapter provides the start to that understanding.

If you are anything like the undergraduate and graduate students in our arts management and administration courses, this chapter may be the one dreaded the most. The purpose of this chapter is to introduce arts administration students to the basics of financial management. Though spreadsheets, numbers, and basic equations are essential for hands-on budgeting and financial management, no math is required to understand conversational financial management.

---

**LEARNING OBJECTIVES**

By the end of this chapter, learners should be able to:

- Describe the similarities and differences between cash and accrual accounting.
- Explain the three financial statements and their uses.
- Analyze the benefits and risks of a nonprofit arts organization owning a building.
- Discuss the benefits and risks of using admission income in advance of audience attendance.
- Explain why financial transparency is vital in the nonprofit arts.

---

## Financial Management Basics

When you hear the term *finance*, you may think of the management of financial resources, but this function is typically more associated with the term *financial management.*[3] The term finance is most frequently used to refer to the process where an organization (or person) allocates its assets in ways that generate income. In essence, finance generally centers on financial investment. Few nonprofit arts organizations actually handle financial investing to drive profits. Financial management, however, occurs in every organization, regardless of size. *Financial management* is the process of accounting for assets and liabilities and overseeing the organization's financial health. Though it is ultimately the responsibility of the board and its officers to ensure the organization's financial security,[4] typically, an accountant, bookkeeper, chief financial officer (CFO), or other financial management officer is tasked with accounting for financial transactions.

For the arts administrator, an understanding of basic financial management is prudent.[5] Though nonprofit arts organizations primarily focus on service to the community rather than profits,[6] financial management is essential for the sustainability of an arts organization. Even in an arts organization funded by the government or a sole benefactor, the basic ingredients of financial management remain the same.

At its most basic, the financial components arts organizations must manage are the same components an individual must manage in their own life: income and expenses. *Income*, or revenue, is any money that comes into the organization, while *expenses* refer to any money the organization pays out. Nonprofit arts organizations can have many different income streams, but most arts managers divide it into two categories, earned and unearned revenue. *Earned income* is any money paid to an organization in exchange for an arts experience or a service.[7] For example, earned income would include ticket purchases, courses and workshops, merchandise from a gift shop, and even concessions sold in the lobby.

For many nonprofit arts organizations, *unearned income* makes up a large percentage of their overall budget.[8] This income primarily consists of contributions from individual donors, corporations, and grants. Large nonprofit arts organizations often have a development team tasked with developing relationships to support the organization through raised money. Some prefer to call unearned income contributed income because it describes how most of this income occurs more accurately. Unearned income may seem an unfair label to those who work incredibly hard to ensure their organization receives contributed income. However, unearned income also includes passive income earned through investments and any other mechanism designed to generate income beyond the sale of arts experiences and other typically tangible exchanges.

Anthony Rhine and Jay Pension

## Cash and Accrual Accounting

A key element of financial management occurs through the process of accounting. *Accounting* is the tracking of income and expenses and generally occurs through cash or accrual accounting. Small nonprofit organizations often operate on a cash accounting basis.[9] Many large organizations opt to use accrual accounting when tracking income and expenses. Ultimately, the difference between cash and accrual account is when the organization recognizes the income or expense.[10]

*Cash accounting* reviews what is happening with money in an account. For example, if you have a bank account and deposit a check, the total in the account increases. Likewise, if money is spent from an account, the amount in the account decreases. This tracking is cash accounting. Income and expenses are resolved and recognized as they are added to or debited from the account. Many small arts organizations operate this way because it is intuitive and easy for the consistent tracking of income and expenses.

*Accrual accounting* is also the tracking of income and expenses. However, it focuses on when income is earned, and expenses occur.[11] For example, if a donor pledges $1000, but has not yet delivered a check, or the check has not yet been deposited, under accrual accounting, the organization would see that $1000 as income, even though they do not yet have the $1000 in their account. Likewise, if they hire a performer and commit to pay that performer $5000, but they have not yet produced the payment, or the payment has not yet left their bank account, under accrual accounting, the organization would see that $5000 as an expense, even though the $5000 has not yet left their account. The reverse is also true. For example, if a museum sells $10,000 in advanced tickets to an event and has the money in their account, if they use accrual accounting, they will not count the $10,000 as earned until the event occurs because the event is when the income is earned, not when money was exchanged with the purchase of a ticket. In this case, though the company has the money in advance, it is not counted as income until it has actually been earned.

Whether an organization chooses to use cash or accrual accounting, understanding how the accounting occurs helps arts administrators make wise financial management decisions. In many for-profit business ventures, the expense to create a product occurs before the income from the product occurs. An initial capital investment is necessary to produce the product, then the corporation earns income through sales after the product is produced. In many other business ventures, a client pays for a product upfront, and the business uses that payment to create and deliver the product. In the nonprofit arts, the financial arrangement between expenses and income relative to arts experience is rarely that simple.[12]

### CASE STUDY: ACCRUAL VS. CASH ACCOUNTING FOR A NONPROFIT

Between 2010 and 2019, a nonprofit theatre focused on young audiences struggled with financial challenges. The theatre's new executive director and artistic director met with the board and established a new vision for the theatre: to be a national leader in the production of youth plays and musicals and the development of new works for young audiences in the United States. The first step in their strategy was to increase the quality of productions and the venues in which the theatre performed.

Previously, the productions were primarily low budget and in donated performance spaces. To increase the quality, the theatre planned additional money for production expenses and rented one of the nicest performance spaces in the city for their five-show season. Though these changes led to increased expenses, the board deemed the expenses a necessary step to achieving the new vision.

Like many theatres, they held a subscription series where community members could become subscribers and, at a discount, obtain tickets to the full season by purchasing in advance. The organization used cash accounting to track income and expenses. As a result, the theatre saw substantial revenue at the beginning of the season. Since the money was in the account and they used cash accounting, the theatre used it to enhance their productions as planned. Non-subscriber community members also purchased tickets to attend each production, so the organization still saw income.

By the fifth production of the season, however, the theatre's expenses were outpacing revenue because they had used the income acquired early in the season to pay for the higher production expenses. In addition, the theatre had contracts with a performance venue, designers, performers, and technicians but did not have the revenue to pay those expenses. So rather than reducing production expenses, they announced early sales with an early bird price for the following season to encourage buyers. As a result, they increased their revenue (according to cash accounting) and were able to pay for the added expenses for the fifth and final production of their season.

The theatre ran into the same problem in their fourth production the following year. The theatre put the following season on sale even earlier to compensate for the gap. The cycle continued until the sale of the following season of five productions began, almost at the start of a new season.

These issues are not the fault of cash accounting. However, the thought process around financial management may have been different if they used accrual accounting. Accrual accounting would have designated ticket income from season sales as not earned until the production for which the tickets were sold occurred. As a result, the final productions of the season would have the same designated subscription sales income as the first productions. Therefore, the gaps created by the increased expenses may have been more visible earlier in the process, so the problem may not have grown exponentially over time the way it did.

## The Three Types of Financial Statements

Many students in arts administration courses have shared that though they see some value in accrual accounting, cash accounting is more intuitive and thus easier to visualize. Accrual accounting in the abstract can seem difficult to operationalize. Managers use financial statements to track income, expenses, and other elements vital to the organization's financial operation in accrual accounting. Regardless of whether an organization uses cash or accrual accounting, they use financial statements to guide decision-making.[13] The three most common financial statements used are the income statement (some people call the income statement the profit and loss statement or the P&L), the balance sheet, and the cash flow statement.

An arts administrator uses the *income statement* to see how an organization performs over a set period.[14] The period could be a week, month, quarter, or year. The term could also be any duration. For example, the executive director of a dance company might choose to set a duration beginning at the start of a rehearsal and ending at the close of a run of performances. The income statement shows the organization's financial performance for that period. It displays income, expenses, appreciation, and depreciation of assets, and the organization's total profit or loss during that time. It also assesses profitability but excludes total liabilities and assets for the organization outside of the set period. Arts administrators use income statements for accrual accounting and not for cash accounting.

A *balance sheet* provides a single snapshot in time of the financial position of an organization.[15] It presents all of the organization's assets and liabilities. Assets include the current value of anything an organization owns that could be sold, including technology, costumes, buildings, and art owned by the nonprofit. It is called a balance sheet because the sheet's two sides (assets and liabilities) must balance. At first, it may seem impossible that both the assets and liabilities of a company would be perfectly equal. The balance sheet, however, was developed for for-profit companies. Included in the liabilities for the organization is the net equity (the value of the corporation itself). In most for-profit corporations, the company is owned by an individual or shareholders. Equity is the total value of the corporation. For example, if a company has $1000 in assets and $100 in debt, then $900 is the company's equity (which appears on the liability side)—which would make the sheet balance. Likewise, if a company has $100 in assets and $1000 in debt, then $900 shows as negative equity (still on the liability side)— and the balance sheet still balances. Though nonprofit arts organizations do not distribute net revenue to shareholders, for an arts administrator, understanding the equity an organization has may be useful in many circumstances, including determining the organization's potential ability to take on a business loan.

A *cash flow statement* is similar to the income statement but centers on the inflows and outflows of cash during a set period.[16] The statement is used by nonprofit arts organizations for cash accounting. Of the three statements, it may feel most familiar because it functions essentially like a typical bank account. The cash flow statement shows actual money flowing in and out of the organization over a set period. Like the income statement, an arts administrator could choose any period to review cash flow (annual, quarterly, monthly, weekly, based on a specific project, or more). The cash flow statement does not consider assets, liabilities, appreciation, depreciation, or equity. The benefit of a cash flow statement is that it presents a clear picture of the organization's liquidity. For example, a museum may own a valuable piece of art, or a symphony orchestra may own a large hall, but such assets are not easily sold and may only actually be sold if the organization were to close—so those assets are less helpful in determining the day-to-day financial health of an organization.

The good news (or stressful news depending on your perspective) is that arts organizations can use both cash and accrual accounting to gain the most from both perspectives. In the example from the first case, the organization used only cash accounting, so their books looked healthy, and their cash flow statement showed a consistent positive generation of funds because it tracked when money actually came into and out of the organization. A combination of cash and accrual accounting would have provided the executive director and board with a more holistic picture of the organization.

## Credit and Loans

Like individuals, businesses can open a line of credit to borrow money to operate the business. Obtaining a line of credit, however, is frequently more challenging for a business than for an individual. Businesses pose a greater risk than an individual for lending institutions. There are mechanisms to recapture debt if a person fails to repay a loan. If a person does not pay their credit card statement, their credit score drops, and other lenders are less likely to lend to that individual in the future. When a business fails to repay a loan due to low profits, it may close operations and cease to exist, resulting in a total loss for the entity that loaned the business the money.

Individuals can open a line of credit by mail, through the internet, in retail stores, on airplanes, and more. For businesses, access to loans proves a greater challenge. Financial institutions loan money with the expectation that the borrower will return the funds over time with interest. This interest becomes profit for the lending institution, which they use to operate the business and distribute dividends to shareholders. Since lending institutions are responsible to their shareholders, they must carefully assess risk in determining to whom a loan is made, the loan amount, the timeline for repayment, and the interest rate. Since businesses represent a higher loan risk, gaining access to loans is not as readily available to them as it is for individuals.

To assess the risk of loaning to a business, lending institutions review the business's assets, cash flow, and plans for the future. Large businesses can take lines of credit against their assets. For example, if they own a building and take a loan using the building as an asset, the lending institution can force the sale of the building to repay the loan if the company fails to make the payments. Small businesses may have few assets to use as collateral to obtain a loan. Small businesses (and often new businesses) will use a business plan to obtain a loan. The business plan will present the detailed steps the business will take to become profitable and include a timeline of projected profit. The income statement, the balance sheet, and the cash flow statement are often essential components of applying for a loan.

The barrier to loans is higher for businesses than for individuals and even higher for nonprofits. Since the function of a nonprofit organization is mission driven rather than profit driven, finances are often too bleak for a financial institution to be willing to risk loaning the organization money. The challenge becomes greater once the nonprofit *arts* are added into the mix.[17] Financial institutions rarely even loan funds for for-profit commercial arts like Broadway productions designed to earn the largest potential profit possible. Large nonprofit

Anthony Rhine and Jay Pension

arts organizations that own a building do have an asset that a financial institution could use as collateral, but the organizations must be careful because if they default on the loan, the lending institution may force the sale of their building to repay the loan.

Nonprofit arts organizations should be cautious in taking on debt through loans.[18] Though nonprofit arts organizations often struggle with financial resources, and a loan may seem to solve these struggles, the loan postpones and exacerbates a financial shortfall since the loan must be repaid with interest. To avoid taking a loan, arts organizations should consider using one of the primary benefits of operating as a 501(c)(3): the ability to accept donations and provide a letter the donor can use for a tax deduction. Donations do not have to be repaid and may be readily accessible in the community if the organization's mission or projects can touch those with the means to donate. By focusing on donations from individuals, the organization can also develop more meaningful connections with people in their community and develop lifelong relationships.

## In-kind Contributions

In addition to cash, individuals can make in-kind contributions to a nonprofit and receive the same tax benefit. An in-kind contribution is any contribution that is a non-cash donation. They can be physical items, services, or even expertise. For accounting purposes, physical in-kind donations are seen as income and are added as assets to the nonprofit arts organization.[19] When a nonprofit receives an in-kind contribution, they must determine the value of the gift and produce a letter notating the value of the donation to the donor. The donor may indicate the value, but nonprofit arts organizations should do their due diligence to confirm that value by assessing the price the organization would pay for such an asset if they purchased it from another source. The donor can then use the letter and take a tax deduction based on the value of the contribution, just as they could if they had donated cash.

For-profit corporations can also make in-kind contributions to nonprofits.[20] Many for-profit corporations will donate lightly used technology, legal expertise, or even provide catering for an event to nonprofit arts organizations as an in-kind contribution.

The for-profit receives that same benefit as an individual: the ability to deduct the valued worth of the contribution from their taxes. Nonprofit arts organizations that desire in-kind donations can develop relationships with for-profit organizations just as they develop relationships with prospective individual donors.[21]

Determining whether to accept an in-kind contribution can be a more challenging task than it initially seems. Certain gifts may not be appropriate for a nonprofit arts organization. For example, if a community member offered their local symphony orchestra a rowboat, the symphony may not need or want a rowboat. Though they could sell the rowboat and use the income from the sale, there are two issues with this. First, they may not have the staff or time to undertake the sale of the rowboat. Second, since the income from the sale of a rowboat is not associated with the organization's mission, the income from the sale may be taxed. More challenging are in-kind contributions from the community that are directly related to the organization's mission. For example, a local community member may want to donate a painting that they have loved to their local museum. If the museum has no intention of displaying or using the painting, they ought to reject the in-kind donation, which could harm the relationship with the community member. A good practice for nonprofit arts organizations is only to accept in-kind contributions they know they will use and decline other in-kind donations with tact, grace, and transparency.

### Communication with Bookkeepers and Accountants

Bookkeeping is a part, but only a part, of the accounting process.[22] Most nonprofit arts organizations have a bookkeeper (or team of bookkeepers) and an accountant. Staff members may fill these roles, or the organization may hire a company to help with accounting. *Bookkeeping* is the process of recording and classifying transactions. These transactions consist of all of the income and expenses for an organization. The organization gains valuable data about expenses and spending by recording and classifying transactions. Through recording transitions, the organization can pull financial reports (including the income statement, the balance sheet, and the cash flow statement).

*Accountants* review the statements that the bookkeeper prepares for accuracy. They also interpret the statements and turn them into a report, complete with an analysis of the organization's financial position. Accountants also advise arts administrators about the organization's financial health and assist in making wise financial decisions.

As noted, most arts administrations have backgrounds in the arts rather than in business. Many arts administrators never communicate with an accountant until they are in a position of financial decision-making for the organization. However, while studying to be accountants, many students work on communication skills to support their approach to communicating about financial matters.[23] Many accountants come prepared for communication with executives with minimal financial background. There are key differences in the training of artists and accountants of which arts administrators should be aware. In the arts, creativity is a value essential to the industry; accounting is an industry focused on facts, numbers, and clearly defined laws and policies. Arts administrators involved in a conversation with an accountant who already understands the three financial statements are ahead of many arts administrators who only understand the functioning of their personal bank account.

The essential component to communicating with anyone, especially an accountant, is seeking clear understanding. Many accountants and bookkeepers will presume that arts administrators have little understanding of accounting practices at first. Arts administrators should feel comfortable asking questions about the accounting process and for clarification on points that the accountant shares. Accounting is not abstract, and so, if an arts administrator does not understand what the accountant is attempting to communicate, it is prudent to ask for clarification until a clear understanding is gained. Arts administrators should be wary of making financial decisions for the organization without a clear understanding of the organization's financial position.

## Communication with Staff Members

Financial transparency with stakeholders, including staff members, is a crucial component for the health of arts organizations.[24] Though arts administrators who manage the finances may not need to share every detail of what bills are paid when sharing an organization's financial standing, it can help promote confidence and understanding in how decisions are made. Many arts organizations have a department head who manages the budget for the department's activities. No department head wants to be surprised if their budget is unexpectedly cut. Unfortunately, budget cuts are often necessary for an organization's financial health, especially during times of change. By communicating transparently about the organization's financial position, an arts administrator can reduce the emotional toll budget cuts can have on a department. At best, when department heads hear about a significant deficit, they may look for ways to adjust their spending or increase potential income to help the organization at large. Creating transparency around financial management can help teams work together with a clear picture of the organization's needs, assets, risks, and opportunities.

### CASE STUDY: TRANSPARENCY AND COMMUNICATION

Over time, the youth theatre from the previous case fell further and further behind in what ticket income was paying for materials. Eventually, they were nearly a full season behind, selling tickets for the following season to pay for the first productions of the current season. However, the financial books looked generally healthy because they only used cash accounting.

Around the executive director's fifth year, financial matters started to slip. Bills from creditors began to go unpaid—or they were paid very late. Though the executives and the board were aware of the financial challenges, those challenges were not effectively communicated to the staff. Department heads would place orders that would never arrive because the theatre had not paid for previous orders. These delays often came as a surprise to the staff members who were left to make alternative arrangements, often at greater expense, further exacerbating the problem.

Soon, these financial issues spread to include independent contractors. Contractors working for the theatre would not receive payment for months. Understandably, most declined to return to work until they received payment. Though most would eventually receive their pay, over time, fewer and fewer skilled workers were willing to work for the company. Full-time staff members found their work increasingly challenging as the executive staff and board failed to communicate the organization's financial standing. The cycle continued until the organization failed to make the full payroll every two weeks. Staff members often received only a portion of their pay or none at all. Even then, they were rarely told why the organization could not pay their bills.

Irresponsible financial management was exacerbated by a lack of transparency around the organization's finances, which turned staff and stakeholders into enemies. Ultimately, the organization declared bankruptcy because the mounting debt and operating costs were too great to continue. However, organizations can increase loyalty and understanding even during difficult financial times by increasing financial transparency.

## Financial Audits

An *audit* is a review of financial information and the tracking of that information.[25] An audit may be conducted by the arts organization itself through an external company hired by the arts organization or the government. The purpose of an audit is to review the organization's financial history over a set period to confirm that the financial reports and movement of funds match. The audit can enhance the arts organization's ability to track its funds by finding errors and oversights. It can also identify illegal activity, such as theft, if the financial records do not match the movement of funds in the organization's bank accounts.

As shown in previous chapters, nonprofit organizations function with a set of established mandates that require the organization to conduct certain activities to maintain its status as a nonprofit. For some nonprofits, one of these mandates is an annual audit by an independent firm. Often this determination is made based on the nonprofit's annual gross revenue and is determined by the state in which the organization is based. Independent auditors review the organization's finances and bookkeeping to create a report about the organization's financial health. Like the organization's internal audit, the independent auditors look for errors and possible theft. In addition, since nonprofit organizations belong to the community, the process of independent audits helps to ensure that staff and board members with access to finances are honest and transparent in their financial management.

Regardless of state audit requirements, conducting an annual audit is an excellent practice.[26] Though the prospect of an audit may be frightening, audits help to correct financial management issues and provide evidence that the board is protecting the nonprofit's assets for the community it serves.[27] In addition, audits are often required for nonprofits that apply for grants through corporations, foundations, and government agencies, even if not government mandated.

### To Lease or Buy, Considerations for Nonprofit Arts Organizations

Purchasing venue space for performances or gallery events may seem like a wise financial move; after all, renting space is often one of the costliest expenses nonprofit arts organizations face.[28] An organization can certainly reduce rental expenses and potentially build equity by owning the property. Unlike a business loan to pay for operating expenses, mortgages on a property can be more accessible provided the organization has the resources for a down payment. Also, the building becomes a form of collateral for the lender; therefore, if the organization cannot make its payments, the lending institution can take the property to satisfy the loan.

Though a mortgage on a building may be attainable, an arts organization should carefully consider the risks and rewards of taking on a mortgage and the costs of owning the property. The initial down payment and the mortgage payments are only a part of the financial burden of property ownership. The nonprofit will also need to insure the property, provide maintenance and security for the building, and incur costs related to decoration and event supplies. When all expenses are considered, arts administrators may find that renting event space for short periods might actually make better financial sense. Over time, property values change. In 2008, property values across the

Anthony Rhine and Jay Pension

United States dropped significantly. A great change in property values can damage the equity in a company and reflect poorly on the organization's balance sheet. These challenges may not exclude purchasing a property, but they are considerations that every nonprofit arts organization should be aware when making such a decision.

### Programming Finances, Producing, or Presenting?

Most nonprofit arts organizations serve their community by providing arts experiences.[29] For some organizations, this means creating something from scratch that can be experienced in a performance venue, gallery, school, or even on the street. For others, it means welcoming a touring artist (or artists) who comes with a fully prepared arts experience for an audience. Finally, other organizations provide creative works based on the intellectual property of an artist uninvolved in the specific experience, such as plays, musicals, symphony concerts, ballets, and more.

For arts administrators, understanding the financial differences in and responsibilities of *producing* and presenting is essential. When an organization produces an original work that they pay a person or group to create, they must manage all elements of the arts experience from beginning to end. Financial arrangements are made in advance, and an agreement is executed as to who will own the art (or who owns what pieces) at the contract's conclusion. Producing a work that is someone else's intellectual property typically means that the organization will pay a royalty for the right to perform the work (more on this in the chapter on intellectual property). However, the organization still must manage all elements of producing the work. Generally, the nonprofit arts organization retains the gross income from ticket sales in these circumstances.

*Presenting* creative works has very different responsibilities and a very different financial arrangement.[30] Presenting means cultivating and welcoming artists from outside of the organization to perform for a local audience. Frequently, when a nonprofit presents, they are presenting work by a for-profit producer. The team that does the event typically brings their own sets, costumes, performers, lighting design, technical staff, and more (or less depending on the event's needs). The organization presenting the event generally works to promote it, coordinates the needs of those involved, has control over programming, is responsible for event finances, and has decision-making authority over the performance offerings. Arrangements for presenting vary, but often, the event's creator charges a fee to guarantee attendance and secure a percentage of the box office income from the presenter (the nonprofit arts organization).

Following the event, representatives from the producer and the presenter meet to review the sales and finances. The income divided is termed the *net adjusted gross box office receipts (NAGBOR)*.[31] Gross box office receipts are comprised of the income from customers to attend. Typically, the adjustments are related to ticketing fees and credit card processing. Determining what can be deducted as part of the net sales adjustment before signing a contract is vital for a nonprofit arts organization.

There are financial management pros and cons to producing and presenting for nonprofit arts organizations. Producing involves significantly more personnel activity and tracking of expenses than presenting. However, the organization maintains greater control of the experience and the finances by producing. When presenting, the organization must collaborate with a producer (often for-profit) seeking the best possible financial arrangement for their work. In this instance, the benefit to the nonprofit arts organization is that they can minimize financial risk by not creating the event but only promoting the event and coordinating the venue. Ultimately, deciding whether to present or produce should not be made from a financial perspective alone. The arts organization's responsibility is to serve their community, so programming decision-making is best achieved by determining what will better serve the community.

### Final Thoughts

Throughout this textbook, it is made clear that arts administrators are actively involved in a variety of activities. Ultimately, arts administrators are not accountants, nor are they responsible for the organization's financial health—the board of directors holds that responsibility. However, it is wise for arts administrators to have a basic understanding of financial

Anthony Rhine and Jay Pension

management. Among other reasons, this level of financial literacy is a step in preventing theft from the organization. In addition, understanding financial management helps arts administrators become more effective and helps them to protect their organization's assets.

## DISCUSSION QUESTIONS

1. Search online: What type of common financial challenges do you find for arts organizations.
2. What elements of financial management make you most nervous, and why do you think that is?
3. If you were an arts administrator, though you can use both, would you choose to use cash or accrual accounting more, and why?
4. What type of bookkeeping and accounting software can you find currently available? If you were an arts administrator, how would you select the best fit?
5. Of the three financial statements, which do you believe best presents the current financial positioning of the organization, and why?
6. If you were an arts administrator leading an organization, would you prefer a bookkeeper that works for the organization or a company that would provide bookkeeping services? What do you think are the benefits to each?
7. Have you ever worked for a company that was very, or was not very transparent about finances? What was the result?
8. What type of nonprofit arts mission do you think works best for organizations that would produce their own work? How about organizations focused on presenting?
9. What other types of financial statements could you use as an arts administrator that not covered in this chapter?

## FURTHER READING

Coe, Charles K. *Nonprofit Financial Management A Practical Guide.* Hoboken, N.J: Wiley, 2011.

Coe's text is a guide for nonprofit organizations and paths for their financial management. Though not focused on arts organizations, the guide provides practical advice and steps an any nonprofit organization can take to improve their financial management practices.

**Jean-Francois, Emmanuel.** *Financial Sustainability for Nonprofit Organizations.* **Springer Publishing Company, 2014.**

Jean-Francois's book provides an essential examination of developing financial stability for nonprofit organizations. It uses clear examples to describe the practical steps nonprofits can take in times of financial crisis to develop a greater foundation to continue serving their community.

**Kieffer, Elise Lael. "Riding the Seesaw between Artist and Administrator." American Journal of Arts Management 6.2 (2018): 1–22.**

Kieffer's article describes the work of the arts administrator and the shifting efforts between their work as artists and their work as administrators. It addresses how most arts administrators come into the field. The reading may be useful to consider the many roles arts administrators must play.

## Notes

1 Kieffer, Elise Lael. "Riding the Seesaw between Artist and Administrator." *American Journal of Arts Management* 6.2 (2018):1–22.

2 Rhine, Anthony S., and Jay Pension. "The MFA in theater management and the MBA: A replicative study of perspectives of decision-makers at theaters in the United States." *The Journal of Arts Management, Law, and Society* 51.6 (2021): 351–364.

3 Drake, Pamela Peterson, and Frank J. Fabozzi. *The basics of finance: An introduction to financial markets, business finance, and portfolio management.* Vol. 192. John Wiley & Sons, 2010. https://doi.org/10.1002/9781118267790.

4 Cargo, Russell A. "Changing fiduciary responsibilities for nonprofit boards." *The Journal of Arts Management, Law, and Society* 27.2 (1997): 123–138.

5 Balfour, Dan., and Ramanath, R. "Forging Theatre and Community: Challenges and Strategies for Serving Two Missions." *Public Voices*, XII(1) (2011): 46–66.

6 Jung, Yuha. "Diversity matters: Theoretical understanding of and suggestions for the current fundraising practices of nonprofit art museums." *The Journal of Arts Management, Law, and Society* 45.4 (2015): 255–268.

7 Jung, Yuha. "Diversity matters: Theoretical understanding of and suggestions for the current fundraising practices of nonprofit art museums."

8 Jung, Yuha. "Diversity matters: Theoretical understanding of and suggestions for the current fundraising practices of nonprofit art museums.

9 Coe, Charles K. *Nonprofit financial management: A practical guide.* Vol. 4. John Wiley & Sons, 2011.

10 Coe, Charles K. *Nonprofit financial management: A practical guide.*

11 Coe, Charles K. *Nonprofit financial management: A practical guide.*

12 Rhine, Anthony. *Theatre management: Arts leadership for the 21st century.* Macmillan International Higher Education, 2018.

13 Francois, Emmanuel Jean. *Financial sustainability for nonprofit organizations.* Springer publishing company, 2014.

14 Coe, Charles K. *Nonprofit financial management: A practical guide.*

15 Coe, Charles K. *Nonprofit financial management: A practical guide.*

16 Coe, Charles K. *Nonprofit financial management: A practical guide.*

17 Schumann, Jennifer Diane. "Facing the music: How seven theater companies respond to economic challenges." PhD diss., Drexel University, 2014.

18 Charles, Cleopatra, Margaret F Sloan, and John S Butler. "Capital structure determinants for arts nonprofits." *Nonprofit Management & Leadership* 31.4 (2021): 761–782. https://doi.org/10.1002/Nml.21454.

19 Samu, Sridhar, and Walter W. Wymer Jr. *Nonprofit and business sector collaboration: Social enterprises, cause-related marketing, sponsorships, and other corporate-nonprofit dealings.* Routledge, 2013.

20  Austin, James E. "Strategic collaboration between nonprofits and businesses." *Nonprofit and Voluntary Sector Quarterly* 29.1_Suppl (2000): 69–97. https://doi.org/10.1177/0899764000291s004.

21  Austin, James E. "Strategic collaboration between nonprofits and businesses."

22  Coe, Charles K. *Nonprofit financial management a practical guide.*

23  Hassall, Trevor, Jose L. Arquero, John Joyce, and Jose M Gonzalez. "Communication apprehension and communication self-efficacy in accounting students." *Asian Review of Accounting* 21.2 (2013): 160–175. https://doi.org/10.1108/ara-03-2013-0017.

24  Harris, Erica E., and Daniel Neely. "Determinants and consequences of nonprofit transparency." *Journal of Accounting, Auditing & Finance* 36.1 (2021): 195–220. https://doi.org/10.1177/0148558x18814134.

25  Coe, Charles K. *Nonprofit financial management a practical guide.*

26  Rhine, Anthony. *Theatre management: Arts leadership for the 21st century.*

27  Dicarlo, Christopher, *Nonprofit transformation: 100 keys to breakthrough results for every board and chief executive.* Archway Publishing, 2016.

28  Segers, Katia, Annick Schramme, and Roel Devriendt. "Do artists benefit from arts policy? The position of performing artists in Flanders (2001–2008)." *The Journal of Arts Management, Law, and Society* 40.1 (2010): 58–75. https://doi.org/10.1080/10632921003603919.

29  Borwick, Doug, and Barbara Schaffer Bacon. *Building communities, not audiences : The future of the arts in the United States.* Winston-Salem, N.C: Artsengaged, 2012.

30  Micocci, Tony, *Booking performance tours: Marketing and acquiring live arts and entertainment.* Skyhorse Publishing, Inc., 2013.

31  Micocci, Tony, *Booking performance tours: Marketing and acquiring live arts and entertainment.*

# Intellectual Property and Licensing and the Arts

## Elaine Hendriks Smith

## Chapter 6

**INTRODUCTION**

Students focused on arts marketing often believe that "fair use" of copyright means a certain portion of copyrighted materials can be used to promote art. This misconception is raised when a theatrical production wants to use promotional materials from someone else's production or create an advertisement using video clips of a scene from the play. The reality is that if those video clips include dialogue from the play, that dialogue is protected, and none of it can be used without being licensed specifically for that use. The confusion likely comes because the "fair use" doctrine allows for some copyrighted materials to be used for educational purposes, so in a classroom, the copyright protection has a slightly different set of teeth.

We felt that one of the often most misunderstood topics, then, was copyright protections, and we turned to Elaine to flesh out what we felt was an extremely vital part of the book. Elaine spent over 20 years as an arts administrator managing various arts

DOI: 10.4324/9781003207535-7

organizations in Detroit. Her background includes nonprofit, touring, and educational productions. Beyond her work as an arts administrator, she is also a sought-after lighting designer and has recently worked in higher education. This combination of experiences resulted in Elaine encountering many intellectual property conflicts. In this chapter, she shares vital information for artists and arts administrators about how art is protected by law in the United States.

This chapter explores copyright and intellectual property and introduces how those relate to licensing. The chapter focuses on copyright basics and how copyrights, patents, and trademarks protect intellectual property. Next, the chapter examines intellectual property, why it can and should be protected, and how this is more vital in the arts than ever. The processes for protection of property are discussed, and the case of Joe Mantello's *Love! Valour! Compassion!* lawsuit is presented. The chapter concludes by shifting focus to introduce licensing and how it is used to access intellectual property.

## INTELLECTUAL PROPERTY AND LICENSING AND THE ARTS

*A Contribution by Elaine Hendriks Smith*

Imagine a performing artist completing their work of art. Can you imagine Martha Graham completing the choreography for *Lamentation* or David Bowie listening to a completed track of *China Girl* for the first time? Maybe you can imagine Lin-Manual Miranda completing the score for *Hamilton*. What is the relationship between the artist and the completed artwork? Is the completed artwork theirs? Who has ownership rights over the work once they share it with the public? Should an artist be compensated for another's use of their work?

When an artist creates a piece of work, be it a script, a piece of music, choreography, or an element of theatre, the art belongs to the artist. What that means for each artist depends on their contracts and the industry in which the art is experienced. This chapter explores the ins and outs of ownership, rights, and licensing in the performing arts.

**LEARNING OBJECTIVES**

1.  Demonstrate an understanding of how copyright protects artists and their artwork.
2.  Illustrate the importance of intellectual property in the performing arts.
3.  Identify the processes for the protection of artist's property and why it is vital today.
4.  Demonstrate knowledge of different ways to license art for the performing arts.

## WHAT IS COPYRIGHT?

Many countries around the world protect intellectual property. This chapter focuses on copyright and intellectual property. Though many of the concepts in this chapter apply in other countries, the specifics relate directly to the United States for one simple reason. In the United States, the right for an artist to own their original work is addressed in the US Constitution. Article 1, Section 8 gives Congress the right to "promote the Progress of Science and useful Arts by securing for Limited Times to Authors and Inventors the exclusive Right to their respective Writings and Discoveries."[1] So, the same article of the Constitution that gives Congress the ability to raise taxes and declare war also gives artists (and scientists) the right to own their creations (and discoveries). Throughout US history, several laws attempted to clarify who is considered an "author" and what type of art is covered by the Constitution. However, the passing of The Copyright Act of 1976 shaped copyright law into what it is today.[2] Copyright is "a form of protection grounded in the US Constitution and granted by law for original works of authorship fixed in a tangible medium of expression. Copyright covers both published and nonpublished works."[3] This means artists have legal ownership over their new works from the moment they create them, provided they can prove authorship in a court of law.

## What Can Be Copyrighted?

What about the part of the US Code that says "tangible medium of expression" (17 U.S.C. §102 (1988))? "Tangible mediums of expression" include written works, paintings, music, photographs, architecture, film, maps, and computer software. However, the definition of tangible gets a little more challenging with performing arts. For example, copyright does not cover simple dance moves, social dances, or improvisational scenes. It also does not cover titles, short phrases, procedures, ideas, concepts, or discoveries. So, for copyright to cover an artist's work, the art needs to be recorded in some form that proves the art's fixity and the artists' ownership.

## Works for Hire

An important exception to copyright is "works for hire" which means work that is created under one of two circumstances. The first is an employee whose job is to create artwork as a part of their daily duties. In this case, the employer is the author and the copyright holder for the work created. So, in what situations is a work considered a "work for hire"? One example would be a musician creating a new jingle for a commercial as a part of their full-time employment at an advertising agency. Thus, the jingle copyright goes to the advertising agency and not the artist.

The second is when an artist enters into a written agreement with any hiring party to create work specifically for commissioned use as one of the following: a compilation, a contribution to a collective work, a part of a motion picture or other audiovisual work, a translation, a supplementary work, an instructional text, a test, answer materials for a test, or an atlas. For example, this chapter of this textbook is part of a larger text. I am only writing this chapter, which is part of an instructional text, so my writing for this book checks off a few items on the list.

These exceptions should always be agreed to before work begins, in writing, so that all expectations are clear for everyone. If you are an artist who is not sure about your current agreement with an employer or contracting agency, check your contract for specific language that addresses ownership, or speak to your employer—the clearer the understanding for everyone, the better the working environment for everyone.

Elaine Hendriks Smith

## ARTIST'S RIGHTS UNDER COPYRIGHT LAW

Five exclusive rights come with an artist's copyright are as follows:

1. Artists have the right to reproduce their work.
2. Artists have the right to adapt or derive other works from their work.
3. Artists have the right to distribute copies of their work.
4. Artists have the right to display their work publicly.
5. Artists have the right to perform their work publicly.

These rights establish the ability for an artist to make a living and are meant to encourage creativity, but they do have restrictions. Three such restrictions on the rights named above are: (1) Rules of Fair Use, (2) First Sale, and (3) Duration.

## RULES FOR FAIR USE

The Rules For Fair Use are outlined in Section 107 of the US Copyright Act in order to allow use for the purpose of "criticism, comment, news reporting, teaching (including multiple copies for classroom use), scholarship, or research, is not an infringement of copyright."[4] Fair Use was created in an attempt to avoid the suppression of creativity due to oppressive copyright laws, which is the opposite of the intent of the laws. There are four factors that need to be reviewed when considering if the use of a copyrighted work falls under the Rules For Fair Use.

1. For what purpose is the artwork being used?
2. What is the nature of the copyrighted work?
3. How much of the work is being used, and what is the substance of the piece being used versus the entire copyrighted work?
4. What effect does the use of the copyrighted work have on the potential market value of the work itself?

   It is important to also note a few examples of what Fair Use **does not include:**

1. **It does not** allow for presenters to use copyrighted artwork for marketing materials. Even if a video clip is

only nine seconds long, or a copyrighted clipart is found on the internet without a watermark.

2. **It does not** allow for a designer to use copyrighted artwork within a performance. That means playing seven seconds of a song as a transition in a play, or using a clip from a television broadcast or news report is not covered by Fair Use.

3. **It does not** allow for producers to use artwork from another production of the same show. That means using the Broadway poster when staging a local community theatre production is not covered by the Rules of Fair Use.

## FIRST SALE DOCTRINE

The First Sale Doctrine

> provides that an individual who knowingly purchases a copy of a copyrighted work from the copyright holder receives the right to sell, display, or otherwise dispose of *that particular copy*, notwithstanding the interests of the copyright holder. The right to distribute ends, however, once the owner has sold *that particular copy*.[5]

This applies to all arts. For example, a director purchases a CD of a show that they are rehearsing, once the show is done, they sell the CD to another director that is interested in the play. This is covered by First Sale. However, once the director sells their original CD, they infringe on the artist rights if they sell any copies or digital backups they may have made. The same goes for scripts and scores that were purchased, either from a bookstore, online store, or purchased (not rented) from a licensing company. Only the physical script or score can be sold to someone else. What cannot be sold is any scans, backups, or physical copies that were made of the original. This also applies to artwork that can be found on the internet, including photographs and paintings. The purpose of the First Sale Doctrine is to protect the artist who created the copyrighted art so they can make a living creating more art.

Elaine Hendriks Smith

## Duration

The copyright on any artist's work begins upon creation and continues for the remainder of the artists' life plus 70 years after their death for anything created after January 1, 1978. If an artist chooses to remain anonymous, the copyright lasts for 95 years from its first publication or 120 years from its creation, whichever comes first. Anything created before January 1, 1978 varies depending on the work. Chapter 3 of title 17 in the US Code explains more about anything from before 1978.

Under copyright law, the copyright owner can transfer ownership only in writing and signed by the owner or their authorized agent. Owners can also bequeath their ownership to their heirs. Though it is not required, it is good to file the transfer of ownership with the United States Copyright Office, which registers who has the current rights to the art, in case there is a legal dispute over the rights of an heir.

## What Is the Difference between Copyright and a Patent?

To be covered by copyright, the artwork itself has to be original and *nonuseful,* or *nonfunctional.* Once something becomes useful or functional, it is considered a tool for work that requires a patent instead of copyright. In addition to work, board games are considered functional and so are covered by patents, as are elements of video games.[6]

## What About a Trademark?

Trademark is "any word, name, symbol, or device, or any combination thereof, adopted by a manufacturer or merchant to identify her goods and distinguish them from goods produced by others (15 U.S.C. §1127 (1988))."[7] Trademarks do not cover anything that is a part of everyday language. For example, the word "and" cannot be trademarked because of the English use. Neither can the @ or # symbols. Here are a few examples of trademarked words that are becoming part of everyday language, though the trademark has not expired on them just yet.

1. When you receive an item in the mail, what is it wrapped in? Bubble Wrap® or would you call it packing material?

2. Have you ever ridden on a Jet Ski® or would you call it a personal watercraft?
3. When you crave an icy treat, do you want a Popsicle® or an ice pop?

Trademarks can add to the perceived legitimacy of a product or business for the consumer, and so it has been used by nonprofit organizations to establish themselves for potential donors and grant funders. An article in *The Non-Profit Times* detailed how the "Make-A-Wish Foundation of America logo is one that has wide public recognition and is a registered trademark." This gives them the ability to protect their logo from being replicated and used by another organization or individual who is attempting to benefit from their hard work. For nonprofit organizations, it is advisable to "consider obtaining trademark protection for their organizational name and logo, as well as for the names of major charitable programs" for the organization.[8] This allows for stable fundraising and allows legitimization of the logo and product.

### What Is Intellectual Property?

Intellectual property is not necessarily as tangible as a book or a script. The Stanford Encyclopedia of Philosophy describes it as "generally characterized as a non-physical property that is the product of original thought." It is important for artists to protect their intellectual property so they can make a living by creating artwork. The rights for intellectual property "surround the control of physical manifestations or expressions of ideas." The purpose of intellectual property is to allow an artist (and scientists) to create something completely original without having to register it with an office, like the copyright office. Once a work of art is completed and is automatically copyrighted the artist "has the ability to take legal action to exclude others from invading the boundaries of the property."[9] In other words, the artist can set the rules or "boundaries" for their artwork. This leads to the ability for artists to be paid for their artwork, which means they are able to create new artwork to earn a living.

### Registering for Copyright

Since March 1, 1989, it has not been required for artists to register for copyright but it does afford an artist some benefits.

Registration "establishes a claim to copyright with the Copyright Office."[10] The copyright application has three elements: (1) a completed application form, (2) a nonrefundable filing fee, and (3) a nonreturnable deposit which is a copy of the artwork that is "deposited" with the Copyright office.

Once approved, the registration certificate creates a public record of crucial facts about the author and owner of the claimed work and date of registration which can be helpful when disputes over ownership arise. If a dispute over copyright ownership arises, the registration is a public record of the copyright. This must be completed before legal action begins. For an artist who has already registered their work, this may serve as a form of protection from anyone who has claimed prior copyright but does not have their completed artwork on file with the Copyright office.

To find out more about the rights of artists, visit the website of the Artists Rights Society (https://arsny.com/). They were founded in 1987 and work to protect the intellectual rights of artists.

## CASE STUDIES: COPYRIGHT IN THE COURTS

### Mantello vs. Hall

In 1996, Joe Mantello, the director of the original production of *Love! Valour! Compassion!* saw a regional production of the show in which he claimed, "Ninety to ninety-five percent replication of the staging we had done" on Broadway. Mantello's union, the Society of Stage Directors and Choreographers filed a lawsuit against the Caldwell Theatre claiming that their production's director, Michael Hall committed copyright infringement. This became a three-year court battle that ended with an out-of-court settlement in 1999.

The article that appeared on Playbill.com stated, "In the settlement, Hall agreed to acknowledge the unauthorized use of 'certain elements' created by Mantello."[11] Because the case was settled out of court, no final decision was made about the copyrightability of a directors blocking or staging in the case. The case is still noteworthy because as the courts worked to decide if a director's staging can be copyrighted, this case established the idea that a director can try to protect their staging by filing a lawsuit that considers copyright.

**Einhorn vs. Mergatroyd Productions**

In the John Marshall Review of Intellectual Property, Jennifer Maxwell wrote about an interesting case about play directors. In August of 2004, Nancy McClearnan, the playwright of *Tam Lin*, and Jonathan X. Flang, the producer of *Tam Lin*, hired Edward Einhorn to direct and choreograph the show. Einhorn created a script that tracked his blocking (instructions for how actors move around the stage) and choreography. He directed all of the rehearsals, including technical rehearsals until the day before opening when McClearnan and Flang fired him from the production, refusing to pay him his director's fee. Einhorn brought a lawsuit against them claiming that when the production opened, it used the staging, choreography (including fight choreography), and shadow puppetry as he had directed the cast to do. Before he filed the lawsuit, Einhorn registered his blocking and choreography script for copyright, depositing a copy of his script with his staging and choreography notation as a "work of Performing Arts."[12]

The judge asked both sides to provide the answer to five questions. (1) Was the staging fixed in a tangible form? (2) What was the scope of the copyright registration? What did it cover? (3) Is there a way to tell a distinction between a blocking script and stage movement? (4) What were Einhorn's total alleged contributions to the final production? (5) What is the applicability of the Doctrine of "scenes a faire"?

Maxwell wrote that *scenes a faire* "specifically deals with dramatic conventions." It applies when theatrical incidents, settings, or characters are "so standard in the treatment of a given topic that they should not be protected by copyright."[13] Much like how a trademark eventually expires when a word becomes part of daily use in language, stock characters, standard movements, or common locations on stage cannot be covered by copyright because they should not limit the ability of use by other performers, directors, and designers.

In the end, the judge dismissed the case because neither party could answer his questions. The case is important because it has established the elements needed for a judge to rule on copyrighting a director's staging script. Jennifer Maxwell believes that as long as "stage directions can be shown to fulfill the copyright requirements" they "should be copyrightable."[14]

## LICENSING

So, now that you know what can and may one day be copyrighted, how do you produce or present performing arts without infringing on the copyright laws or rights of artists? Artists, arts organizations, schools, producers, and anyone who would like to use copyrighted material must license the music, dance, play, musical, or any artwork before use.

### Licensing Music

Determining how to license any artist's music can be a burden if the presenter does not understand the ins and outs of music licensing. Music licensing works the same way across all genres of music, including classical music. To play music in the lobby of a venue, as a sound effect or transitional piece in a play, to write a jukebox musical, to create a dance to copyrighted music, to play music in a gym, or even to perform a cover of music, the rights must be obtained for the use of the music. This may sound like a big job, however, with access to the proper resources, finding who holds the rights to any music can become normalized over time. Currently, one of the quickest ways to find out who owns the right for an artist's music is to ask their musical agent. The most reliable starting place to find an artist's agent is by using the Internet Movie Database's (IMDB) paid service. The paid service gives access to many performer's agents who manage their music, appearances, speaking engagement, performance, etc. Be careful, doing a simple Google search for an artist's agent will bring up several pages of false agents who are more than willing to contact an agent or licensing company for you with a very high upcharge. Learning how to find the agent and licensing agency for any artist is important when searching for licensing rights.

### Three Important Performing Rights Organizations

The three major performing rights organizations (PROs) for music are American Society of Composers, Authors, and Publishers (ASCAP), Broadcast Music Inc. (BMI), and The Society of European Stage Authors and Composers (SESAC). Each of these PROs has annual fees as well as individual use fees. Learning how each agency works is an important part of licensing music. The fees and potential legal issues, not to mention the reputation a presenting organization can get for not paying the fees can prove to be monumentally more detrimental than paying the licensing fees for music upfront.

1. **ASCAP** is a nonprofit PRO that licenses the music for over 845,000 musical artists across all genres of music and at all stages in their careers. Members of ASCAP receive royalties (approximately 88 cents per dollar they collect) that are split evenly between the writer and the publisher of the music. They license over 16 million songs and scores and have annual licensing fees for organizations playing the music as a part of ambiance or having it performed live (www.ascap.com).[15]

2. **BMI** has been licensing all genres of music for over 80 years. They "currently represent more than 1.1 million copyright owners and their over 17 million musical works" (https://www.bmi.com/).[16]

3. **SESAC** invites artists from Europe and the United States to join its ranks of licensed music. "SESAC currently licenses the public performances of more than 1 million songs on behalf of its 30,000 affiliated songwriters, composers, and music publishers." SESAC represents music publishers as well as film and television composers (https://www.sesac.com).[17]

Some music is not included in any of the PRO's named here. Often the music is owned and licensed by the artist or their descendants. This is the case with anything created by The Mamas & the Papas. To use their music, the licensing requests go directly to the artist's representatives. You can find out who an artist's music representative is by contacting their agent directly.

It is important to note that many classical compositions have expired copyrights. When this is the case, the music enters the public domain and can be played without obtaining musical licensing rights. However, it is essential to confirm the age of any classical piece of music played by an orchestra before assuming it is not covered. If an orchestra is playing a modern version of a classical work, it is strongly suggested that presenters confirm the age of the music from the artist representative and ask for the details for the program. It is a long and helpful tradition to cite the artists, including the composer and year of composition in the program for classical music audiences.

But, what about licensing for plays and musicals? That is a different set of licensing agencies.

## Theatrical Licensing

Obtaining the license to produce a play requires a small amount of research, but once you get the hang of licensing for plays and musicals, the search to find the licensing organization for a play usually leads presenters to one of several theatrical licensing houses. A few of the most influential licensing houses are:

1. **Concord Theatricals** who have recently acquired the catalog of Samuel French to add to their Rodgers & Hammerstein collection, their Andrew Lloyd Weber collection, the Tams-Witmark collection, and the work of Lin-Manual Miranda. They claim to be the "only firm providing truly comprehensive services to the creators and producers of plays and musicals, including theatrical licensing, music publishing, script publishing, cast recording and first-class production"[18] (www.concordtheatricals.com).

2. **Dramatic Publishing** was established in 1885. They are "committed to developing and serving authors, artists, and

educators"[19] by licensing both full-length, one-act plays, and some musicals (www.dramaticpublishing.com).

3. **Musical Theatre International (MTI)** grants "theaters from around the world the rights to perform the greatest selection of musicals from Broadway and beyond."[20] They were established in 1952 and hold the most popular musical theatre titles, such as *Disney's Newsies* (and all of Disney's musicals), all versions of *Annie, Billy Elliot, Hairspray, Godspell, West Side Story,* and many more (www.mtishows.com).

## Licensing for Other Forms of Art

Arts administrators, agents, producers, presenters, and artists come together throughout the year at conferences that have an arts marketplace where artists have booths and short 15-minute performances take place. The largest of the US conferences is the annual meeting of the Association of Performing Arts Professionals (APAP) in New York City. Their website (apap365.org) also offers extensive information, training, lectures, and a job bank that all arts administrators can benefit from, even if the annual trip to New York is outside the budget. In addition, smaller conferences showcase the artists' work in the state or region of the country in which they live. Another type of conference that showcases artists is created by genre. The list of agents and agencies who grant rights is immense and ever-changing. Even the most prominent agencies change drastically from year to year. So attendance at multiple conferences becomes vital for artists, agents, presenters, producers, grant funders, and anyone who is part of the performing arts to come to know what kinds of works, innovations, and trends are happening in various fields of the performing arts, and who the major rights granting agencies for each of the various fields is. This is where individual research is important, but being a part of the state-wide consortiums for the arts will be essential to keeping up to date with who is doing what each season.

## Final Thoughts

Copyright is a right guaranteed to people who are creating something new, from new life-saving medicines to the latest Broadway show, creativity in the arts and sciences has the protection of the US Bill of Rights (which includes the First Amendment to the US Constitution). The ownership protections of artists result from the goal to encourage innovation and creation. Since its creation, copyright has been litigated in the court system, but the most recent law that has shaped today's copyright is the Copyright Act of 1976. The legal system will continue to define copyright as long as artists continue to create new forms of art.

Artists gain copyright protections from the moment they create new works if it is published or not, as long as it is in a form that is tangible and can prove the arts fixity in a court of law. The exception to the rule is when an artist creates new work as part of their job duties or as a work for hire. In this case, ownership would go to the entity that paid for creating the artwork unless expressly stated otherwise in the contract. Copyright gives artists the ability to reproduce their work, adapt or derive other work from their original work, distribute copies of their work, display their work publically, and perform their work publicly. But these rights do have limits and restrictions.

It is important to remember that because a work is easily accessible for an artist, arts administrator, producer, presenter, director, or designer, that does not give anyone but the artist the right to use their work without express permission, unless one or more of three restrictions are met: fair use, first sale, and duration. Each of these restrictions allows for conversation and education. Bear in mind that when invoking any of these restrictions, they are still meant to protect the artist and will not protect an arts administrator from attempts to abuse them.

Many examples exist of theatrical producers who edited a play, even though the copyright (or rights) agreement expressly stated that script (and score for musicals) is required to be performed in its complete, original form. I could give a specific example here, but to respect the privacy of others, I will refrain. Instead, I will generally say that presenting the artwork in full is protected by copyright law in theatrical productions. Additionally, it shows respect for the artwork of the playwright and composer. When a rights granting agency finds out that copyrighted material has been cut and willfully violated, they will protect their artists first and levy a heavy fine. They have even been known to suspend the rights of an organization or an individual to produce their works, which can be an extensive catalog of musicals and/or plays. This is the same for rights to any kind of artwork.

Copyright infringement is not taken lightly by artists or the courts. The "additional reading," includes an article about the $600,000 settlement the rap artist, Eminem, received from the Nationalist Party of New Zealand who used his music without his permission. It is an interesting case of an artist with the means to take on an entire political party and win. But not all legal cases are so glamorous or have such decisive outcomes. Even so, each case is critical as it shapes the laws that protect artists' work, with the same goal that spurred copyright in the First Amendment, to encourage creators to continue to create.

## DISCUSSION QUESTIONS

1. Why do you think the founding fathers added this right to the United States Constitution?
2. In what situations would an artist's work fall under "work for hire"?
3. When does the use of copyrighted art fall under the Rules For Fair Use? What are some examples of when the artwork does not fall under the Rules For Fair Use that are new to you?
4. When does an item move from artwork to functional? Are there examples of this that you can name?
5. Can you think of words or symbols that are trademarked and are becoming part of everyday language?
6. Do you think a director should be able to protect their staging for any given production? Are there limits to what could be covered by copyright?
7. What do you do if you want to play pre-show music in your lobby that has a copyright on it?
8. How do you find out how to license a performing arts work? Where do you start?

## FURTHER READING

Artists Rights Society. 2020. "Artists Rights 101." https://arsny.com/artists-rights-101/.

Grow, Kory. "Paul McCartney Sues Sony over Beatles Music," *Rolling Stone Magazine*, January 18, 2019. https://www.rollingstone.com/music/music-news/paul-mccartney-sues-sony-over-beatles-music-191827/.

Elaine Hendriks Smith

Hull, Geoffrey P. 2009. "Fair Use." The First Amendment Encyclopedia, Middle Tennessee State University. https://mtsu.edu/first-amendment/article/956/fair-use.

Ugwu, Reggie. "Eminem's Publisher Triumphs in New Zeland Copyright Battle," *The New York Times*, October 15, 2017. https://www.nytimes.com/2017/10/25/arts/design/eminem-new-zealand-copyright.html

The United States Copyright Office. https://www.copyright.gov/.

The United States Patent and Trademark Office. https://www.uspto.gov/.

## Notes

1 United States Constitution, Article 1, Section 8. *The U.S. Constitution and other Key American Writings.* San Diego, CA: World Cloud Classics, 2015. (pg. 40)

2 "Copyright Law of the United States and Related Laws Contained in Title 17 of the United States Code." (n.d.)

3 US Copyright Office. "Copyright in General." *Copyright.gov.* https://www.copyright.gov/help/faq/faq-general.html#what

4 United States Copyright Office. "Subject Matter and Scope of Copyright." U.S. *Copyright Act*, vol 92, 19. https://www.copyright.gov/title17/92chap1.html#107

5 "1854. Copyright Infringement – First Sale Doctrine." The United States Department of Justice. https://www.justice.gov/archives/jm/criminal-resource-manual-1854-copyright-infringement-first-sale-doctrine

6 "Cooperative Patent Classifications." United States Patent and Trademark Office. https://www.uspto.gov/web/patents/classification/cpc/html/cpc-A63F.html

7 Moore, Adam and Ken Himma, "Intellectual Property." *The Stanford Encyclopedia of Philosophy* (Winter 2018 Edition), Edward N. Zalta (ed.). https://plato.stanford.edu/archives/win2018/entries/intellectual-property/.

8 Staff writer. "Trademarks: Protecting Your Nonprofit's Brand." *The NonProfit Times*, December 8, 2013. https://www.thenonprofittimes.com/npt_articles/trademarks-protecting-your-nonprofits-brand/

9 Moore, Adam and Kim Himma. "Intellectual Property." *Stanford Encyclopedia of Philosophy*, October 10, 2018. https://plato.stanford.edu/entries/intellectual-property/.

10 "Copyright Basics." *United States Copyright Office.* Library of Congress.

11 Playbill staff. "Mantello and Caldwell Theatre Settle L!V!C! Case; Issues Still Unresolved." *Playbill.com*, April 25, 1999. https://www.playbill.com/mantello-and-caldwell-theatre-settle -l-v-c-case-issues-still-unresolved-com-81475

12 Maxwell, Jennifer. "Making a Federal Case for Copyrighting Stage Directors: Einhorn v. Mergatroyd." *The John Marshall Review of Intellectual Property Law.* 7 J, Marshall rv. Intell. Prop. L. 393. 2008. (pg. 392 – 411)

13 Maxwell, Jennifer. (pg. 400)

14 Maxwell, Jennifer. (pg. 400)

15 American Society of Composers, Authors, and Publishers. (ASCAP). https://www.ascap.com/

16 Broadcast Music Inc. (BMI). https://www.bmi.com/licensing

17 The Society of European Stage Authors and Composers (SESAC). https://www.sesac.com/our-history

18 "Who We Are." Concord Theatricals. https://www.concordtheatricals.com/resources/who-we-are

19 "About Us." Dramatic Publishing. https://www.dramaticpublishing.com/about-dpc

20 "About Us." Music Theatre International. https://www.mtishows.com/about

# Unions and Contracts in the Arts

Julia Atkins

## Chapter 7

### INTRODUCTION

Knowing how unions and their contractual relationships work is vital for understanding how to operate most nonprofit arts organizations. We tend to think of unions as "labor" and companies as "management," however, the reality is that companies are made of management and employees, and unions are simply a way for employees to organize and gain greater control of their work requirements, pay, and benefits.

Decades ago, Anthony was hired to run a large organization, and his first few months included negotiating labor contracts with several major unions. He remembers feeling overwhelmed not by the amount of work, but by a lack of understanding about how the relationships were supposed to work. Some unions were very combative, while others were very congenial and willing to work together. Any lessons learned from one negotiation did little to inform the others. When he transitioned into academia, he realized that the lessons he learned from real-world challenges needed to be addressed in the classroom. Though Chapter 8 addresses negotiations, this chapter describes important foundational material necessary before an arts administrator can even begin the process of negotiating with a union.

DOI: 10.4324/9781003207535-8

Julia Atkins worked with Jay and Anthony on developing the Southeastern Arts Leadership Educators conference while she was a Ph.D. candidate at Florida State University. Her experiences in the arts, specifically in symphony orchestra management, made her a perfect partner for exploring unions and contracts. Having been a professional arts administrator and educator, Julia made clear she had a good perspective on these contractual relationships between management and employees, so we invited her to address the topics. She has developed material in a clear and succinct way.

Chapter 7 describes the formation of key unions with which many nonprofit arts organizations work. These unions established operational rules for the protection of their members. The discussion moves through subcategories of nonprofit arts organizations (theatre, museum, opera, dance, and orchestra) to explore the attributes unique to each field. Unions reviewed in the chapter include Actors Equity Association (AEA), International Alliance of Theatrical Stage Employees (IATSE), Stage Directors and Choreographers Society (SDC), American Guild of Musical Artists (AGMA), American Federation of Musicians (AFM), and American Guild of Variety Artists (AGVA). The reader will learn about the history, purpose, and central demands of each union and then be taken through an exploration of the common challenges between nonprofit management and unions.

## UNIONS AND CONTRACTS IN THE ARTS

*A Contribution by Julia Atkins*

Unions are an important part of business in the arts.[1] No matter what type of arts organization an administrator may work for, they will likely encounter union rules and regulations. In fact, arts organizations tend to follow union guidelines even when they are volunteer or nonunionized. Artists have long recognized the plight of the worker treated unfairly. Understanding the history and purpose of trade unions helps to effectively manage the organization you work for while creating a healthy work environment for artists and other staff. This chapter covers the history and purpose of unions in the arts, the unions one may encounter, and the challenges that sometimes occur between management and unions in arts organizations.

## HISTORY AND PURPOSE OF UNIONS IN THE ARTS

*Labor Unions* are organized groups of workers that make decisions about the working conditions, rights, and interests affecting their members.[2] Unions date back to the eighteenth century in the United States and Europe.[3] During this time, there was a surge of new workers, many of whom were mistreated, undervalued, and underpaid. Wealthy industrialists who owned companies could dictate any requirements to employees, and the employees had little bargaining power to strengthen their position until they realized they could band together. As a group, they posed a threat to management. When workers found safety in numbers—banding together—they realized the power of being "united" or a "union." Until that time, workers were abused and expected to work preposterously long hours in substandard conditions without proper compensation. Workers had no recourse because, as individuals, they were replaceable. Therefore, they needed representation and protection to ensure fair treatment in the workplace.

The art world was no different. For the arts, the need for union representation was as essential as it was for other industries. For example, it was common for musicians to play for hours with no break, no water, and for very little money. With no industry standard of acceptable working conditions for musicians, those who hired them could demand they play as long they wanted and in any environment. An individual artist could not risk offending an employer by asking for changes to their work conditions out of fear of losing the work altogether. Yet, if all musicians asked for changes simultaneously, the employer would have few options and would be put in a position necessitating compliance with the request for better conditions and higher wages. As a result, many artists' unions were established during the nineteenth and early twentieth centuries.

Existing artist unions were originally established to protect members, improve compensation, ensure benefits, and establish contractual rules by which the employer and employee must abide. Over the years, these standards have evolved to safeguard artists' best interests.

Today, thousands of artists are now union members.[4] Specialized unions represent different types of artists. Typically, a union has local branches (Locals) where an artist or employer can join, vote, and participate as desired. Locals are an incorporated part of a union that serves as the local bargaining units for individual employers, corporations, or industries.[5] Members engage with their local union representatives who serve their needs and interests, but ultimately belong to a national union with branches throughout the country.

Collective bargaining negotiations typically result in a collective bargaining agreement (CBA)[6] that serves as an contractual obligation between employer and employee. The CBA is generally limited to two or three years, as unions would like to renegotiate the terms of an agreement as often as possible. Bargaining results rarely become less favorable for workers; therefore, a CBA often provides improved working conditions and better pay for union members when renegotiated. Employers typically prefer longer-term CBAs that provide security in predicting future expenses. At the end of the CBA's duration, the interested parties gather to bargain over the terms of the CBA and adjust them as necessary. The key areas of the CBA typically include:

1. Compensation and benefits
2. Job specifications
3. Procedures and policies
4. Work rules, conditions, and safety
5. Seniority rules

The CBA is a legal contract that outlines negotiated terms between the employer and union members. Any employer that fails to comply with the terms listed in the CBA can result in hefty fines from the union and, sometimes, public scrutiny. Likewise, if a union member violates the terms of the CBA, they are open to termination by their employer under certain circumstances and disciplinary fines or expulsion from the union. Because CBA violations often have strict penalties, most organizations avoid them at all costs and do their best to comply with the terms agreed upon in the CBA. Though the CBA certainly protects the artist and provides them with much-needed working standards, many unions and the terms listed in CBAs have evolved to the point of hand-tying the organizations to what they can and cannot do. This is one reason unions and arts organizations may have conflict. CBAs also limit and specify restrictions for union members to protect them... even though the employer may see it as hand-tying. For example, a performing arts center Holiday celebration may last from 8 AM until midnight. To switch off crews in the middle of that could put the public at a safety risk but requiring those employees to work without special compensation for the extra hours might be unfair. The employer feels hand-tied, but it is done in the sense of fairness and safety. Everything must be weighed against a full spectrum of potential situations, with safety and equitability prioritized with unions. The chapter explores some of these challenges in the coming pages.

### CASE STUDY: GUGGENHEIM MUSEUM WORKERS UNIONIZE

Employees of the Guggenheim Museum organized to form a union to protect their employment and receive better wages. The formation came after a series of events, the first being in 2019. A spreadsheet was dispersed publicly among the museum and the art world that contained anonymous art workers' job titles and salaries alongside museum officials' salaries.[7] The spreadsheet showed that most museum officials made almost eight times as much as their curators, including those at the Guggenheim.

Additionally, when the COVID-19 pandemic hit in 2020, the Guggenheim Museum, specifically, cut more than 10%

of their staff.[8] Conservators, curators, digital marketers, educators, visitor services, and even administrative staff all sought to unionize to obtain greater wage equity, more transparency, and greater job security. In June 2019, the employees voted 57–20 to join Local 30 of the International Union of Operating Engineers (IUOE), which presently represents over 140 employees of the museum.[9] However, it took nearly a year of intense negotiations with the management of the Guggenheim to come to a contractual agreement. During much of the negotiations, employees claimed that management made it clear they understood the importance of their work but had no intention of raising wages.[10] Employees publicly accused management of "dragging their feet" on the negotiations and negotiating in "bad faith."[11] According to one source, management threatened that if employees went on strike they could be replaced permanently.[12] Despite it all, IUOE negotiated on their behalf to win the employees a three-year contract that covers 22 full-time staff and 145 on-call staff. The agreement secured these employees a 10% increase in salaries, annual bonuses for on-call workers, and benefits for full-time employees such as health care and retirement packages.[13]

## DIFFERENT UNIONS IN THE ARTS

There are many different unions for the arts, each representing members' unique skill sets or trades. This section focuses primarily on unions found in the United States, though some have equivalent sister unions worldwide. This section discusses the history of unions, what they do, how they work, how to become a member, and the main services unions provide.

### Actors Equity

The AEA is the US labor union that represents more than 51,000 professional actors and stage managers.[14] AEA serves its members in the live theatre industry by negotiating wages, improving working conditions, and negotiating and coordinating benefits. Similar to other unions, AEA works to negotiate the CBAs of actors and stage managers across the United States.

AEA was founded in New York City on May 26, 1913.[15] Until the early twentieth century, most actors' working conditions were determined by the shows' producers. Rehearsals had no time limit, leading some organizations to hold rehearsals lasting hours without breaks. After its founding, AEA called its first strike in 1919 to demand producers recognize AEA as the main representative and bargaining agent for actors. The strike lasted 30 days across eight different cities. It resulted in the closure of 37 plays and prevented the opening of 16 others. Producers lost millions of dollars. Once the strike ended, producers signed a five-year contract that included most of AEA's demands.

Today, AEA is governed by its members through an elected council.[16] The council represents actors, chorus actors, dancers, and stage managers through regional offices in the Eastern, Central, and Western parts of the United States. When an actor or stage manager joins AEA, they receive contractual and membership benefits. Contractual benefits are part of the CBA and include line items such as a set minimum salary, work rules, health insurance, pension, retirement packages, and dispute resolutions. Membership benefits include audition listings only available via AEA postings, member discounts, and other professional development tools. Each year, AEA has an open enrollment period where any stage manager or actor who has worked professionally on a theatre production in the United States can join. Previously, only stage managers and actors employed by an AEA employer could join. The open-access plan allows anyone to join to make union membership more equitable across the field.

## International Alliance of Theatrical Stage Employees

The IATSE is a union that serves live theatre, motion pictures, television production, trade shows and exhibitions, television broadcasting, and concerts.[17] IATSE's members are primarily the employees the audience does not see—the behind-the-scenes employees such as stagehands, carpenters, and electricians, to name a few. IATSE was founded in 1893 and comprised members from several different major cities across the United States. Within the United States and Canada, over 360 established locals comprise IATSE.

The local branches are organized by district, and each holds its own 501(c)(5) nonprofit entity. A 501(c)(5) nonprofit is different from a 501(c)(3) in that they are focused on labor, agriculture, and horticulture. Each IATSE local establishes its own rules and regulations, including membership benefits, contractual benefits, and dues through a democratic process. The founding members pledged to establish fair wages and safe working conditions for members of IATSE moving forward. Today, IATSE has over 150,000 members, and its mission continues to be about improving all entertainment workers' lives within and outside of the workplace.

## Stage Directors and Choreographers Society

The SDC is a union specifically for these specialized staff members of live theatre across the United States.[18] Their mission is

> to foster a national community of professional stage directors and choreographers by protecting the rights, health, and livelihoods of all our members; negotiating and enforcing employment agreements across a range of jurisdictions; facilitating the exchange of ideas, information and opportunities; and educating current and future generations about the critical role of directors and choreographers in leading the field.[19]

SDC has jurisdiction over venues including Broadway, Off-Broadway, dinner theatres, regional theatres, and regional musical theatres, to name a few. A collective of directors and choreographers founded SDC in 1959, SDC bargains for equitable wages and working conditions for stage directors and choreographers and continues to unite and protect their members to this day. There are two types of membership: full and associate. Full membership includes full protection as provided in CBAs, and full members may participate in the collective bargaining process. Associate members receive the benefits of association with SDC but do not receive the same level of protection from the CBA. Another crucial difference between full and associate membership is that full members are required to file a contract with SDC every time they work, whereas associate members can file but are not required to do so.[20]

## Association of Theatrical Press Agents & Managers

The Association of Theatrical Press Agents & Managers (ATPAM) is a local branch of the IATSE based in New York City that represents press agents, publicity and marketing specialists, company managers, and house and facility managers in staged entertainment of all types.[21] Founded in 1928, ATPAM developed like most other unions due to issues surrounding unfair wages and poor working conditions. However, unlike the other unions previously discussed, ATPAM does not do CBAs. Instead, they negotiate Minimum Basic Agreements (MBA) and Memorandums of Agreement (MOA). The MBA is negotiated with the League of American Theatre Owners and Producers and governs company and house managers who work on Broadway and touring productions.

In contrast, the MOA is negotiated with the Broadway League and is jointly administered by IATSE and ATPAM for press agents who work on Broadway and touring productions. Both the MBA and MOA cover the economic and working conditions of the members of ATPAM. ATPAM also administers other agreements with Off-Broadway organizations and regional theatrical venues such as the Kennedy Center, the Brooklyn Academy of Music, and Carnegie Hall, but they are not considered CBAs.

Any press agent or company manager can become a member of ATPAM.[22] Unlike the other unions discussed thus far, ATPAM has an Apprenticeship Program that allows members to receive certification from the union. The Apprenticeship Program is not required, but ATPAM highly recommends it to hold a contract and become a full member of ATPAM.

## United Scenic Artists

The United Scenic Artists (USA), founded in 1897, is another local branch of IATSE that represents over 5,000 member designers, artists, craftspeople, and department coordinators in film, theatre, opera, ballet, television, industrial shows, commercials, and exhibitions.[23] USA's main mission is to "foster and adopt ways and means for the continuous improvement of the working and living standards of the members of United Scenic Artists."[24] USA aims to secure legislation that benefits its members while also assuring higher wages and better working conditions.

Like other unions, USA's main function is to negotiate and administer CBAs for its members. There are three ways to become a member. One is by applying to become a member should the individual be hired under a CBA.[25] Many of these individuals are required to apply based on the CBA they receive. The second option is to undergo a review process that evaluates an individual's skills to be placed in a specific category.[26] These categories include scenic artist, scenic designer, costume designer, lighting designer, sound designer, projection designer, computer artist, and coordinator. The last option is participating in an Apprenticeship Program similar to that of ATPAM. However, the Apprenticeship Program for USA is only for scenic artists in New York City or St. Louis.

## American Guild of Musical Artists

The AGMA represents artists in opera, dance, and chorus.[27] These categories can include vocalists, dancers, actors, or production staff that work in opera, dance, and choral companies. AGMA's mission is to guarantee that artistic institutions in the United States adhere to fair labor practices that allow for gainful employment and high quality of life.[28]

AGMA was founded in 1936, originally for solo musical artists, although it expanded to include dancers, actors, and production staff later in the twentieth century.[29] Its first members included Frank Chapman, George Gershwin, and Paul Whiteman. The main function of AGMA is to negotiate CBAs that protect its members and improve their working lives.

An application process is required to become a member of AGMA. Membership benefits include gaining access to audition and job listings and other professional development resources.

## American Federation of Musicians

The AFM is a union that represents professional musicians across the United States.[30] Musician members of AFM perform in orchestras, backup bands, festivals, clubs, regional theatres, Broadway, and touring theatre productions. They also perform music for film, commercials, television, and other sound recordings. AFM was founded in 1896 with the same goal as many other unions to "elevate, protect, and advance the interests of all musicians who receive pay for musical services."[31] AFM's mission is to help its members live and work in dignity; seek fulfilling work for its members that is compensated fairly; have a meaningful voice in decisions that affect them; offer its members the opportunity to develop their talents and skills; be the collective voice and power for its members in a democratic process, and help oppose the forces of exploitation.

Individuals can apply for membership through their local AFM branch.[32] Most major cities have a local chapter. Collectively, the AFM has over 80,000 members.

## CASE STUDY: CBA CONDITIONS

An orchestra in the United States prepared to perform an outdoor concert for the Fourth of July. The orchestra's members were part of the union and their union representative present. The concert was sponsored by corporations and donors from the area, and approximately 6,000 people were in attendance. This concert was situated in a southern state in the United States, and the weather was very hot and humid that night. The orchestra's CBA had a line item that said *under no circumstances could the musicians perform in conditions where the temperature was above 85 degrees or less than 65 degrees on stage.* The union representative stood on stage with a thermometer to assess the temperature and found that the temperature read 89 degrees 10 minutes before the concert. Due to the line item in the CBA, the orchestra had to postpone the concert's start.

About 15 minutes after the expected concert start time, the temperature had dropped from 89 degrees to 87 degrees. After 30 minutes, the temperature had dropped to 86 degrees. The primary sponsor of the concert asked if the concert could begin at this time, arguing that there were thousands of audience members waiting for the music and they could not be kept waiting any longer. The union representative said no, they had to wait until the thermometer read 85 degrees. The union representative gave the go-ahead for the musicians to take the stage and start the concert when the thermometer finally read 85 degrees, an hour after the concert should have begun. Additionally, the orchestra had to cut pieces of music from the program because they risked going over time. A separate line item in the CBA indicated how long a service could last. The clock started ticking at the time the musicians took the stage originally. Because the orchestra started an hour late, they could only perform 45 minutes of music.

Though the union representative was there to make sure the musicians were not performing in extreme conditions, the audience and sponsors were unhappy due to the long wait time. As a result, the orchestra would not again be asked to perform at the Fourth of July concert.

## American Guild of Variety Artists

The AGVA represents artists and stage managers in live variety performances.[33] Members include singers and dancers in theatrical revues and touring shows (non-book shows), theme park performers, skaters, circus performers, comedians & stand-up comics, cabaret and club artists, lecturers, poets, monologists, spokespersons, and variety performers working at private parties & special events.[34] AGVA negotiates CBAs for its members to set fair wages, benefits, and safe working conditions. AGVA members include performers at the Disneyland Resort and Walt Disney World, Universal Studios, Cirque du Soleil, and the Radio City Music Hall Rockettes. In addition, cities like Las Vegas and Atlantic City often have performers working under an AGVA CBA.

In order to become a member, individuals must have received an AGVA contract from their place of employment.[35] An application must be submitted through the membership department for independent variety artists and self-produced artists.

## CHALLENGES BETWEEN MANAGEMENT AND UNIONS

Unions are an asset for arts organization employees and contracted artists. Most cannot disagree with that testament, considering the substandard working conditions most artists endured before unions were organized. Indeed, unions exist to ensure employees earn a decent living without worrying about compensation or poor working conditions. However, many challenges exist between unions and arts organizations today. Though compensation, benefits, and working conditions may be highly improved for the employees compared to the pre-union past, working with unions can hinder managers. The negotiating process can feel adversarial, and any change in working conditions or costs will adversely affect an organization's budget. When money is at stake, people tend to tread very carefully.

First, the process of negotiating CBAs with arts organizations can be challenging. Many arts managers and artists know that if they do not agree with the demands of union representatives, managers risk their employees going on strike, creating public scrutiny about the organization, or leaving their organization entirely. This illustration is not meant to say that all bargaining occurs this way—there are union negotiators who are very good at bargaining a CBA that serves the artist's needs as well as management (see the next chapter, which addresses negotiations). However, there are many negotiations that fail to find a resolution and can therefore result in a strike.

Likewise, should management feel the union is demanding too many concessions or benefits that might jeopardize the organization completely, management can decide to "lockout" union members, essentially forcing them into unpaid leave until the disagreement can be resolved. In some cases, a lockout can lead to the permanent termination of union members and replacement with non-union workers. A strike is a collective refusal by employees to work under the conditions set by the employer.[36] Typically, strikes or lockouts are used as a last resort but serve a purpose in negotiating the CBA before the term of the CBA runs out.[37] Many strikes or lockouts are warranted, depending on how one frames the issues involved. Often, one can easily argue for or against the artist or management. Both the employee and employer avoid strikes and lockouts as much as possible as any strike or lockout brings the public eye. However, strikes or lockouts are inevitable if a consensus cannot be reached.

Compensation and benefits packages tend to be a point of contention in many negotiations, largely because money is always a hot topic. For instance, symphony orchestra artist salaries have put many organizations into difficult financial positions. Artistic costs such as musician, guest artist, and conductor salaries have risen so that they amount to over half of an orchestra's expenses; rising from the start of union negotiations that began in 1962.[38] With the addition of inflation over the past several decades, the minimum annual salary for a musician in the Los Angeles Philharmonic in 2017 was $154,336.[39] Though excellent for employees, large minimum annual salaries may hurt some nonprofit arts organizations that must find alternative means to raise more money to afford their services.

For management, ever-rising costs against income are difficult to predict. Economic fluctuations, inflation, donor contributions, and public demand can shift regularly and become problematic. Imagine that a symphony has two years left before renegotiating its CBA. When the CBA is negotiated, ticket sales are robust, and union musicians rightly feel they deserve a large share of the income since their artistry is the primary driving factor for attendance. However, if ticket sales dry up for an extended period—or a season—that does not release management from salaries negotiated based on a higher anticipated income. You can see the obvious challenge for management. In the CBA, management must promise to provide a certain amount of money and benefits to union members without an assurance that the money will be available to pay out. Many artists claim this is how it needs to be as there is no arts organization without the artist themselves.

Artists have long struggled to demonstrate that their value is worth livable wages and benefits, a reasonable demand for any employee. Artists are indeed vital to arts organizations. An orchestra does not exist without musicians, and theatre productions do not exist without directors and actors. Understanding this truth is why most managers fear the possible strike or walk-out if they do not agree with what is presented at the bargaining meeting. Though we would like to think that arts organizations will not keep their artists in a six- to

Julia Atkins

seven-hour-long rehearsal with no breaks, it must be clarified. Tensions run high as opening night approaches, and oftentimes the rehearsal required goes beyond what would be considered a normal 9-to-5 workday.

However, the challenge is not with the foundation of the CBA, it is with the finer details. Unions are very much needed since they establish a standard in which all arts organizations follow to take care of their artists and employees. However, as with anything, unions certainly do not come without their challenges.

## CASE STUDY: THE MINNESOTA ORCHESTRA LOCKOUT

The Minnesota Orchestra endured a 15-month labor dispute between its musicians and management in 2012, marking it one of the longest labor disputes in American classical music history.[40] The Minnesota Orchestra was in financial distress, announcing large deficits in 2011 and 2012. It was drawing funds from its endowment to stay in business. The orchestra's leadership proposed to lower musician salaries by 30%–40% to cut back on their expenses. Inevitably, musicians refused to accept the stark decrease in salary, and negotiations with the union occurred. When both parties failed to find an agreement, a lockout ensued. The lockout was very divisive. Some felt the musician salaries were far above what they should be making, as many were earning six-figure salaries and felt the cut would benefit the organization.

In contrast, others were outraged that management could so flippantly lower salaries and felt the organization was insensitive to the well-being of its musicians. Finally, after 15 months, both parties came to an agreement to lower musician salaries by 15%. This outcome kept the Minnesota Orchestra one of the top 10 best-paid orchestras in the United States. However, the scrutiny that came from the lockout will remain with the Minnesota Orchestra for many years to come.

## CONCLUSION

This chapter gave a brief overview of unions in the arts. By this point, it should be clear why unions exist, what types of unions exist, and how they serve employees in the arts. As a whole, unions set a standard by which the arts industry must abide. Even non-union organizations follow standards set by the union to take care of their employees and operate from best practices. Though challenges certainly exist, unions ensure a safe and equitable work environment and help employers build trust with employees and a more productive, secure workforce.

## DISCUSSION QUESTIONS

1. If given a free choice and was not required by an employer, would you join a union? Why, or why not?
2. What are the positive and negative impacts of a unionized arts organization?
3. What are the positive and negative impacts of a non-unionized arts organization?
4. How would you approach collective bargaining if you were a union negotiator at the bargaining table?
5. If you were an arts manager at the negotiating table, how would you come to an agreement with the union that would serve both the organization and the artist?

### FURTHER READING

"A Brief History of Unions," Union Plus: https://www.unionplus.org/page/brief-history-unions

This website discusses the history of labor unions generally as they pertain to the US. This website is an ideal place to learn about how unions were and are formed.

Any websites of the unions discussed in this chapter. These websites are ideal for understanding more about each union and how they work within the arts:

Actors Equity: https://www.actorsequity.org/

American Federation of Musicians: https://www.afm.org/

American Guild of Musical Artists: https://www.musicalartists.org/

American Guild of Variety Artists: https://agvausa.com/

Association of Theatrical Press Agents & Managers: https://www.atpam.com/

IATSE: https://iatse.net/

United Scenic Artists: https://www.usa829.org/

Julia Atkins

# Notes

1  William Byrnes, *Management and the Arts*. Routledge, 2014.

2  "What Is a Union?" Union Plus, accessed on November 1, 2021, https://www.unionplus.org/page/what-union.

3  "A Brief History of Unions," Union Plus, accessed on November 1, 2021, https://www.unionplus.org/page/brief-history-unions.

4  "Actors Equity: Association 1913," Actors Equity, accessed on November 1, 2021, https://www.actorsequity.org/.

5  "Local Union," Local Union and Legal Definition, US Legal, accessed on November 1, 2021, https://definitions.uslegal.com/l/local-union/.

6  William J. Byrnes, *Management and the Arts*.

7  Elizabeth A. Harris and Robin Pogrebin, "Inside Hushed Museum Hallways, a Rumble over Pay Grows Louder," *The New York Times*, last modified on July 22, 2019, https://www.nytimes.com/2019/07/22/arts/museum-pay-unions.html.

8  Alex Greenberger, "Guggenheim Museum Workers Push to Unionize Amid Wave of Organizing across U.S. Museums," *ARTnews*, last modified on August 2, 2021, https://www.artnews.com/art-news/news/guggenheim-museum-union-drive-uaw-1234600541/.

9  Elizabeth A. Harris and Robin Pogrebin, "Inside Hushed Museum Hallways, a Rumble over Pay Grows Louder," *The New York Times*, last modified on July 22, 2019, https://www.nytimes.com/2019/07/22/arts/museum-pay-unions.html.

10  Hakim Bashira, "Guggenheim Signs Contract with Union after a Year of Tense Negotiations," *Hyperallergic*, last modified on February 16, 2021, https://hyperallergic.com/622396/guggenheim-signs-union-contract-local-30/.

11  Hakim Bashira, "Guggenheim Signs Contract with Union after a Year of Tense Negotiations/".

12  Brian Boucher, "After a Bitter Battle, the Guggenheim and Its New Union Have Struck a Deal for Improved Pay and Benefits," *Artnet News*, last modified on February 17, 2021, https://news.artnet.com/art-world/guggenheim-agreement-union-1944606.

13  Brian Boucher, "After a Bitter Battle, the Guggenheim and Its New Union Have Struck a Deal for Improved Pay and Benefits."

14  "Actors Equity: Association 1913," Actors Equity, accessed on November 1, 2021, https://www.actorsequity.org/.

15  "Actors Equity: Association 1913," November 1, 2021, https://www.actorsequity.org/.

16  "Actors Equity: Association 1913," November 1, 2021, https://www.actorsequity.org/.

17  "IATSE: The Union behind Entertainment," IATSE, accessed on November 1, 2021, https://iatse.net/.

18  "SDC: Stage Directors and Choreographers Society," SDC, accessed on November 1, 2021, https://sdcweb.org/.

19  "SDC: Stage Directors and Choreographers Society," November 1, 2021, https://sdcweb.org/.

20  "SDC: Stage Directors and Choreographers Society," November 1, 2021, https://sdcweb.org/.

21  "ATPAM: Association of Theatrical Press Agents & Managers," ATPAM, accessed on November 1, 2021, https://www.atpam.com/.

22  "ATPAM: Association of Theatrical Press Agents & Managers," November 1, 2021, https://www.atpam.com/.

23  "Local USA 829: United Scenic Artists," United Scenic Artists, accessed on November 1, 2021, https://www.usa829.org/.

24  "Local USA 829: United Scenic Artists," November 1, 2021, https://www.usa829.org/.

25  "Local USA 829: United Scenic Artists," November 1, 2021, https://www.usa829.org/.

26  "Local USA 829: United Scenic Artists," November 1, 2021, https://www.usa829.org/.

27  "AGMA: American Guild of Musical Artists," AGMA, accessed on November 1, 2021, https://www.musicalartists.org/.

28 "AGMA: American Guild of Musical Artists," November 1, 2021, https://www.musicalartists.org/.

29 "AGMA: American Guild of Musical Artists," November 1, 2021, https://www.musicalartists.org/.

30 "American Federation of Musicians," American Federation of Musicians, accessed on November 1, 2021, https://www.afm.org/.

31 "American Federation of Musicians," November 1, 2021, https://www.afm.org/.

32 "American Federation of Musicians," November 1, 2021, https://www.afm.org/.

33 "AGVA: American Guild of Variety Artists," American Guild of Variety Artists, accessed on November 1, 2021, https://agvausa.com/.

34 "AGVA: American Guild of Variety Artists," November 1, 2021, https://agvausa.com/.

35 "AGVA: American Guild of Variety Artists," November 1, 2021, https://agvausa.com/.

36 "Strike," Britanica, accessed on November 18, 2021, https://www.britannica.com/topic/strike-industrial-relations.

37 "Union Negotiation Tactics," Organized Labor Relations, Lumen, accessed on November 1, 2021, https://courses.lumenlearning.com/boundless-business/chapter/union-negotiation-tactics/.

38 Jeffrey Pompe and Lawrence Tamburri, "Fiddling in a Vortex: Have American Orchestras Squandered Their Supremacy on the American Cultural Scene?" *The Journal of Arts Management, Law, and Society,* 46, no. 2 (2016): 63–72.

39 Jeffrey Pompe and Lawrence Tamburri, "Fiddling in a Vortex: Have American Orchestras Squandered Their Supremacy on the American Cultural Scene?"

40 Anne Midgette, "Minnesota Orchestra Lockout Ends After 15 Months as Musicians Approve 3-Year Contract," *Washington Post,* January 15, 2014, https://www.washingtonpost.com/entertainment/music/minnesota-orchestra-lockout-ends-after-15-months-as-musicians-approve-3-year-contract/2014/01/15/d42c4014-7e10-11e3-93c1-0e888170b723_story.html

# Negotiations in the Arts

Anthony Rhine and
Jay Pension

# Chapter 8

## INTRODUCTION

The focus of Chapter 8 is negotiating, a vital talent in the job
of an arts administrator. If you recall from the introduction to
Chapter 7, Anthony once had to coordinate negotiations with
several unions immediately after starting a new job. The board
instructed him that the labor negotiations were immediately
required as contracts were about to expire. It was Anthony's first
time negotiating labor contracts, and he was ill-prepared. After
understanding the foundations of unions, the largest challenge
in labor negotiations is how to interact with an opposing side in
a way that leads to positive results for everyone.

Though the chapter addresses union negotiations, it also
addresses other forms of negotiations. Certainly, we all negotiate
regularly over simple, daily things, but the arts administrator
negotiates salaries, contracts, royalty agreements, donor
agreements, marketing trades, and more. The frequency of
negotiation that occurs at a nonprofit arts organization is probably
higher than for most traditional businesses, as the organization
both relies upon and works for the benefit of the community. By its
very nature, the structure of a nonprofit arts organization implies
that negotiating is an important talent to possess.

The chapter discusses negotiation basics such as the
bargaining zone, information, objectives, outcomes, time, and

DOI: 10.4324/9781003207535-9

needs versus wants. Digging deeper, the reader is then led through an explanation of relationships in negotiations, and why it is essential to focus on them. A lengthy discussion of the BATNA is followed by consideration of Fred Jandt's Win–Win Negotiating process. As an extra pedagogical tool, this chapter also includes case studies for readers to consider the detailed challenges with union contract negotiation.

## NEGOTIATIONS IN THE ARTS

Negotiations are not just for big business or politicians. Each day we make internal negotiations about what we should do and how we should do it. We weigh the pros and cons of multiple sides of a decision, interpret all the relevant input, and make a decision based on this internal negotiation. Likely, we also negotiate with other people almost every day. "Where do you want to go to lunch?" is not just a simple query but an opening salvo in a negotiation. Of course, some negotiations are more intense than others. Typically, higher stake outcomes lead to a greater intensity of negotiation. However, regardless of the intensity of negotiation, the same basic tenants are true for the process, and they all relate to human nature.

Formal and informal negotiations frequently occur in arts organizations. An arts administrator may negotiate internally in planning their day to determine what tasks to complete and when. Employees negotiate with the arts organization regarding their pay and benefits. A marketing director may negotiate the timeline for announcements within their department. Departments frequently negotiate with each other for resources and time. Arts organizations themselves negotiate with external organizations, government offices, and frequently—unions. Union negotiations may be the first type of negotiation that comes to mind in conjunction with an arts organization. Regardless of the level of negotiation and whether the negotiation is formal or informal, the basics of negotiation hold true in all circumstances for arts organizations.

### LEARNING OBJECTIVES

By the time you have finished reading this chapter, you should be able to...

Anthony Rhine and Jay Pension

- Describe how BATNAs can be used in arts organization negotiations.
- Prioritize potential negotiating strategies for different types of negotiations.
- Explain the value of silence and how an arts administrator could use it during a negotiation.
- Define why it is essential to understand both parties' needs in a negotiation.
- Illustrate how an arts administrator could mirror back tentative understandings during a negotiation and why it is useful.

## Negotiating Basics

Though many experts provide recommendations on the best negotiating practices, this chapter explores the most commonly suggested approaches to an effective negotiation that you can apply to arts organizations. Most experts agree that the best negotiations are those where the negotiators have conducted detailed and explicit research and preparation for the negotiation. This chapter includes three cases that illustrate how a new executive director of the Santa Barbara Civic Light Opera led three separate union negotiations in his first year.

## BATNA

BATNA is an acronym for the *best alternative to a negotiated agreement*. A BATNA is applied when negotiations occur between two entities and is planned in advance of negotiation.[1] Essentially, it is the bottom line for the negotiator who establishes how far they are willing to compromise before the compromise becomes ineffective. It sometimes makes walking away from the negotiations a better alternative to a less-than-satisfactory result.

The BATNA serves several purposes. It provides a bottom line for the negotiator, so they can withdraw when negotiations are unsatisfactory. The BATNA also provides bargaining strength in knowing where a good result and a poor result diverge. Finally, the BATNA also provides a backup solution in case the negotiations simply fail.

A great strength of the BATNA is that it clarifies goals, provides strategic planning, and guides negotiation from the perspective of both parties. Contemplating the other party's BATNA strengthens a negotiation because it allows you to discern where the two parties might find agreement. For example, imagine that Helen works as a stage manager and could be hired at a new arts organization. Helen believes that the salary should be at least $1,000 per week. Vinny, the executive director of the new arts organization, has seen stage managers hired for $850 per week in similar organizations. Though Vinny would prefer to pay only $650 per week, one alternative to negotiating a price with Helen is to hire someone else for $850. So, Vinny's BATNA is $850, and the goal in negotiating is to get a price closer to $650. If it goes over $850, Vinny walks away and can hire someone else. Helen would like to get $1,250 per week but knows that some stage managers are willing to work for less. Helen explores what other stage managers receive and decides that the BATNA is when the negotiation gets the salary below $900 per week because Helen knows another company will offer them $900.

In this case, the buyer's and seller's BATNAs have no overlap. Vinny's BATNA starts once the weekly rate drops to $850, but Helen's BATNA walk-away rate is anything below $900. However, if Helen decides that the lowest acceptable weekly rate is $800, there is a window of overlap between the two BATNAs in the weekly rate of $800–$850. Any negotiated agreement that lands in this range will be acceptable to both parties. This sweet spot is sometimes referred to as the *ZOPA*, which stands for the *zone of potential (or possible) agreement.*[2]

To determine a BATNA, a negotiator must consider all alternatives to a negotiated result.[3] They may ask themselves: what are the possibilities if a negotiated agreement cannot be reached? How many alternatives exist, and what are they? The negotiator then considers every possible alternative and its value to them. The BATNA is derived by examining the value of each alternative and selecting the alternative that would provide the greatest value. By knowing the value of the best alternative, the negotiator can then decide what amount of value must be derived from a negotiation to exceed the value derived from the alternative.

Anthony Rhine and Jay Pension

One additional note about the BATNA: determining one's own BATNA is vital in the negotiating process. Likewise, attempting to discern the BATNA of the opposing party is an additional preparation that negotiators use to help ensure successful bargaining. By understanding both BATNAs, negotiators can navigate the tricky waters of negotiation much more successfully.

Though we have addressed the BATNA as a number that can set a maximum and minimum acceptable tradeoff in a negotiation, the BATNA can often be used for individual pieces of a larger negotiation. On a performing arts union contract negotiation, for example, issues like health care, retirement, salaries, and the like can all be separate issues with separate BATNAs, and together they form a single negotiation that has its own BATNA. Thus, the amount of preparation for a significant negotiation can be lengthy but vital if the negotiators wish to succeed.

### Bargaining Zone

The bargaining zone is the area of overlap between the BATNAs of both parties.[4] This zone is the place where the negotiation will land successfully. Because negotiations can have hundreds of areas where the parties establish BATNAs, they sometimes change during the negotiation process. As a result, a certain amount of give-and-take is required from one issue to the next, as they are interconnected in a lengthy or expansive negotiation.

### Information Is Power

It is a long-held axiom that information is power and that sentiment holds true in negotiations. Therefore, the more information you have about the issues in the negotiation, the better off you will be as a negotiator. Understanding the depth of financial issues, the challenges facing the opposing party, presumed BATNAs for both sides, and a host of other information will allow the negotiator to be prepared to navigate the bargaining table.[5]

Though negotiators can and do much research before entering a negotiation, the negotiation in itself can also be a source of information for the savvy negotiator. Certainly, in advance of negotiation much preparatory work can be done, including studying the competition, their other competitors, market stakeholders, and any other relevant collaborators. The better one knows the opposing party, the more likely the resulting negotiation will produce a stronger result for the negotiator.[6] Information can also be gleaned from the opposing party during negotiation by asking pointed, planned, and specific questions designed to reveal at least some idea of the opposing party's position. Also, the clever negotiator can analyze nonverbal cues and interpret spoken responses for glimpses that might reveal when a negotiation is getting close to the opposing party's walk-away position.[7]

## CASE STUDY: SANTA BARBARA CIVIC LIGHT OPERA AND ACTORS EQUITY ASSOCIATION

Information is power, and sometimes providing complete transparency and sharing information with the opposing party can turn a negotiation in an arts organization's favor. When the Santa Barbara Civic Light Opera (SBCLO) company hired its new executive director, the arts organization was already in dire financial straits. The organization's financial challenges meant that to survive, significant cuts to their annual budget were necessary.

After reviewing the financials, the executive director recognized that one of the theatre's largest expenses was the union performers. After exploring multiple other options, they decided to reduce the number of Actors Equity Association (AEA) contracts for actors in half and hire non-union actors in their place for the following year. The SBCLO and AEA soon coordinated their formal negotiation for the performers' contracts.

Initially, AEA was resistant to any change in the number of union performers and came in requesting a raise for all the performers. The SBCLO was prepared with research about their organization and presented the financials to AEA, disclosing that they had briefly considered becoming a non-union company. They invited AEA to examine their financials so that AEA could have full knowledge of the challenges. This clarity provided the opportunity for AEA to partner with the SBCLO to find possible solutions. Ultimately, AEA agreed that current terms were not sustainable for the theatre at that time. They worked together with the understanding that if they moved to cut the number of AEA contracts in half, they would return to the previous agreement once the organization's financial concerns were reduced.

By providing full transparency, the SBCLO was able to show that they were not trying to avoid the union contracts but rather that the union contracts would sink the organization. This transparency brought the union and the organization more closely together and strengthened the relationship. When the news was announced to the union members, some wanted to picket the first production, but AEA came to the SBCLO's defense and prevented the picket line since AEA had co-created the arrangement.

## Know Objectives from Both Sides

Knowing the BATNA is incredibly valuable in the negotiating process, but knowing or having some understanding of the opposing party's objectives is equally as useful. Typically, the objectives, or major objectives, are of the greatest importance to each party. Knowing major objectives makes it easier to dispense with smaller issues or use some of those smaller issues and their associated BATNAs as bargaining tools, used as giveaways to provide strength for negotiating major issues.

Many negotiators in arts organizations enter the discussion with one or more items or issues that they feel they can "give away" to the opposing party as both a gesture of goodwill and in exchange for other tradeoffs in the process.[8] When entering a negotiation, it is always wise to know what you are willing and capable of giving away to the opposing party. Occasionally, these giveaways can even be used as decoys to divert attention from more major issues, or as intentional focus grabbers that can be satisfied in favor of the opposing party. These decoys are typically items of little or no consequence to the negotiator.

Also, an important objective is to know what you want and ask for it. Too many negotiations end with an undesirable result because one party was too afraid to tip their hand and, as a result, never asked directly for what they wanted or needed. Always be sure to ask, and make the ask aggressive. Negotiations are never about "no" until it is determined that the two parties are too far apart and unwilling to compromise any further.

### Be Prepared for Any Outcome (and Be Okay with It)

One long-held theory in negotiating is that you need to be prepared for any number of possible outcomes from the perfect negotiation, to a walk-out cannot be rectified. Because a negotiator is dealing with many unknowns and the human behavior attached to them, any possible outcome can occur at any time. The savvy arts administrator is always prepared to deal with any contingency.

In order to demonstrate that preparedness, it is often wise to make a move that demonstrates a strong mastery of negotiation at the start of the process. By demonstrating strong skills, the negotiator creates a foundation upon which to build. If the opening salvos of the negotiation are weak, it is very difficult to change course and establish a different position. There is no "catching up" in negotiating around arts issues.

The strong negotiator must always be prepared to put an end to the negotiations as well. This scenario is most common when arts organizations negotiate with unions, but arts administrators may stop negotiations in other high-stakes situations. Sometimes that may be a temporary stop to allow time for discussions to sink in and have their impact, and sometimes that may be a hard stop that includes walking away never to return. Canceling negotiations is never ideal and defeats the purpose of the negotiation, but just as risky is an attempt to continue negotiations when one or more parties cannot move into an area of agreement. Identifying stumbling blocks is important, but shutting down negotiations when there is no chance of compromise is essential. Likewise, if the conditions, terms, or behavior of the other party makes the negotiation difficult, challenging, intense, or problematic, it is always appropriate to ask for a break. If the conditions of

Anthony Rhine and Jay Pension

negotiation created by the other party are unacceptable, it is essential to be clear with an unwillingness to participate in that fashion and to walk away, leaving the other party to wonder if you will return. Sometimes this process leaves the opposite party hanging and in need of a completed negotiation, and by having them "on the hook," they will be more inclined to reach an amicable conclusion and accept less favorable terms than they otherwise might have.

## Schedule Enough Time

Many arts administrators have shared that they have too little time to complete their day-to-day responsibilities. This perspective may impact their decision-making when it comes to scheduling negotiations. They may underestimate the amount of time a serious, dedicated discussion and negotiation will take. A timing issue such as this inevitably leads to major decisions being pushed off until the last minute when the stakes are highest, the pressure is greatest, and the opportunities for failure lie everywhere. Both parties will be better off by allowing sufficient time to complete the negotiation and scheduled topic discussions throughout the negotiating period.

## Needs versus Wants

Many negotiators differentiate wants and needs regarding specific issues within a negotiation. Needs are items that must be achieved for the negotiation to be considered successful, and wants are items that would make the result feel favorable but are not required to reach a mutually agreeable conclusion. Distinguishing between the two allows the negotiator to focus their energy on the most vital issues, as with the BATNA, a negotiator who seeks to understand both sides' wants and needs will be better prepared for any negotiation.

## Relationships

To some people in the arts, the concept of negotiation may seem adversarial in nature. It is often easy to portray the opposing party as an enemy or someone to beat. There is a certain amount of truth in the idea that one is attempting to outmaneuver and perhaps even manipulate the opposing party into a subordinate position. It is rarely the case, however, that the person on the other side of the table, given the totality of the relationship, is an adversary. On the contrary, the person on the other side of the table likely has a mutual interest in finding a solution that will be satisfactory to both parties. Of course, we want the resolution to be most satisfactory for our interests, but the best solution is to find common ground and then compromise as a means to achieve our goals.[9,10] Compromising does not mean that the opposing party is not trying to end the negotiation with a better hand than you, but that both parties have a mutual goal. Often, a negotiation occurs with someone we already work with or with whom we want to work. For example, consider an arts union negotiation. In that instance, non-union management talks with their staff, the union labor, about working conditions. It is in the best interests of both parties to have the best possible working conditions, so the negotiation is about what constitutes the best possible working conditions and what is manageable from an administrative perspective. Certainly, there is plenty of room for disagreement about what constitutes the best possible working conditions, and in fact, there can even be disagreement about what is feasible to accomplish. However, both parties are attempting to create a better work environment for everyone involved. Losing sight of this commonality and making the opposing party an enemy can make the negotiation more difficult. The opposing party is a partner in finding a solution, not an adversary to defeat.

It is easy to say "put yourself in someone else's shoes" and much more difficult to do it. However, if you have done adequate research, crunched numbers, and compared positions, you are in a much better place to consider how and what your opposition thinks in a negotiation. Attempting to understand the other party and their desires helps to make way for a collaborative negotiation.

### Dealing with Objections

There will most certainly be a time in arts negotiations when the other party either formally or informally objects to something or demonstrates serious disapproval of a position you hold or a statement you make. That is okay. Part of the negotiation process is to learn and understand the thoughts and feelings of the other party. Even if the objection is insulting, a negotiator need not take that approach personally. Instead, they may ask for clarification to learn more about their position and how the opposing party is approaching it. Asking questions is one of the strongest ways to successfully complete a negotiation, as it is the best way to gain knowledge. Ask for very specific answers to topics. Try to tease out details of where, when, and how much the other party wants to negotiate. When an opposing party objects to something, it is an opportunity to listen carefully and gain important knowledge if you approach the situation thoughtfully.

Never interrupt the other party. If they are speaking, they are sharing valuable information with you. Allow them to finish, ask for further clarification and details, take time to absorb the information, and then embark on a more robust discussion. Remember that if you focus too much on small details, you may fail to succeed in your larger aims. Fighting rarely, if ever, ends in a successful result.

### Know When to Stop

Many negotiators are skilled at talking, asking questions, gaining clarity, fleshing out details, and getting to yes, but they do not know when to stop talking. A poor negotiator may not take the time to listen genuinely. In negotiations, keep your voice in check, and know that what you hear is going to serve you far better than what you say. Negotiations are not about trying to prove your point, and if you are constantly speaking, you are trying to prove your point. Step away from the negotiation, regroup, and move forward with questions. Great negotiating is far less about talking and more about listening.[11]

Finally, remember that anything you say cannot be eliminated from the conversation after being said. Choose your words carefully, as the other party will hear and remember everything that you say. Consider writing down what points you wish to discuss, ensuring that you do not share unnecessary information in the process.

### Win–Win Negotiating

In 1985, Fred Jandt released the book *Win–Win Negotiating: Turning Conflict into Agreement*, which became a very popular title among management professionals.[12] Though Jandt addressed the issues and topics explored so far in this chapter, he added a folksy quality and made it clear that some more important details must be considered in the negotiation process.

Jandt went to great lengths to describe the many options one might choose from in a negotiation. He started by indicating that winning everything and having your opponent lose everything is just as unacceptable as if you were to lose everything and your opponent won everything. In neither of these cases is the solution a good, workable one that leaves relationships intact.

What mattered for Jandt, and should matter for all negotiators, is the value of the relationship. Because a negotiation should never damage or even mar the relationship, particularly when the relationship is strong and the stakes are high. It is vitally important to keep in mind the value of winning when held against the value of the relationship. This perspective can help keep negotiations productive.

### CASE STUDY: SANTA BARBARA CIVIC LIGHT OPERA AND THE AMERICAN FEDERATION OF MUSICIANS

As the new executive director prepared for a negotiation with the American Federation of Musicians (AFM), he thought back to the negotiation with AEA. Though he was not proposing to cut the number of union musicians, he prepared all the same paperwork to show why the SBCLO would not be able to offer raises and would need to maintain the existing financial arrangement to stay solvent. Though it was his first negotiation with the AFM, he felt prepared for the challenge having just successfully completed the AEA negotiation.

Upon sitting down with the AFM representatives, however, the conversation took an unexpected turn. Though AFM did ask for a raise, their request was meager compared with what the executive director expected. More surprising, their primary concerns were less about pay and more about the working conditions of the orchestra pit. First, they complained that they had not been provided with new chairs as promised in the last negotiation. The musicians felt that the chairs were old and uncomfortable. AFM shared that they felt they had not been heard and respected. SBCLO's executive director seized the moment, recognizing that solving this issue could be a token of good faith in their relationship. He shared that he was unaware of the issues and committed to providing new chairs before the next production three weeks from then. AFM also noted that a dripping pipe above the brass section was unacceptable. As with the chairs, the executive director shared that he was unaware of the plumbing issue and pledged to solve it before the next production. The AFM was so thrilled by these commitments that they willingly accepted that raises would have to wait.

Ultimately, for the SBCLO, the issues addressed were not actual concessions but more routine maintenance that should have been provided in terms of safe and stable working conditions. The SBCLO acquired new seats at a minimal cost. These adjustments had almost no impact on the organization's financial situation but significantly improved the relationship between the SBCLO and AFM. By focusing on what the SBCLO could provide and responding with (genuine) surprise about the musicians' conditions, the new executive director ushered in a new depth to the relationship and created a win–win result to the negotiation.

## Don't Rush

Though one may be inclined to ink a deal as quickly as possible when it seems a decision has been reached, but particularly in instances where the other party must concede something, they need to be allowed time to accept the surrender. Human nature instantly causes us to fight when we feel we will lose. Pressuring the other party to move forward before emotionally accepting a position can spur them to fight. However, cooler, calmer heads always prevail. When emotions are ratcheted up by a seemingly close culmination to a negotiation, it is wise to allow time to step away, let participants collect their thoughts, and then move forward. Though this can lead to a response to re-open discussions and shift positions, that risk is a far better option than one where a surrendering party instead chooses to fight.

## Control and Power

Power is the ability to control someone else's dependency on something. If you have something another person wants or depends on, like a salary, for example, you have power over them. Likewise, if someone has something you desire, they have power over you. Power struggles are rampant in nonprofit arts organizations. Power works when someone provides something to another or when they withhold it. In order to gain power in a negotiation, you must recognize what the other party desires. Sometimes what they want may not be what they say they want. Determining the other party's needs requires a certain amount of personal judgment that skilled talent negotiators hone through practice.

So how does one make these judgments and adjust the power dynamic in a negotiation? For beginners, the key to establishing the power dynamic is to understand your own needs and the needs of the opposing party. It often makes sense to list all your needs and then consider why you need them. Often, there are solutions other than the specific things you identify as needs. Do you truly want them, or do you want what they represent? If it is the latter, you may very well find ways of satisfying that need without a negotiation.

Once you have determined your needs, it is vital to rank them in order of importance. This process allows you to make logical and weighted decisions in the negotiation process that will not jeopardize more important needs for less important ones. Once the list is created, it becomes a relatively simple task to determine who controls what you need and who may be standing in the way of acquiring those needs.

It then becomes the task to determine what resources you control and who would like those resources. In this way, the entire negotiation can be broken into its respective parts and studied thoroughly before the negotiating begins. Knowing who has what, who wants what, and the importance of each paves the way for a much easier negotiation. At that point, it becomes a matter of trading items that you have in exchange for things you want. Understanding these elements is key to a strong negotiation.

Anthony Rhine and Jay Pension

## The Other Party's Reasoning

One of the biggest mistakes we can make when going into a negotiation is to assume the other party or parties are reasonable. By reasonable, we make an assumption that, given the same circumstances, the opposing party will make decisions the way we would. Even if you have an idea of what the opposing party wants or needs are, those numbers only have value to the person assigning them. An unreasonable person may go into the negotiation with all intended sincerity and be surprised (and unreasonable) when you push back. Sometimes defiance or unreasonableness is shown, often due to a lack of preparation. However, even if it is just a show of bravado, it is an aspect of the negotiation you must navigate. As a result, that means attempting to learn the opposition's real desires and why their requests may seem unreasonable.

## Reflecting Tentative Understandings

Reflecting is an invaluable tool in negotiation. Instead of asking questions or directing the opposition, reflecting allows the opposing speaker to hear their words echoed back to them and helps them to focus on the topic at hand and center their thoughts. It will also encourage them to continue their stream of thought. Opening the way for the speaker to continue is vital in securing the utmost understanding of the opponent's message and creating goodwill in the proceedings by showing that the negotiator is present and actively listening to the opposition's concerns. Reflecting is demonstrated as either mirroring or paraphrasing the speaker's words.

Mirroring what the person has stated involves repeating exact words or phrases used by the speaker. It is best to note only a few essential words or phrases, or perhaps the last words spoken if they epitomize the statement made. Mirroring too much can come to sound condescending or irritating to the speaker. It is also important to match the inflective tone of the statement.

Reflective paraphrasing uses your own words to repeat the statement or offer as you understood it. You must be concise and direct. Do not try to change, distort, or alter what the other person has presented or proposed. When paraphrasing, be simple and sincere. Do not interject your feelings and emotions into the statement or imply judgment. The only objective is to ensure clarity and make certain that both parties are being heard and understood.

It is easy for one party to misunderstand a topic and spend vast amounts of time discussing something based on an inaccurate foundation. By reflecting, you reiterate the arguments on their position or what it is they are offering. Too frequently, in the heat of a negotiation, someone will make an offer, only to come back later and say that it is not what they intended or meant. Reflecting allows the other party to clarify or make adjustments to their statements and ensure you are both on the same page.

Finally, expert negotiators know the value of silence. They will drop a piece of information and then remain silent, allowing the opposing party to fill the silent void, as humans are wont to do, with questions and statements that may fuel the negotiation. The negotiator who remains silent tips no hand and shares no information. Though skilled negotiators know the value of silence, many nonprofessional negotiators lose their foothold quickly by revealing too much when attempting to fill a silent void.

**Tokening**

In some instances, a small concession can satisfy a major want or need. For example, consider a long-time museum guard who is earning as much as newer hires. Though the guard may feel some disparity, the greater concern could also be that the seniority is not clear. This employee, however, does not need or want more money. They have a different desire than that. The employer can offer a *token* to satisfy the real desire, that of the recognition of seniority. The token could be as simple as providing a more senior title to the employee, a special badge, or a uniform. This gesture could easily satisfy the desire without having any cost effect on the nonprofit museum. The employee might also be satisfied with extra days off, a name plaque on their door, or another concession that creates satisfaction. This strategy is known as *tokening*.

**Think Outside the Box**

We consider what the issues represent to us and what we believe they represent to the opposing party because it frees us from thinking about the strictness of specific items. However, to successfully navigate a negotiation, sometimes it is important to look for solutions far from the obvious choice. Those outside-the-box ideas usually arise because the parties have taken the time to consider what their needs represent.

Consider a negotiation between labor and management. Labor wants a full union workforce, which management cannot afford. Management wants to hire only a percentage of their workforce as union labor. The union decides to suggest two different tiers of pay structure, not changing the current non-union take-home pay, but adding them to the union at a new pay rate. This structure solves the represented needs of both parties. In this particular instance, there may be a long-term ramification to unionizing a workforce, but the strategy of adding a new pay structure tier is most definitely outside the box.

### CASE STUDY: SANTA BARBARA CIVIC LIGHT OPERA AND THE INTERNATIONAL ALLIANCE OF THEATRICAL STAGE EMPLOYEES

In the new executive director's first year, the SBCLO had a third contract negotiation with a union. You may recall from Chapter 7 that the International Alliance of Theatrical Stage Employees (IATSE) covers stagehands across many performing arts disciplines. Most of the technical staff at SBCLO were members of IATSE. This year, the collective bargaining agreement between IATSE and SBCLO was due for renegotiation. More than AEA and AFM, the negotiation between SBCLO and IATSE had the potential to be explosive.

Even before the negotiation, the new executive director knew that the BATNA would involve reducing or, at most, maintaining expenses of IATSE member employees. He had also heard that IATSE was contemplating striking the organization if SBCLO did not authorize a significant raise and the hiring of additional IATSE employees to support the existing work being performed. Despite conducting a significant amount of research and being prepared with the overall budget to share with IATSE negotiators, the executive director had no idea how the negotiation would land.

The IATSE representatives were skilled negotiators and quickly took a stand regarding their demands: a 5% pay increase each year for the following three years and full-time IATSE member assistants for each of the three technical department heads. The new executive director knew that such an arrangement was far outside of the BATNA. He presented the representatives with the budget as he had AEA. The result could not have been more different. IATSE blamed the financial situation on the executive management and insisted that their demands be met, or the union members would strike and picket the organization.

The executive director began asking questions to understand IATSE's position better. The representatives explained that they felt they had been underpaid and that the amount of work was too great for department heads without additional union help. Though they recognized the financial obstacle for the SBCLO, they insisted that no less than what they proposed was fair. As he listened, the executive director developed an idea. Perhaps they could work together to solve the issue of each department head having a union assistant.

After a lengthy dialogue, IATSE and the SBCLO came to an arrangement that neither had considered prior to the negotiation. The SBCLO would become a training ground where non-union members could work under the guidance of IATSE union members and eventually earn their union membership. The non-union members would serve as assistants to the department heads, and though they would earn less than union members, they would follow all union policies and procedures on their path to union membership. Once they earned their membership, a new non-union technician would fill their place, and the process would begin again. As a result, each department head would have the help they needed, SBCLO would not be required to pay the union rate given their financial position, and IATSE would eventually have more dues-paying union members than ever before.

This level of collaboration between IATSE and SBCLO showed IATSE that SBCLO was acting in good faith. They accepted SBCLO's offer to raise union members' pay 2.5% annually for the following three years of the collective bargaining agreement. This agreement kept the pay increase for IATSE members below the predicted 3% inflation. By thinking outside of the box, both entities were able to come together to find an alternative to meet both of their needs.

## Final Thoughts

One final note about negotiations: Never say "never." Though it is easy to establish minimum requirements for a negotiation to move forward, it is generally not wise to consider them inflexible. Often, when one or both parties can develop a solution outside the traditional norms or structures of an agreement but is mutually satisfactory, the traditional minimums and maximums might fall by the wayside to make room for better solutions. Taking a position and not being willing to consider other options rarely leads to a win–win result. Knowing the minimums and maximums and the reasoning behind those decisions often makes it easier to be flexible in a discussion. Perhaps you cannot pay more than $25 an hour for your employees and set that as a maximum. If the other party can show you a way to do so and save money in the long run, that is a better solution than sticking to the $25 maximum. There are many ways one might find such a solution. It is always better to stay flexible and keep an open mind in negotiations.

## DISCUSSION QUESTIONS

- Think about a time you have worked in the arts; this can either be at an arts organization or school. What examples of negotiations (formal or informal) did you see there?
- Search online or through the library, what other negotiation strategies not included in this chapter do you find?
- When have you participated in an informal negotiation either with someone else or with yourself? What happened in the negotiation?

- What examples can you find of famous negotiations in the arts? What was the result and why do you think the negotiation ended the way it ended?
- If you were to lead a formal negotiation, would you want to handle it alone or have co-negotiators to collaborate with? Why?
- What elements of negotiation make you most nervous? Why do you think that is?
- If you could do one thing to prepare for a negotiation not mentioned in the chapter, what would it be, and why?

### Notes

1  Spangler, B. (2003). Best alternative to a negotiated agreement (BATNA). Guy and Heidi Burgess, eds., *Beyond Intractability. Conflict Research Consortium*, University of Colorado, June.
2  Cordell, A. (2018). Zopa. In *The Negotiation Handbook* (pp. 39–41). Routledge.
3  Sebenius, J. K. (2017). BATNA s in negotiation: Common errors and three kinds of "No". *Negotiation Journal, 33*(2), 89–99.
4  Schaerer, M., Loschelder, D. D., & Swaab, R. I. (2016). Bargaining zone distortion in negotiations: The elusive power of multiple alternatives. *Organizational Behavior and Human Decision Processes, 137*, 156–171.
5  Galinsky, A. D., Schaerer, M., & MAGEE, J. (2017). The four horsemen of power at the bargaining table. *Journal of Business and Industrial Marketing, 32*(4), 606.
6  Kim, P. H., Pinkley, R. L., & Fragale, A. R. (2005). Power dynamics in negotiation. *Academy of Management Review, 30*(4), 799–822.
7  Lincoln, M. G. (2000). Negotiation: The opposing sides of verbal and nonverbal communication. *Journal of Collective Negotiations, 29*(4), 297–306.
8  Coehoorn, R. M., & Jennings, N. R. (2004, March). Learning on opponent's preferences to make effective multi-issue negotiation trade-offs. In *Proceedings of the 6th International Conference on Electronic Commerce* (pp. 59–68).
9  Beers, P. J., Boshuizen, H. P., Kirschner, P. A., & Gijselaers, W. H. (2006). Common ground, complex problems and decision making. *Group Decision and Negotiation, 15*(6), 529–556.
10 Putnam, L. L. (2004). Transformations and critical moments in negotiations. *Negotiation Journal, 20*(2), 275–295.
11 Brodow, Ed (2013). *Ten Tips for Negotiating in 2013.* https://www.labwrench.com/article/33969/ten-tips-for-negotiating-successfully-in-2013
12 Negotiating, W. W. (1985). *Turning Conflict into Agreement.* Wiley.

# The Engagement Edge

Anthony Rhine and
Jay Pension

# Chapter 9

### INTRODUCTION

Chapter 9 discusses the relatively new concept of engagement in the arts by describing the engagement edge. The engagement edge theorizes that traditional marketing schools of thought must be fully reconstructed to maximize success for arts organizations. Several years ago, we began examining two related concepts and how they work together: marketing and engagement. It seemed that given a recent push in arts administration to interact more intimately with our communities through engagement, there was much yet to be explored, understood, and explained. The idea of engaging with consumers is not new, but in many sectors, the idea of engagement is taking a firmer hold. It happens to be paramount in the nonprofit arts, where the organization's function is to serve the community. As a relatively new concept, many scholars have proposed definitions for engagement, especially as arts organizations move away from the concept of outreach.

Marketing, however, is well understood. Marketing is centered on the construction of the marketing mix, a combination of product, price, promotion, and place (distribution networks).

DOI: 10.4324/9781003207535-10

We struggled to align these four Ps with what actually happens in the nonprofit arts. For example, an art "product" does not necessarily function in the marketing mix as a traditionally understood "product" does. Likewise, pricing strategies that work in retail do not effectively apply to the nonprofit arts. Similarly, arts distribution (place) is vastly different from traditional distribution channels, leaving "promotion" as the only concept applied to the arts the way it is explained in the marketing mix. Furthermore, the marketing mix does not work well without balancing all four parts. As a result, we developed a theory about how engagement is the more appropriate method for serving the arts to a community by focusing on a balance of the concepts of education, environment, ease of access, and experience.

The chapter leads the reader through how the engagement edge works and varies from traditional marketing strategies. The discussion then shifts to the details of the edge: promotion and how it shifts to education and why, product and how it shifts to experience and why, place and how it shifts to environment and why, and finally price and how it shifts to ease of access and why.

## THE ENGAGEMENT EDGE

Arts organizations have embraced the concept of engagement for many years. Recently, it has begun to take hold as a paradigm important for the vitality of nonprofit arts.[1] What is engagement, exactly, and how can it help the nonprofit arts? As simple as this question appears to be, answers are complex and multifaceted. The concept appears in discussions of civic engagement, audience talk, cultural engagement, community engagement, and audience engagement, to name just a few. Beyond the arts, one can find myriad ways to consider or use engagement as a concept.

These multiple uses confuse the term, and its function, in relation to the nonprofit arts. However the term is applied, the notion of person-to-person engagement and how we as humans need and take advantage of that interaction appears to be increasing as technology and the internet take greater hold of society.[2] Perhaps this is because the nature of our relationships

Anthony Rhine and Jay Pension

with each other has shifted as a result of the internet. Society continues to look for more ways to engage with one another—and more intense ways to engage when we do. Therefore, the topic of engagement deserves focused attention, particularly in the arts, where social interaction is a vital part of the experience.[3]

The engagement edge is that attention. It is a way of thinking about the dividing line between the concepts of marketing and engagement. It is also a model for how commercial marketing practices can reflect the engagement edge as a means to bring nonprofit art to communities through an innovative adaptation of approaches found within the marketing mix, the cornerstone of the marketing paradigm.

Engagement has been identified as person-to-person interaction, but it should also be considered functionally related to outreach and service. In the concepts of service or community service, one party goes to the second party and provides something of value in terms of intangible labor or other offerings. One might also provide a tangible product in service to another. In this process, one party is the giver, and one is the receiver. More importantly, in service, the control of the process belongs to the recipient. Next, consider outreach or community outreach. In this process, one party reaches out to another—*Where they are*—so that they can be served and provided with something to which they otherwise may not have access.[4] In the arts, outreach may feel like an extension of the idea of promotion, except that apart from simply sending a message, it proposes doing something in a more intimate and relationship-oriented way.[5] In the concept of outreach, the control belongs in the provider's hands, who makes decisions regarding how the process will unfold and be delivered.

Engagement, however, requires two parties to meet in the middle and share their resources for mutual benefit. The idea that both parties will participate in how the mutually beneficial results occur is inherent in engagement. Engagement implies the partnering of two entities in roughly equal ways. Unlike service, where one party controls what the other provides, or outreach, where one party provides what they think the other party needs, engagement involves shared efforts and benefits.

In the nonprofit arts, this means arts organizations meeting with potential audiences and sharing the process of creating and distributing the art. It is no coincidence that the publication ArtSearch,[6] which posts jobs in the arts for management, has seen an uptick in listings like "Engagement Director" and "Engagement Officer."

It then becomes a question of how the concept of engagement operationally fits into a nonprofit arts organization. The engagement edge proposes that engagement is an adjunct to the other functions of a nonprofit arts organization and is the replacement for the traditional notion of marketing. This is not to suggest that one department within an arts organization can simply retitle itself to fit the nuances of a twenty-first-century marketplace. Instead, the engagement edge requires an organization to be focused on its engagement with the community.

For-profit organizations have a single primary function; the marketing of their products and services.[7] The development and creation of those products and services through the guarantees and customer service provided after the sale are all parts of marketing and are associated with various parts of the marketing mix. In the arts, commercial marketing concepts run afoul of many of the mission-driven functions of the arts organization. The engagement edge solves this problem.

### Marketing versus Engagement

In order to understand where the engagement edge fits into nonprofit arts organizations, it is vital to understand the basic mechanics of marketing, particularly since the engagement edge proposes replacing (at least to some degree) the functions of marketing. Before the 501(c)(3) (nonprofit) tax code was established as we now know it, Neil Borden, a respected marketing researcher, published *The Concept of the Marketing Mix*, which was his way of explaining the work of management: that of marketing.[8] The writing was based on work Borden had been doing since the 1940s and followed his previous publications that defined the marketing mix and how it works. Borden studied food ingredients and their costs to improve the marketing ability of food service providers. He equated

Anthony Rhine and Jay Pension

the work of the manager to that of a chef who has to mix ingredients in just the right quantities to achieve the optimum result. For Borden, the idea of the marketing mix was that every organization needed to have a recipe or mix of quantities of the ingredients he identified to be most successful in their marketing endeavors.

Though a bit clunky, Borden's discovery considers 12 potential ingredients that must be considered in combination to maximize the results of the marketing mix. Those 12 are product, planning, pricing, branding, channels of distribution, personal selling, advertising, promotions, packaging, displays, servicing, physical handling, and fact-finding and analysis.[9] Borden's approach was revolutionary in that it became the foundation for what is considered the marketing mix today.

Borden left open the possibility that his list of 12 ingredients may require alteration at some future point. It was important for Borden to note that, regardless of how many of his 12 pillars were addressed, they impacted one another. This point is vital for the nonprofit arts because it suggests that every piece of marketing impacts every other piece *and the product*—such as the art in a nonprofit arts organization. The product then affects the rest of the marketing mix, and every ingredient in the marketing mix has some effect on the product. In the nonprofit arts, however, the creation of the art remains the sacrosanct realm of the artist and tends not to be beholden to market economics. As a result, in the nonprofit arts, the determination and creation of any product are often not considered in the marketing mix. When this one piece of the marketing mix is removed, the recipe struggles for maximum efficiency. Borden saw the practice of marketing as more of an art than a science and noted, "Marketing and the building of marketing mixes will largely lie in the realm of art."[10] Though he was referring to the artistic "gut" that is used to make certain decisions based on experience rather than data, his words seemed to set up the twenty-first-century advances in marketing, and particularly the relationship between marketing and the arts. It is from this place that the engagement edge emerges.

Jerome McCarthy is one of the founding fathers of today's marketing mix approach, and he published his findings in 1960 in *Basic Marketing: A Managerial Approach*.[11] In his approach, McCarthy used Borden's foundation to inform his four Ps of the marketing mix. He was particularly interested in using sociology and the psychology of human behavior in market transactions, and his approach provides managers with a systematic way of breaking down the function of marketing: product, price, place, and promotion. In his approach, the one that still resonates today, the manager could use data to adjust each of the four Ps to maximize marketing effectiveness. McCarthy's framework of the four Ps was much easier to understand and work with than Borden's 12 pillars, and the result was an almost universal acceptance of the marketing approach. The concept is extremely effective for marketing most tangible goods and has had great success in marketing services. There is great adaptability in the model that allows this to occur, but that adaptability has never proven sufficient to the satisfactory marketing of the nonprofit arts.

We have noted that the notion of "product," as it is used in the marketing mix, is not necessarily something that falls in the realm of the marketing manager in the nonprofit arts. Likewise, the notion of place, which refers to the distribution channels and pathways of products and some services, is a poor way to represent the process of adding value and creating a pathway to our product in the nonprofit arts. Price is an elusive concept, as it is the one pillar where revenue is generated, and pricing strategies that might work in other industries often fail the nonprofit arts for reasons presented later in this chapter.[12] This leaves us with the P of promotion, which is where the vast majority of nonprofit arts organizations invest their marketing time, effort, and money. For the nonprofit arts, the recipe made from the marketing mix includes only one ingredient: promotion.

It is easy to imagine why the processes that Borden and then McCarthy developed that work so well for commercial business do not fit the nonprofit arts. If you follow the timeline, you will see that the marketing mix and its generally accepted design were founded and developed through the 1940s–1960s. The nonprofit arts organization was not considered in the design of this paradigm, partially because 501(c)(3) nonprofit arts organizations as we know them today did not exist until 1969. The marketing mix design never incorporated the

Anthony Rhine and Jay Pension

unique and subtle differences between nonprofit and for-profit organizations. Some businesses and even researchers have modified, adapted, and even proposed different marketing mix models to successfully navigate the market given unique business circumstances. Still, this cannot be said for the nonprofit arts, where there continues to be a struggle to align organizations with the marketplace. The engagement edge proposes a paradigm shift that works more effectively for the nonprofit arts.

## The Engagement Edge

The engagement edge is a model for considering how nonprofit organizations can interact with their market in ways that will help to grow and expand the reach of the nonprofit arts organization in the marketplace. In the engagement edge, four components remain that all work in tandem, and though some pieces may have more bearing on other pieces, and some work almost independently, the four Es of the engagement edge help define how nonprofit arts organizations can reach out to their markets.

The four Es begin with *education*. In the engagement edge, education more closely aligns with the functions and processes of nonprofit arts organizations than promotion functions. Though there are some similarities, simply announcing that art is available or making certain people are aware of it is insufficient.

The second E in the engagement edge is *experience*. As noted, the experience extends far beyond simply attending the art, reaching into a number of occurrences both before and after the consumption of the art that affects the community member. The concept of experience is also broader in that what we would consider the artistic product is only a piece of the full picture within the experience. Products are tangible goods or services (or sometimes ideas or concepts) that satisfy the needs and wants of consumers. Consumers do not have to know that they need or want a product, but promotion is used to help them to that understanding. For the nonprofit arts organization, the artistic product itself is incomplete until it has an audience to experience it, and the quality of that experience is determined internally by the consumer, who is actually a part of the artistic product. So, the engagement edge sees the myriad elements of the art experience as something much broader, more internal, and of greater scope than the mere notion of product. In the nonprofit arts, the artistic product remains largely the purview of the artists and is not structured, altered, or adjusted to fit the needs or wants of the consumer, a task which would fall to the marketing manager in a commercial enterprise.

The third E in the engagement edge is *environment*. Everything we experience in life occurs within an environment, just as the distribution channels in the notion of place exist within an environment or several environments. However, the concept of place includes distribution channels where warehousing, transportation, servicing, support, and the like are value-added to the original product. In the nonprofit arts, it is rare to have a collection of distribution channels beyond, perhaps, a ticket agency. Even if one were to think of the ticket agency as a distribution channel, it does not actually distribute the art but provides a leasehold on the space where the art will be presented. Touring productions may be seen as more closely aligned with the concept of place than of environment; however, those are typically commercial, for-profit productions, rather than nonprofits serving their community, so the comparison falls flat. *Environment* is the place in which the consumers' experience occurs. As this chapter will present, that environment extends far beyond the walls of the arts organization, as the experience begins at the moment the consumer becomes aware of the art, and occurs at multiple experiential points, including components like traveling through an environment to get to the art, enjoying a meal in an environment as a prelude to the art, sharing an after-dinner drink at a bar to discuss the art, and any number of occurrences that exist in observance of the experience afforded by the arts organization and the art itself.

The final E in the engagement edge is the concept of *ease of access*. In the arts, the price of a ticket sometimes buys access (though not always), but providing access constitutes many other elements that reach beyond the scope of most pricing strategies. Pricing strategies work on the principle that price is designed to maximize revenue to the organization, resulting in a profit. Because of the struggles in determining pricing for the arts, the engagement edge considers that the true framework in this area for the nonprofit arts is less about setting a price and more about creating uncomplicated access for consumers. For the nonprofit organization, the monetary value that provides access (if one exists) is mediated by donations to the organization, which offset some of the actual costs of creating the art. The idea of price is incapable of looking at a structure that relies upon the largesse of donors on a recurring basis to mediate monetary cost. Pricing strategies do not fit the nonprofit arts well as a model. However, when nonprofit arts organizations work toward ease of access for their community, the model makes much more sense.

## Promotion and Shift to Education

People often have different definitions of education, as the nature of education is somewhat fluid. Nearly 600 years ago the printing press changed the way much of education occurred. Students began reading information, coupled with the information a teacher would share. To ensure that the student had retained the information, a test or paper was often required to make an assessment of that retention. This downloading of information is known as the banking model, and what the banking model does is it reduces the student from being a critical and independent thinker to being a receptacle for facts.[13] The process of the banking model raises the power and control of the teacher while failing to recognize that students are more than simply unthinking blank slates. The concept, then, is placed squarely into the minds of students, who are taught that they are subservient and beholden to the keeper of information. As a result, students have little control over their own thinking and their own education.

A different learning theory is constructivism, which posits that knowledge is constructed individually by every single learner in their own way, using their own unique experiences to frame their new knowledge.[14] Every individual has a distinct set of experiences and knowledge with which to shape inputs, and the constructivist approach promotes that students should think critically about information within the framework of the life they have already lived. This model encourages teachers to consider that every student has an individualized educational experience. It falls to the teacher to ensure that they are creating experiences and opportunities for the student to explore concepts within their personal framework.

Following constructivism is a relatively new concept called learner-centered teaching which suggests that the function of education is one that falls to the student, coordinated by the teacher.[15] In the learner-centered teaching model, the teacher prepares work for the student to engage with (note the term engage), and then stands back and lets them explore the ideas and concepts. In a learner-centered teaching classroom, it is common to see the teacher sitting quietly in the background as the students do the actual work of learning. The teacher's role is to answer questions, keep the students on track, and let them learn from whatever they have been given to work on. After all, it is the one doing the work who is doing the learning.

The concept of promotion is the process of communicating about a product or service to persuade the buyer to make a purchase and move them to act.[16] It is not a process where the potential buyer is encouraged to explore the concepts and uses of a product or service, imagine and test it within their sphere of knowledge and experiences and see how it can and does apply to their life. Promotion seems to fit neatly with the banking model of education, which does not engage its students but rather tells them what to believe. Promotion is a way to tell people what to think, while learner-centered education encourages people to critically think about something in a way that fits with their perception of the world around them. *Education* is engaging.

For the arts, education is a means to allow our communities to explore what an individual artwork can mean to them if they witness the art and is also an opportunity to stimulate thinking about art forms. Part of the education of our potential audiences is about allowing them to consider what an art form is, how and why it may be relevant to them, what it may mean for their lives and their existence, and how they might best enjoy, use, and appreciate the art. This position suggests that educating our potential audiences begins by creating opportunities for our communities to learn about the value of art in general, allowing people to explore what it is, adapt it to their lives, and make it their own. Promoting that the arts are valuable to every human being is simply attempting to download information onto the masses. However, if the people have no context with which to appreciate the information, they merely bank it and never act. Instead, educating people about the value of art in all its forms allows them to explore concepts in their own way.[17] For people who view the world through a for-profit lens, this may be difficult to see. However, an arts organization's education is as equally successful for community members who choose to attend as it is for community members who encounter the education and decide the experience is not for them. In both circumstances, the community member receives valuable service from the nonprofit.

The big trick on the shift from promotion to education is in ensuring to gather the necessary information to know what the needs, wants, desires, concerns, and attitudes of the community are, at least to the degree that we can accurately provide opportunities for them to interact with the art form in ways that are satisfactory to them. In the twenty-first century, we are buried in promotions and advertising. In the shift to education, arts organizations do not generate buyers. They encourage lifelong awareness. For arts organizations, it is not only the specific artistic product they present, but the arts in general.

## Product and Shift to Experience

We tend to think of *an* experience as a unique moment filled with an emotional response. Experiences are exciting, disturbing, compelling, exhausting, special, upsetting, endearing, or any other term that describes an emotional reaction.[18] Experience is also something that we gain after repeated practice, as in, "they have lots of experience." Sometimes we refer to those who have academic training as having experience. However, in the arts, it is *an* experience that is vital.[19]

Experience is the way a person senses their surroundings. It is a perceptual process and requires sensory input, as it is that input that shapes our response. As we take in this sensory input, our brains create new memories, and the emotional response to those inputs helps create the experience as something memorable. For example, though we may say that we experience a bottle of shampoo, the experience does not generate a new collection of sensory responses and emotional reactions strong enough to build and maintain new memories about the experience. The distinct process of shampooing one's hair could become memorable, but one would hardly classify hair washing as *an* experience on a regular basis.

In the nonprofit arts, there is a social nature to how an experience occurs. Because we experience the arts with others, we also have a shared set of norms, customs, values, and roles that exist during the experience. Therefore, social interaction is as vital to the arts experience as the art itself.

It is not lost on commercial businesses that the experience is vital to the sales process. Commercial enterprises now see that experience is more than a simple transaction but a culmination of all the critical touchpoints the consumer encounters leading to, during, and after the actual transaction. It is the same way for the nonprofit arts. Every touchpoint of importance in advance of, during, and after the art is a component of the experience, which means the art is only a part of the experience. One may think of the artistic director as the one who supervises and guides the creation of the art, but arts organizations should seek to cultivate the whole experience, including how the art unfolds within that experience.

Product as a framework works exceptionally well to develop physical products or services for the for-profit sector. However, the experience (or even product) of art does not occur until the audience member has *an* experience. The audience member is as much a part of the product in the arts as the art itself. The experience that occurs within audience members as they interact with the art is the ultimate goal of most nonprofit arts organizations. Traditional projects exist with or without the consumer, but the ephemeral nature of arts experiences requires an audience member to internalize the experience as it unfolds to its culmination.

### Place and Shift to Environment

When we think of the term "environment," we tend to think of the vastness of the planet earth, its natural beauty, its beaches and forest, deserts, and mountains. However, the term environment refers to our surroundings. Any individual, group, organization, gathering, or even entire system exists and functions within an environment. So, the notion of the environment is not about nature or beauty, but rather the space surrounding us and how its components interact. It is this interaction that helps define any unique environment. Those interactions also often affect the environment, which affects its components to the degree that they are interrelated. This interrelationship within an environment is vital to understanding the engagement edge.

Environments can be created and adjusted by human beings and human activity unintentionally or intentionally. However, we cannot control every aspect because various living and nonliving things affect the environment. Scholars often look at how entire systems function, and this is called a *systems analysis* approach. A systems analysis approach sees how elements (which may seem solitary) may impact other elements, and in turn, impact the entire system of which the elements are a part. Within an environment, each element has some interplay with the next. The engagement edge proposes that arts organizations take greater control over the environment(s) in which the arts experience occurs. Arts organizations can explore how one environment can interplay with and affect the workings of other environments. For example, a poor environment in a venue's lobby can impact how someone will experience a performance in a theatre.

Environmental management is the process of attempting to control and maintain an ecosystem. In arts organizations, engagement managers operate at the environmental management level as they attempt to alter the ecosystem of the arts experience and the environments in which it will take place. Although it would be inaccurate to say that environmental management's function is to control an ecosystem, as it does not always allow for control, with intention and purpose, engagement managers can change the way interactions occur within environments in an *attempt* to control them.

In a human-designed environment, the engagement manager attempts to determine how participants will experience elements within the environment. The engagement manager focuses on aspects of the environment that satisfy functionality as part of the experience and design elements that create spaces with varying aesthetic values that can influence the emotions of those within the environment. The engagement manager is concerned with developing and modifying environments through which a patron will pass as part of their artistic experience.

### Price and Shift to Ease of Access

There are dozens of different pricing strategies, all using slightly different approaches to determine the appropriate amount to charge a consumer for a product or service. Pricing determination can require a vast amount of research and input from the market, but generally, the price somewhat relates to the cost of developing and creating the product. Price can also result from studying the competition's pricing, desired profit, and how consumers perceive the product or service's value. In addition, factors like discounts, seasonal effects, and the lifecycle of any given product or service can affect pricing. Ultimately, McCarthy's price is a paradigm centered on earning the greatest profit through product sales.

Since nonprofit arts organizations' primary focus is on mission and service, traditional pricing strategies do not work. Many of these organizations provide free service for their community. The engagement edge encourages a focus on the process of accessing the artistic experience. This lends itself to making the functional process of accessing an artistic experience easier, and concerns access for those who have been limited from participation due to societal distinctions. Unlike an experience, an environment, or an education, ease of access is not a concept readily understood, particularly because its concept is richer and deeper when the words ease and access are used together. For this reason, the definitions of those two words and how they relate to the engagement edge will be explored.

The word ease brings relaxation, comfort, and freedom from anxiety, stress, and pain to mind. Though we do not wish our arts patrons discomfort, most arts organizations do not focus on alleviating strife from the arts experience as a primary goal. Even relaxation is something arts managers are loath to promise because though some arts experiences may be relaxing, that is typically not an intentionally designed result. However, relieving stress and anxiety surrounding the process of attending the arts is a vital part of the work of an engagement manager.

When looking at a suitable substitution for price in the engagement edge, the logical E seems to be "exchange." After all, price is a concept that has to do with all the things each party trades in exchange for what the other party is trading. The notion of exchange seems to be at the heart of what nonprofit arts organizations currently do with price. However, as noted, the fact that nonprofit arts organizations have two products, the art and the donation, there is a strange mediation between the two. Donations mediate where pricing can and should be set for paying customers. The exchange becomes muddy because we actually do not make an exchange of items of equal value. What the nonprofit arts seek is some financial contribution (price) toward the cost of creating the arts experience, but donations allow us to charge prices that are well below the actual cost of creating or presenting the art. What arts consumers require is not an ability to participate in an exchange but an ability to access, as easily as possible, the experience that the organization offers.

To ease access, nonprofit arts organizations examine common obstacles that reduce access to community members. Obstacles initially worth considering include time, location, self-efficacy of the community, accessibility in venues, and even price. Each of these factors (and more) can be considered to enhance the diversity of the audience a nonprofit arts organization serves.

Though time is a constant factor for all people within a community, the ability to control how a person spends their time varies from person to person. Some community members (especially those who seem to frequent arts organizations) have ample time to explore the world and experience art. Others in the community may have many competing interests for their time; perhaps they work multiple jobs or cannot afford childcare. The duration of a performance or the time it takes to move through a gallery is only one factor to consider in the obstacle of time. Ordering tickets, preparing to attend, travel time to and from the event, and many other factors go into the time commitment each community member must expend to participate. Those with ample time may attend the arts more right now, but the engagement edge begs the question: shouldn't arts organizations strive to create greater ease of access to those with less control of their time?

Arts organizations can conduct this form of examination with many factors that impact ease of access:

- Location of the arts experience: How far must people travel? Is there existing public transportation? Parking availability for people with cars?
- Self-efficacy: How can the arts organization discourage elitist practices that may hinder participation? How can they encourage an understanding of what it takes to attend an arts experience?
- Accessibility in venues: How can the organization ensure that everyone in the community has equitable access within the venue?
- Price: What strategies can the arts organization use to reduce the obstacle of ticket price (if they charge a ticket price)?

In examining these paragraphs, the difference in the spirit of price and ease of access should stand out as nonprofit arts organizations have no business in attempting to capture the most profit possible from the community members they serve.

### Final Thoughts

Though much has been said about marketing strategies and how they can be manipulated for the nonprofit arts, for 50 years, those manipulations have proven to be less effective than in the for-profit corporate sector. The engagement edge seeks to solve this problem by changing the focus from selling to educating consumers and engaging with potential audiences. Education and engagement require effort by all parts of the organization, as every aspect of the operation will have some bearing on the experience.

The engagement edge works by using education to create ease of access into the environment(s) where the experience will occur. As a company focuses on the engagement edge, they should begin to see continual growth, as the growth comes from the efforts of those within the organization and is expanded to those with whom we engage.

## Notes

1   Borwick, Doug, and Barbara Schaffer Bacon. *Building Communities, Not Audiences : The Future of the Arts in the United States.* Winston-Salem, N.C: ArtsEngaged, 2012.

2   Firth, Joseph et al. "The 'online brain': how the Internet may be changing our cognition." *World Psychiatry* 18.2 (2019): 119–129.

3   Wheatley, Daniel, and Craig Bickerton. "Measuring changes in subjective well-being from engagement in the arts, culture and sport." *Journal of Cultural Economics* 43.3 (2019): 421–442.

4   The University of Kansas Center for Community Health and Development. The Community Toolbox. Chapter 23. ctb.ku.edu/en/table-of-contents/implement/access-barriers-opportunities/outreach-to-increase-access/main

5   Walker-Kuhne, Donna. *Invitation to the Party: Building Bridges to the Arts, Culture, and Community.* New York: Theatre Communications Grou, 2005.

6   Theatre Communications Group. ArtSearch online publication artsearch.tcg.org/home

7   McCarthy, E. Jerome. *Basic Marketing: A Managerial Approach.* Homewood, IL: Richard D. Irwin, 1960.

8   Borden, Neil H. "The concept of the marketing mix." *Journal of Advertising Research* 4.2 (1964): 2–7.

9   Goi, Chai Lee. "A review of marketing mix: 4Ps or more." *International Journal of Marketing Studies* 1.1 (2009): 2–15.

10  Borden, Neil H. "The concept of the marketing mix." *Journal of Advertising Research* 4.2 (1964): 2–7.

11  McCarthy, E. Jerome. *Basic Marketing: A Managerial Approach.*

12  Seaman, Bruce A. "Static and dynamic pricing strategies: how unique for nonprofits?" *Handbook of Research on Nonprofit Economics and Management.* Cheltenham; Northampton, MA: Edward Elgar Publishing, 2018.

13  Freire, Paulo, Myra Bergman Ramos, and Donaldo P. Macedo. *Pedagogy Of The Oppressed.* 30th Anniversary Edition. New York: Bloomsbury, 2012.

14  Vygotskiĭ, L. S. (Lev Semenovich), and Michael Cole. *Mind in Society the Development of Higher Psychological Processes.* Cambridge, MA: Harvard University Press, 1978.

15  Doyle, Terry. *Learner-Centered Teaching : Putting the Research on Learning into Practice.* 1st Ed. Sterling, VA: Stylus Pub., 2011.

16  McCarthy, E. Jerome. *Basic Marketing: A Managerial Approach.*

17  Walmsley, Ben. "The death of arts marketing: a paradigm shift from consumption to enrichment." *Arts and the Market* (2019).

18  Latulipe, Celine, Erin A. Carroll, and Danielle Lottridge. "Love, hate, arousal and engagement: exploring audience responses to performing arts." *Proceedings of the SIGCHI Conference on Human Factors in Computing Systems.* 2011.

19  Dewey, John. *Art As Experience.* New York: Capricorn Books, 1959.

# Rural and Regional Arts Organizations

Elise Lael Kieffer

## Chapter 10

### INTRODUCTION

Chapter 10 explores issues specifically related to regional arts organizations, as local region will affect everything an arts organization does, from marketing to artistic creation. The chapter uses two cases to illustrate issues facing these smaller, local organizations: first, the Appalachians, defined by persistent poverty and reduced economic opportunity, where issues are, in fact, regional issues, and second, the southeastern United States. The Southeastern Arts Leadership Educators (SALE) is an annual conference dedicated to challenges specific to the region. Members of SALE share the sentiment that current arts administration organizations do not meet the specific needs of the southeastern United States, a region confronting the effects of its history of racial and social injustice. This chapter explores the value of regional arts organizations and the common challenges they face.

Jay and Anthony first met Dr. Elise Kieffer at the first annual SALE conference, which they organized and founded. Dr. Kieffer was then a Ph.D. student, just beginning her academic journey as a researcher. She demonstrated her deep interest in regional arts organizations, their value, and their contribution to society at the regional level. Like us in our founding of SALE, she found that the arts may often be mistakenly understood in an aggregate fashion, looking at data and information provided from national or

DOI: 10.4324/9781003207535-11

international sources. Even at the statewide level, the value of the arts can sometimes be misunderstood. Regional issues affect the arts and spur the arts to address local regional issues in ways that are unique to their regions. This area of focus has lacked attention but will become vital as our world continues to globalize and interconnect. The physical social interactions we need as human beings will be based more on activities that require gatherings of people in the same region. The arts have a unique opportunity the help grow and strengthen local communities in ways that our electronically globalized world cannot.

## RURAL AND REGIONAL ARTS ORGANIZATIONS

*A Contribution by Elise Lael Kieffer*

Though many of the following themes are applicable to any locale, it is important for readers to be aware that this chapter specifically addresses the intricacies of rural and regional organizations within the United States. The chapter will discuss the National Endowment for the Arts (NEA) in the United States and the concept of State Arts Agencies. This might differ from international Ministries of Culture and the like.

I recently spent a lot of time reading through arts administrator job postings. A position at the University of Alaska Southeast specified, "Experience in the rural Circumpolar North preferred." Another job listing, for a New York institution, required, "Knowledge of local theatre scene is a must." These are two quite different locales, but both require particular awareness of their immediate region. Why? It seems like common sense. In order to work in a community, you need to know about the community. Whether that community is in Manhattan or Appalachia, awareness of the locality is requisite for successfully navigating as an arts administrator.

Accepting that necessity as truth, this chapter presents a case for the benefits of regional arts organizations and conferences to collectively approach common concerns within regions. It will also dive into the unique peculiarities of working specifically in rural communities. Through an exploration of two distinct regional arts organizations, this chapter makes the case for the importance and value of arts and culture organizations that focus on regional issues. By combining forces with other local arts organizations, regional organizations find strength in numbers. However, by strategically limiting impact to the surrounding region, these organizations are able to tackle those issues that perpetually define and challenge the regions in which they operate.

According to the United States Census, approximately 97% of the United States' land area is within rural counties.[1] Operating an arts organization in a rural community requires a largely different skill-set than doing the same job in a metropolitan setting.[2] For example, a small-town arts organization promoting a summer camp might be able to send a representative to every school. Often in small towns, there are only three schools: the elementary, the middle, and the high school. However, an arts organization in a major city would be hard-pressed to make site visits to every district school. The basic skills and education required to run an arts organization are held in common, but the intricacies of the local population and environment require attention. Marketing strategies have to change based on local internet usage and availability, broadcasting and print opportunities, demographics, and education. Fundraising strategies, likewise, need to be modified to be effective in different socioeconomic communities, with differing local priorities, needs, and opportunities. This chapter exposes the special importance of the unique skills and awareness required to operate a rural arts organization. The information contained in this chapter holds particular significance for three populations: arts administration educators, arts administration students, and arts administration practitioners.

**LEARNING OBJECTIVES**

By the end of the chapter, readers will have the ability to:

- Examine the regionally specific challenges facing arts administrators.
- Consider the importance of regionally specific arts collaboration.
- Weigh the role of arts administrators as active participants in their communities.
- Recognize how the arts operate in rural communities.

## National Endowment for the Arts

A 2013 report from the NEA revealed that only 2% of all arts and culture institutions in the United States received nearly 60% of funding.[3] Fewer than 1,000 organizations are included in that 2% and every one of them boasts an annual budget greater than 5 million. Included among those institutions are opera and dance companies, symphonies, regional theatres, and art museums. The majority of these institutions promote traditional Western European fine art.[4] This reality leaves many regionally specific arts organizations behind.[5]

This information begs the question, why does the situation exist, and how might the choices and perceptions of arts administrators be affected when operating among specific populations? Despite the seeming inequities of public funding, arts organizations exist and serve unique populations. Here, we will explore the reasons behind the relevance of two such organizations, and how those regional organizations navigate their unique place in their communities. The organizations in this chapter are: SALE a new and growing conference of academics; and Appalshop, an Appalachian arts and culture organization that is over 50 years old and still going strong.

The NEA promotes a policy of "Art for All Americans" and to execute that policy they strategically fund every congressional district but there is no specific standard of equity in the amounts given to each district or the type of organizations receiving funding. Additionally, metropolitan districts are much smaller geographically than rural districts which often leads to funding in more populous areas, leaving the rural areas without support.[6] Further, state and federal government entities (including State Arts Agencies (SAAs)) often do not have a realistic portrait of the realities facing arts organizations in isolated, rural communities.[7]

Meanwhile, isolated, rural communities often do not realize what public services they are missing. For this reason, Swanson recommended that local stakeholders be included when decisions are being made with regard to resource allocation.[8] Other research reinforces that notion by finding that it is often at the state level where disagreements between federal information and local realities become muddled.[9]

Elise Lael Kieffer

## State Arts Agencies

SAAs provide resources for arts and culture institutions within their states. Historically, the NEA and its policies reflect and respond to the national environment, while SAAs do the same at the state level.[10] By being more closely connected to local institutions and citizens, SAAs can set appropriate arts and cultural priorities for their constituencies. Being closer to their citizenry, SAAs can often anticipate, rather than react to trends and challenges. SAAs do for their states what the NEA is mandated to achieve nationally and most SAAs are supported by both their states and the NEA.

Although much funding originated with the NEA (and also the National Endowment for the Humanities (NEH)), SAAs ensure more equitable allocation of national resources than those two national agencies can provide.[11] SAAs also provide representation for their states at both the NEA and NEH, giving a voice to their own state's arts and culture sectors. SAAs are better positioned to advocate for the individual communities in their states, by considering that resources be equitably allocated and distributed to organizations across disciplines and localities.[12]

SAAs serve a broader constituency than any one small, isolated, rural, and arts organization. As part of that service, they often see the need for small organizations to improve the professionalization of their services. SAAs do not have boundless resources and to allocate them across their states, they choose based on predetermined criteria, established by their individual state mandates and the priorities of their current administrations. These criteria inform what and where to fund, and how to select recipients of their resources.

## THE APPALACHIAN REGION

The United States Federal Government does not strictly designate regions of the country. Instead, regions are defined by organizations, states, and communities. Some subscribe to define the regions of the United States into five categories: Northeast, Southeast, Midwest, West, and Southwest. Others divide the country into time zones to indicate regional areas. Some consider the cultural practice as the division between different regions. However, when we define regions, each region has its own distinct challenges and opportunities. For arts administrators, identifying how the federal and state governments support regional issues is essential. This part of the chapter explores the arts in the Appalachian region of the United States to provide an example of regionally specific considerations.

Established to promote sustainable economic growth, The Appalachian Regional Commission (ARC), operates in specific counties in 12 states: Alabama, Georgia, Kentucky, Maryland, Mississippi, New York, North Carolina, Ohio, Pennsylvania, South Carolina, Tennessee, Virginia, and in all of West Virginia.[13]

The ARC was founded in 1965 by congress and mandated with five objectives. These priorities are "increasing economic opportunities within the region, improving workforce readiness, developing and maintaining critical infrastructure, utilizing and leveraging natural and cultural assets within the region, and developing leadership and community capacity."[14] This region continues to be characterized by perpetual poverty and decreasing economic opportunity.[15] In a study of Appalachian Ohio, Millesen determined that issues within individual communities of Appalachia are often shared by other towns within the region. Local issues are Appalachian region issues.[16] The purpose of the ARC was to confront these very issues, but relevant to this conversation, the ARC does not regularly fund arts and culture activities.

ARC has been operating since 1965 and yet poverty, population decline, access to services, and low education still exist within the Appalachian region. Not much has changed to improve life for those living in the region, even through the first two decades of the twenty-first century.[17] "Practical, working solutions based on thorough research are necessary to understand and approach these problems, including the issue of access to the arts."[18]

The arts are uniquely valuable to rural communities. Often facing extreme out-migration of youth and growing senior populations, rural areas tend to lose access to once-held opportunities and services. This causes reduced tax revenues, leading to diminishing support for infrastructure repairs

Elise Lael Kieffer

and improvements. In turn, residents face poor employment conditions if they remain in the area, greater commute times to higher-wage employment, and low levels of entrepreneurship.[19] The arts facilitate a sense of community and growth in rural areas. Collaboration on arts programs and projects aids the building of capacity in a community. Deliberate creative placemaking efforts supported by the NEA and SAAs have achieved advances toward enhancing and enriching rural communities with access to the arts.[20]

The arts in Appalachia originated largely from the geographic isolation that defines the region.[21] If there was a need, people built, crafted, or made something to serve that need. This resulted in a robust tradition of crafting. Historic settlers in the region needed blankets. This resulted in a strong heritage of quilting. They began wood and metalworking because they needed tools. They made clay ware because they needed pots and dishes. Everything made had a function.

Things began to change when the railroad came to parts of the Appalachian Region. With it came tourists to communities like Berea, Kentucky, and Gatlinburg, Tennessee.[22] In these communities, the historic arts and crafts of the region became sources of revenue for artisans who now had incoming tourists desiring their handiwork. This benefit did not reach all of Appalachia, however. The Cumberland Gap region, for example, still hosts many communities with K-12 public schools struggling to include any arts curriculum in their schools.[23]

> These remaining isolated communities are so economically depressed that they have lost pride in their cultural heritage, making the need to preserve their artistic traditions and promote artistic innovation more necessary. This gap in public arts education makes the impact of nonprofit arts organizations even greater in these isolated communities.[24]

**CASE STUDY: APPALSHOP**
Leciejewski and Perkins studied procedural inequities of mining processes within Appalachia. They discovered that residents of Appalachia still believe that their state

governments do not care about them or their challenges.[25] Appalshop is a thriving, successful organization located in Whitesburg, Kentucky. Founded in 1969 in an effort to promote regional development and fight the War on Poverty, Appalshop provides a useful example of a regional nonprofit arts organization.

Originally called the Appalachian Film Workshop, it was one of ten Community Film Workshops that were initiated through a collaboration between the federal Office of Economic Opportunity and the American Film Institute.[26] In 1974, Appalshop became a nonprofit and was rebranded with its current name. It became a center for filmmaking in Appalachia, producing projects on the regionally important subjects of environmental responsibility, coal mining, the economy, and traditional culture.

In addition to films, Appalshop also produces works of music, spoken word, theatre, books, multimedia, and photography. They also operate a local radio station serving central Appalachia that features regionally relevant programming. According to their own promotional materials:

> Appalshop's goals are: to document, disseminate, and revitalize the lasting traditions and contemporary creativity of Appalachia; to tell stories the commercial cultural industries don't tell, challenging stereotypes with Appalachian voices and visions; to support communities' efforts to achieve justice and equity and solve their own problems in their own ways; to celebrate cultural diversity as a positive social value; and to participate in regional, national, and global dialogue toward these ends.[27]

**Regional Importance.** The concept of "outsider" status is thoroughly researched with regard to communities in Appalachia. Particularly of note is the idea of "educated outsiders," which causes challenges for teachers coming to the community from other regions to teach at public schools.[28,29,30,31,32,33]

Elise Lael Kieffer

"Outsider" status in an Appalachian community not only includes someone not originally from the community, but also might include former insiders who left and later returned.[34] Appalachian natives often think that outsiders come into their communities with self-serving agendas. This sentiment is reinforced by the often negative stereotypes of Appalachian people pervading popular culture. An unfortunate result of this stereotyping of Appalachian locals as hillbillies is the resulting perpetuation of local narratives that "insiders are 'good' and outsiders are 'bad'".[35] Generations of Appalachian locals have watched outsiders enter their communities with their own agendas and then leave without improving anything for those remaining.[36]

For this reason, perhaps more than any other, Appalshop has succeeded. Appalshop proudly proclaims that "Appalachian people must tell their own stories and solve their own problems."[37] Being worker-run and worker-centered, Appalshop has allowed the people of the Appalachian region to trust their name, their information, their motives, and their disseminated products. If an outside organization had released the same products, it seems unlikely those products would have been met with the same acceptance. Within Appalachia, being an "insider" matters. Being founded and dedicated to the region accounts for Appalshop's historic and continued success.

**Application.** Appalshop provides a useful example of the impact an arts organization can have through awareness of its locality and deliberate engagement within its region. Identifying the specific needs of your community and region is essential to ensure sustainable, effective, and impactful arts of any discipline. Looking at other organizations in your region to determine what problems they have faced, or from what opportunities they have benefited is a very useful first step in planning for your own organization.

## SOUTHEASTERN ARTS LEADERSHIP EDUCATORS

The value of regional considerations extends beyond the practice of arts administration into academia. Institutions of higher education work in and around their communities and regions. Just as in the earlier example of Appalshop, those higher education institutions must navigate the unique climates of their regional cultures, concerns, and priorities. For academic programs training future arts administrators, these regional particulars become part of their programming. A national professional association might not be equipped to tackle specific issues faced by regionally similar member institutions. In this spirit, a professional association was created in the southeastern region of the United States.

### Regional History

It seems unnecessary to explain the racial and social history of the Southern United States. Though none of the nation is without blemish in its race relations, the South (particularly those original 11 states that seceded from the Union during the Civil War to form the Confederate States of America) has particularly dark histories. Those 11 states were South Carolina, Mississippi, Florida, Alabama, Georgia, Louisiana, Texas, Virginia, Arkansas, Tennessee, and North Carolina.

More than any other region in the United States, the South perpetuated the enslavement of Black citizens. Following Emancipation, the South continued to withhold equal opportunities to people of color through the Jim Crow era's laws and restrictions. Still decorated with monuments honoring the men who fought to maintain the right to enslave others, the South has yet to face a true reckoning with its past and the implications of that past on the present and future. Arts administration educators and practitioners work in the midst of this complicated environment. The challenges they face might not be entirely unique, but they are uniquely potent.

### *Founding of SALE*

"Southeastern Arts Leadership Educators (SALE) supports the definition, teaching, theory, and practice of transformative arts administration in the southeastern United States."[38] At their first

Elise Lael Kieffer

conference, held in Atlanta, Georgia in April 2018, a gathering of arts administrators from Florida, Georgia, Kentucky, South Carolina, and North Carolina met and drafted the above mission statement. They shared the feeling that current arts administration professional organizations did not meet the specific needs of the southeastern United States, a region always confronting the effects of its history of racial and social injustice. That group of educators negotiated, haggled, and discussed until they finally settled on that one significant word, "transformative."

The profound feeling in the room from arts leadership educators was that the status quo did not and would not work to meet the needs of the diverse population of arts administration students in the Southeast. Likewise, in order to responsibly prepare those students for future success, the arts could not just "be." The arts, like most other aspects of life in the South, had to be strategic. They have to be transformative.

Through sharing and collaboration, the founding members of this organization discovered that many of the problems they faced individually are, in fact, regional. As they began building the SALE conference, they discovered connections in unexpected relationships and learned from the successes and failures of others confronting similar obstacles.

At their third conference, held in February of 2020 at the College of Charleston in South Carolina, the members confronted a choice. The conference had grown substantially since its founding. The question posed was this, "Should we continue to grow by reaching out beyond the Southeast, or do we maintain our specific geographic focus?" After discussion, members reached the conclusion that the reasons the organization came to be persisted. In order to fight the long shadows of the Southeastern region's racial past, the organization had to remain focused. Problems of racial inequity and injustice faced at one Southern university would likely be similar or the same as the struggles at a small Southern private liberal arts college. Many of those challenges come from the shared history of the region, rather than from the type of institution.

The conference concluded that only by remaining geographically focused on the southeastern United States could they continue to tackle the specific stumbling blocks faced by arts leadership educators in their region. Certainly, some lessons on creative justice, diversity, equity, access, and inclusion are broadly transferable, even internationally. The truth remains, however, that the Southern United States shares a unique responsibility for reconciling those struggles they were so integral in creating.

It is not unusual that the struggles one organization within a region faces are also faced by others. The evolution of SALE as an example of a successful and impactful regional gathering provides a model that other regions might consider replicating to confront their own shared difficulties.

SALE facilitates difficult and timely conversations among its member institutions. These conversations would likely be few at national or international conferences with much more geographically broad participation. Just as organizations focus their missions around regional issues, higher education and its supporting professional memberships do likewise to appropriately and sufficiently prepare future arts administrators.

### Final Thoughts

In 1989, Keller published *The Arts Manager's Social Responsibility*. In it, he enforced the responsibility of arts managers to administer, coordinate, and promote activities that incorporate the arts into their communities. Keller argued that it is the arts administrator's duty to ensure the arts they are facilitating remain (or become) both impactful and relevant to the communities served. If large portions of the population are disenfranchised from involvement with their arts and culture organizations, then the administrators at those organizations are to blame. Keller argued that the public cannot be held responsible for their lack of inclusion or participation. If they remain unserved or underserved, their institutions have failed them. "If today's institutions tend to be more the symbol than the cause of the inequities of society, what role should the institutions play in rectifying the imbalance"? This article was written in 1989 and yet the sentiment is just as urgent and relevant today.[39]

Elise Lael Kieffer

The successful arts administrator needs to know their community and their region. This chapter introduced a model organization that highlights the importance of networking within a common region. The chapter also explored the distinct characteristics of managing the arts in a rural setting. Location matters and context is key. Every other chapter in this book provides valuable information on one aspect of managing an arts organization. This chapter served to illustrate how all of those skills need to be assessed and reassessed based upon the individual characteristics of the arts manager's community.

## DISCUSSION QUESTIONS

1. Think about where you are located and identify challenges that are unique to your community.
2. What strategies can the arts manager execute to successfully navigate their community?
3. Do you think arts organizations should operate independently or is collaboration a good idea?
   a. Why do you feel that way?
   b. Identify the positive and negative potential for working independently and collaborating.
4. In what ways does the region in which the arts organization operates influence or inform the art produced at the organization?
5. Assume the arts are uniquely susceptible to the challenges and pitfalls of local influences. Identify several reasons why that might be and provide guidance for how the arts manager might mitigate them.

## FURTHER READING

Appalshop.org.
   Visit their website to learn more about Appalshop and its 50-year history working within the Appalachian region.
Grossman, D. S., Humphreys, B. R., & Ruseski, J. E. (2019). Out of the outhouse: The impact of place-based policies on dwelling characteristics in Appalachia. *Journal of Regional Science, 59*(1), 5–28. https://doi-org.proxy.lib.fsu. edu/10.1111/jors.12398.

This article explores the ARC and its deliberate efforts designed to identify regional challenges and improve economic conditions in the Appalachian region.

Keller, A. S. (1989). The arts manager's social responsibility. *Arts Management and Law, 19*(2), 44–54.

This is a must-read for understanding the strategic and deliberate steps required of the arts administrator and organization to be relevant within their communities.

Kieffer, E. L. (2018). I landed a U.F.O. on Main Street: An autoethnography of the founding of an arts education organization in Appalachian Kentucky. *The International Journal of Social, Political and Community Agendas in the Arts, 14*(1), 3–15.

This article provides a first-hand encounter of the regional difficulties confronting one arts administrator as she attempted to transfer her education and experience into a new locale. The struggles are specific but the lessons of relevance and adaptability are universal.

Millesen, J. (2015). Understanding collective impact in a rural funding collaborative: Collective grantmaking in Appalachian Ohio. *The Foundation Review, 4*, 128.

Millesen provides another example of regional collaboration and its benefits for the nonprofit sector as a whole.

Swanson, L. E. (2001). Rural policy and direct local participation: Democracy, inclusiveness, collective agency, and locality-based policy. *Rural Sociology, 66*(1), 1–21.

For more information about the intricacies of regionally and geographically specific policy-making, Swanson provides an exploration of the importance of local social, economic, and physical infrastructures in mediating effective policy implementation.

## Notes

1 "Explore Census Data." United States Census. Accessed March 22, 2018. http://data.census.gov/.
2 Kieffer, Elise Lael. "Exploring Relationships Between Arts Administrators in Appalachian Kentucky and Tennessee and Their State Arts Agencies: A Qualitative Narrative Inquiry." ProQuest Dissertations Publishing, 2020.
3 "Quick Facts - Arts.gov." National Endowment for the Arts, 2016. https://www.arts.gov/sites/default/files/nea-quick-facts.pdf?source=post_page.
4 Ibid.
5 How a nation engages with art: Highlights from the 2012 survey of public participation in the arts (Report No. 57) § (2013).
6 Kieffer, Elise Lael. "Exploring Relationships Between Arts Administrators in Appalachian Kentucky and Tennessee and Their State Arts Agencies: A Qualitative Narrative Inquiry." ProQuest Dissertations Publishing, 2020.
7 Ibid.
8 Swanson, Louis E. "Rural Policy and Direct Local Participation: Democracy, Inclusiveness, Collective Agency, and Locality-Based Policy." *Rural Sociology* 66, no. 1 (2001): 1–21. https://doi.org/10.1111/j.1549-0831.2001.tb00052.x.
9 Miewald, Christiana. "Making Experience Count in Policy Creation: Lessons from Appalachian Kentucky." *Journal of Poverty* 7, no. 1-2 (2003): 163–181. https://doi.org/10.1300/J134v07n01_09.
10 Rosenstein, Carole, Vanessa Riley, Natalia Rocha, and Tyler Boenecke. "The Distribution and Policy Implications of US State Government General Operating

Support to the Arts and Culture: Lessons from the Great Recession." *Cultural Trends* 22, no. 3-4 (2013): 180–191. https://doi.org/10.1080/09548963.2013.817648.

11  "About State Arts Agencies." National State Arts Assemblies, 2018. https://nasaa-arts.org/state-arts-agencies/.

12  Ibid.

13  "Subregions in Appalachia." Appalachian Regional Commission, 2009. https://www.arc.gov/research/mapsofappalachia.asp?MAP_ID=31 on January 14, 2019.

14  Ibid.

15  Grossman, Daniel S., Brad R. Humphreys, and Jane E. Ruseski. "Out of the Outhouse: The Impact of Place-based Policies on Dwelling Characteristics in Appalachia." *Journal of Regional Science* 59, no. 1 (2019): 5–28. https://doi.org/10.1111/jors.12398.

16  Millesen, Judith. "Understanding Collective Impact in a Rural Funding Collaborative: Collective Grantmaking in Appalachian Ohio." *The Foundation Review* 7, no. 4 (2015): 128–. https://doi.org/10.9707/1944-5660.1271.

17  Sarnoff, Susan. "Central Appalachia-Still the Other America." *Journal of Poverty* 7, no. 1-2 (2003): 123–139. https://doi.org/10.1300/J134v07n01_07.

18  Kieffer, Elise Lael. "Exploring Relationships Between Arts Administrators in Appalachian Kentucky and Tennessee and Their State Arts Agencies: A Qualitative Narrative Inquiry." ProQuest Dissertations Publishing, 2020.

19  Balfour, Bruce, Michael W-P Fortunato, and Theodore R Alter. "The Creative Fire: An Interactional Framework for Rural Arts-Based Development." *Journal of Rural Studies* 63 (2018): 229–239. https://doi.org/10.1016/j.jrurstud.2016.11.002.

20  Frenette, Alexandre. "The Rise of Creative Placemaking: Cross-Sector Collaboration as Cultural Policy in the United States." *The Journal of Arts Management, Law, and Society* 47, no. 5 (2017): 333–345. https://doi.org/10.1080/10632921.2017.1391727.

21  Horwitz, Elinor Lander. *Mountain People, Mountain Crafts*. Hagerstown, MD: Lippincott Williams & Wilkins, 1974.

22  Barker, Garry. *The Handcraft Revival in Southern Appalachia, 1930–1990.* Knoxville: University of Tennessee Press, 1991.

23  Elissa R. Graff. "Preserving Traditional Culture in the Cumberland Gap Region." *Journal of Appalachian Studies* 18, no. 1/2 (2012): 234–243.

24  Kieffer, Elise Lael. "Exploring Relationships Between Arts Administrators in Appalachian Kentucky and Tennessee and Their State Arts Agencies: A Qualitative Narrative Inquiry." ProQuest Dissertations Publishing, 2020.

25  Leciejewski, Mary, and Harold A. Perkins. "Environmental Justice in Appalachia: Procedural Inequities in the Mine Permitting Process in Southeast Ohio." *Environmental Justice*, 4 (2015): 111–116.

26  "Who We Are." Appalshop, 2021. Appalshop.org.

27  Ibid.

28  Amy Price Azano, and Trevor Thomas Stewart. "Exploring Place and Practicing Justice: Preparing Pre-Service Teachers for Success in Rural Schools." *Journal of Research in Rural Education* 30, no. 9 (2015): 1–.

29  Amy Price Azano, and Trevor Thomas Stewart. "Confronting Challenges at the Intersection of Rurality, Place, and Teacher Preparation: Improving Efforts in Teacher Education to Staff Rural Schools." *Global Education Review* 3, no. 1 (2016): 108–128.

30  James David Vance. *Hillbilly Elegy: A Memoir of a Family and Culture in Crisis.* New York: Harper, an imprint of Harper Collins Publishers, 2016.

31  Fisher, Stephen L., Barbara Ellen Smith, Fran Ansley, Yaira Andrea Arias Soto, Dwight B. Billings, M. Kathryn Brown, Jeannette Butterworth, Paul Castelloe, Aviva Chomsky, and Dave Cooper. *Transforming Places: Lessons from Appalachia.* Baltimore, MD: University of Illinois Press, 2012. https://doi.org/10.5406/j.ctt1xcjnd.

32  Si Kahn. "Organizing, Culture, and Resistance in Appalachia: Past, Present, and Future." *Journal of Appalachian Studies* 18, no. 1/2 (2012): 8–24.

33  Grimes, Lee Edmondson, Natoya Haskins, and Pamela O. Paisley. "'So I Went Out There': A Phenomenological Study on the Experiences of Rural School Counselor Social Justice Advocates." *Professional School Counseling* 17, no. 1 (2013): 40–. https://doi.org/10.1177/2156759X0001700107.

34  James David Vance. *Hillbilly Elegy: A Memoir of a Family and Culture in Crisis.* New York: Harper, an imprint of Harper Collins Publishers, 2016.

35  Fisher, Stephen L., Barbara Ellen Smith, Fran Ansley, Yaira Andrea Arias Soto, Dwight B. Billings, M. Kathryn Brown, Jeannette Butterworth, Paul Castelloe, Aviva Chomsky, and Dave Cooper. *Transforming Places: Lessons from Appalachia.* Baltimore, MD: University of Illinois Press, 2012. https://doi.org/10.5406/j.ctt1xcjnd.

36  Ibid.

37  Flood, Bill, and Beth A. Vogel. "The Arts in Cross-Sector Collaborations: Reflections on Recent Practice in the US." In *Regionale Kooperationen im Kulturbereich*, pp. 347–362. transcript-Verlag, 2015.

38  "Mission Statement." Southeastern Arts Leadership Educators, 2018. https://artsleadershipeducators.com

39  Keller, Anthony S. "The Arts Manager's Social Responsibility." *The Journal of Arts Management and Law* 19, no. 2 (1989): 44–54. https://doi.org/10.1080/07335113.1989.9943120.

Elise Lael Kieffer

# Partnerships and Collaborations in the Arts

Yifan Xu

## Chapter 11

### INTRODUCTION

Some of the biggest challenges we face as arts administrators are the different people with whom we regularly interact. Some need things from us or our organizations, some want to work with us, others have no idea how we might interact. The savvy arts administrator knows that every potential contact is a potential means to serve their mission. Unfortunately, precious few academic resources readily discuss the most valuable types of partnerships arts organizations can develop. Though a single chapter cannot be exhaustive on the topic, this chapter addresses partnerships and collaborations describing how they occur and can be vital for nonprofit arts organizations.

Chapter 11 guides the reader through the intricacies of collaboration and partners involved in the collaborative process. The chapter covers detail such as working and partnering with governmental agencies and how to value stakeholders. The chapter then addresses for-profit and nonprofit alliances, corporate partnerships, and community partnerships, as well

DOI: 10.4324/9781003207535-12

as launching into a futuristic look at international partnerships and collaborations in the arts, as well as innovation and entrepreneurship. Finally, the chapter concludes with some practical guidance for spotting opportunities, selecting partners, taking risks, and sharing rewards.

We needed someone who would have a broad perspective on interactions in different environments, with different types of people, so we reached out to a collection of colleagues to see if anyone had the right personal and professional background to address this chapter's topics and met Yifan Xu. Dr. Xu holds a Ph.D. in Arts Administration, Education, and Policy from The Ohio State University and has studied and worked in arts administration with foci in both China and the United States. In addition, her cultural industry management degree made her an even more equipped candidate for the chapter, and the past several years of scholarly activity as a colleague demonstrated her strong ability to develop content on this critical topic.

## PARTNERSHIPS AND COLLABORATIONS IN THE ARTS

*A Contribution by Yifan Xu*

To fulfill their missions, nonprofit arts organizations collaborate and partner with their stakeholders to access financial resources, share costs, build an audience, promote social values, and get inspired for artistic and arts management innovations.[1] It requires arts managers to be entrepreneurial and creative in identifying partnership opportunities and building strategic partnership relations. This chapter identifies major stakeholders that arts nonprofits collaborate with, including governments, for-profit arts companies, corporates, community organizations, and international partners. Nonprofit arts managers are encouraged to challenge their stereotypical perceptions of collaborations and to consider developing strategic partnerships with a diversified group of stakeholders.

After introducing major nonprofit arts partners, this chapter discusses the reasons and benefits for nonprofit arts organizations to collaborate with them as well as their expectations from nonprofit arts partnerships. The chapter describes common types of partnerships built between nonprofit arts and their partners, particularly sponsorships, artistic commissions, community-wide arts education coordination, and international touring and exchange. Arts managers can use these discussions as a nonprofit arts partnership and collaboration design toolbox to address financial concerns and artistic and social impacts. The last section of this chapter offers some food for thought on adopting arts entrepreneurship mindsets and skills like opportunity spotting and risk-taking in selecting partners and building strategic and sustainable partnerships.

---

**LEARNING OBJECTIVES**

When they have completed reading this chapter, learners should be able to:

- Identify and describe the reasons major stakeholders engaging in collaborations and partnerships with nonprofit arts organizations.
- Illustrate and articulate the types and characteristics of nonprofit arts partnerships and collaborations, as well as their changes over time.
- Apply the arts entrepreneurial mindsets and skills to build strategic partnerships between nonprofit arts organizations and their increasingly diversified stakeholders.

---

## THE STAKEHOLDERS OF NONPROFIT ARTS ORGANIZATIONS

Stakeholders are groups or individuals who have the power to influence or are influenced by the operation of an organization.[2] Nonprofit arts stakeholders possess resources critical for the operation of nonprofit arts organizations, like funding, venues, and artistic expertise. Their expectations also challenge nonprofit arts organizations' legitimacy.[3] For example, donors and community members might not willingly support a community-oriented arts organization if they perceive that the organization's missions and impacts are not congruent with their values. Nonprofit arts organizations hence build partnerships and collaborate with different stakeholders to sustain their operations, fulfill their missions, and create spillover impacts.

They frequently interact with stakeholders in their immediate local contexts.[4] Given the accelerated globalization, nonprofit arts organizations have also been increasingly exposed to the international environment. Five important nonprofit arts partners stand out among the various nonprofit arts stakeholders: governments, corporations, for-profit arts companies, community groups, and international organizations.

Nonprofit arts organizations develop different types of inter-organizational relationships with stakeholders in their external environment. Among these relationships are collaborations and partnerships, often used interchangeably in the nonprofit arts sector.[5] Nonprofit arts organizations often find themselves using "collaboration" as a general term when building different types of partnerships. The nature of partnerships is collaboration, which includes both informal networking critical to generating collaboration ideas and more formal partnerships based on contracts or agreements. Partnerships thus differentiate from each other according to the degrees of formality in inter-organizational relationships and the accountability of each partner involved. Nonprofit arts organizations collaborate with their stakeholders with varying degrees of organizational integration in managerial aspects like branding, programs, finance, and administration.[6]

Nonprofit arts organizations often use stakeholder mapping to identify important stakeholders in different circumstances before developing partnerships with them strategically. Arts organizations can rank the power of stakeholders in influencing their management and missions[7] based on their possession of resources.[8] Stakeholders can also be evaluated regarding their perceptions of nonprofit arts organizations, their interests in collaborating with them, and the alignment of their agendas with arts organizations' missions.[9] These different characteristics and profiles of stakeholders reveal their collaboration potential and thus inform arts organizations' partnership strategies.

Developing strategic partnerships requires arts organizations to understand the nature and benefits of collaborations with different stakeholders. In general, nonprofit arts organizations could achieve three types of goals through partnerships and collaborations (Table 11.1). Nonprofit arts organizations usually

Yifan Xu

**Table 11.1** Examples of Partnership Types between Nonprofit Arts Organizations and Their Major Partners in Pursuit of Three Main Collaboration Goals

| Main Goals of Collaboration | Accessing Financial Resources | Supporting Artistic Productions | Fulfilling Social Impacts/ Responsibilities |
|---|---|---|---|
| **Major Nonprofit Arts Partner** | | | |
| **Government** | • Grantmaking | • Artistic program grantmaking | • Social program grantmaking |
| **Corporate/corporate foundations** | • Grantmaking<br>• Sponsorships | • Artistic program grantmaking<br>• Sponsorships | • Social program grantmaking<br>• Sponsorships |
| **For-profit arts companies** | • Sponsorships<br>• Co-promotion partnerships | • Commissions and co-productions<br>• Artist residency programs | • Arts education programs |
| **Community groups** | • Grantmaking | • Artist residency programs | • Community-wide arts education programs |
| **International organizations** | • Grantmaking<br>• Sponsorships | • Touring<br>• Artist residency programs<br>• Co-productions | • Cultural exchange programs |

Source: Author's own summary.

access financial resources by partnering with governments and corporations. They also support artistic innovations and development by collaborating with for-profit arts companies and international peers. These different partnerships often directly or indirectly cultivate cultural diversity and empathy, advance civic and social causes, and enrich community life, particularly when community members and groups are engaged collaboratively. It is also important to take risks and spot opportunities, pick the right timing and appropriate partners, and negotiate resources and responsibilities involved in each specific partnership.[10]

## WORKING WITH GOVERNMENTS

Regardless of the constraints that come with government funding,[11] nonprofit arts organizations could exploit collaboration and partnership opportunities with different actors. Programs like the National Endowment for the Arts' (NEA) Our Town and Challenge America encourage nonprofit arts organizations to partner with state, regional, and local cultural agencies through grant proposals. Governments are also open to initiatives like the Urban Arts Partnership (UAP) StoryStudio Project that are proposed by government officials or arts leaders. Working with governments can be creatively explored to engage local communities and serve the social purpose of arts.

### CASE STUDY: URBAN ARTS PARTNERSHIP STORYSTUDIO PROJECT

UAP is a nonprofit organization that provides students from underprivileged communities access to equal education opportunities through arts.[12] The StoryStudio Project started with a pilot program in 2007, as a part of the Promising Practice grant awarded to UAP by the Center for Arts Education Research at Teachers College, Columbia University. UAP's test of arts education process in fall 2007 with Dr. Sun Yat Sen Middle School 131 in NYC addressed the gaps in existing services for English Language Learner (ELL) students identified by the United States Department

Yifan Xu

of Education Office of Innovation and Improvement (US DEO). The Department later proposed to continue improving StoryStudio as a model of arts-in-education that facilitates English language acquisition for ELL students and to disseminate it to a wider underprivileged community in NYC, in collaboration with UAP.

In conversation with UAP, participating school administrators, certified arts teachers, teachers of EELs, arts coordinators, representatives of NYC DOE school districts, and independent evaluators, US DEO created a narrative for the project. It detailed the significance of StoryStudio, the timeline for the four-year project, project personnel responsibilities and management, as well as project evaluation. Many of the afore-consulted actors who participated in the 2007 pilot StoryStudio were invited to stay in the partnership for the four-year program led by US DEO. The dissemination of the curriculum package and learning results were mainly supported by UAP directors and teaching artists. Additionally, the US DEO narrative of StoryStudio promoted capacity-building and networking among its partners to ensure its sustainable development beyond the four-year financial assistance.

Many government grants require a match of funding from the private sector, which not only cultivates arts–business partnerships but secures more financial support for nonprofit arts organizations. Building on the grantmaking relations, governments are facilitators and coordinators of collaborations among nonprofit arts organizations, corporates, the for-profit arts sector, community groups, and international organizations.

**What Do Governments Want?**

Although arts agencies may support nonprofit arts organizations in areas of artistic development, cultural heritage preservation, and operation, governments have been increasingly invested in the instrumental value of culture. Specifically, the political agendas for arts and culture in the United States prioritize the economic impacts of arts through creative place-making, cultural tourism, cultural infrastructure development, and social values through arts education and serving underprivileged communities. Thanks to Americans for the Arts (AFTA), the value of arts in cultivating cultural diversity, addressing social issues, and encouraging civic participation gained more support from governments. Governments may also be inspired by partnerships with nonprofit arts organizations in public administration and social programs.[13]

### Partnership Types with Governments

Through temporary or permanent committees or informal communication between appointed government officials and arts leaders, nonprofit arts organizations have been mobilized to envision and be a part of a state's economic and infrastructure development. Collaborative networks with educational institutions are built for k-12 arts education projects and professional development programs for the creative workforce. Local arts councils often commission public art projects and murals, preserve local cultural heritage, and support artist residency programs through collaboration with nonprofit arts organizations. Nonprofit arts organizations may also join cultural enterprises and private businesses to promote local cultural tourism and city branding, together with local governments. Though nonprofit arts organizations are usually sought after by governments in creative placemaking initiatives, they enjoy more flexibility in leading government-supported projects, particularly those serving underprivileged groups.

## PARTNERSHIPS BETWEEN NONPROFIT AND FOR-PROFIT ARTS SECTOR

Collaborations and partnerships between nonprofit and for-profit arts are common practices in performing arts, as the production, presentation, and touring of performances require teamwork and coordination among different arts professionals.[14] In effect, nonprofit arts organizations in all artistic fields may benefit from partnerships with the for-profit arts sector artistically, financially, and managerially. Partnerships between different cultural fields and artistic genres, involving both nonprofit arts organizations and arts enterprises, inspire experimental artworks and program innovations.[15] Their collaborations enhance the sharing of risks and critical resources in artistic productions and services and help to distribute them to a wider audience. These partnerships share grants and attract investments, transforming how nonprofit arts organizations solicit funding. By building collaborative artistic and professional relations, for-profit arts companies may also transfer their experiences in arts management to nonprofit arts organizations.[16]

## What Do Arts and Cultural Enterprises Want?

Although sharing similar artistic goals as nonprofit arts organizations, the for-profit arts sector uses arts and cultural products to make profits.[17] Arts enterprises frequently invest in artistic experiments by nonprofit arts organizations and benefit from these creative ideas in the long term.[18] Private arts and cultural enterprises support nonprofit arts organizations' artistic experiments through commissions and co-productions in exchange for increased quality of artistic productions, program innovations, or a growing audience.[19] The for-profit arts sector may also access professional development resources and network with the larger creative community through nonprofit arts partnerships. As an emerging trend in the private sector, fulfilling corporate social responsibilities has become an important factor driving collaborations between cultural enterprises and nonprofit arts organizations.

## Partnership Types with For-profit Arts Companies

Although nonprofit arts organizations collaborate mainly on project mandates and proposals,[20] formal contracts are often used in their partnerships with the for-profit arts sector. Many partnerships between nonprofit and for-profit arts are venue based, through leasing spaces and sponsorships (e.g. The New 42nd Street in NYC).

### CASE STUDY: THE NEW 42ND STREET

In the early 1980s, New York City government and private developers took an interest in transforming its declining theatre district along mid-Manhattan's 42nd Street. The New

York City Economic Development Corporation (NYCEDC) led the 42nd Street Development Project and brought different voices and expertise from the arts and cultural sector. They included Robert A.W. Stern Architects, Disney, temporary arts exhibitions, and more.[21] When planning for the commercial development, the State of NY noticed and addressed the concerns of these experts, planners, and the public regarding the preservation of six historical theatres in the area. The project plan approved in 1984 specified these theatres were to be used for Broadway performances.

Due to the economic downturn in the early 1990s, a nonprofit organization called The New 42nd Street was formed to transform these theatres into offices, rehearsal, and performance spaces for theatre productions. It also partnered with the entertainment sector by leasing the restored theatres for movies. It worked closely with NYCEDC to realize the approved development plan and bring artistic activities and brand values to both new and renovated commercial and cultural venues in this historical theatre district. The New 42nd Street also actively acquired other arts and cultural properties, functioning as an enterprise. Nevertheless, as a nonprofit organization, it kept intact its mission of preserving and studying the historical theatres.

Inspired, supported, and coordinated by the state and NYCEDC, this contact-based partnership between nonprofit arts organizations and various for-profit actors from arts and non-arts sectors achieved desired public results.[22]

Though nonprofit arts organizations may acquire administrative and financial knowledge from their for-profit arts partners to improve their management, their administrative core, and governance structure are rarely influenced.[23] On some occasions, mergers and acquisitions might happen when nonprofit arts organizations encounter existential crises like financial deficits. Most often, the two collaborate on operational aspects like marketing and programming. Co-production and commission are also common nonprofit and for-profit arts

Yifan Xu

partnerships for artistic experiments. Other partners like governments, cultural agencies, and corporations are often invited for additional financial support of artistic productions and operations.

## CORPORATE PARTNERSHIPS

A major source of philanthropic funding for nonprofit arts organizations in the United States is private foundations, usually established by large corporations like the Ford Foundation. Nonprofit arts organizations have also actively sought business sponsorships since the late 1980s to access not only financial support but valuable market resources like audiences, venues, and marketing expertise. With the increasing awareness of corporate social responsibilities,[24] corporations have become more approachable for varying types of nonprofit arts partnerships.[25] Nonprofit arts and businesses often strategically collaborate to foster artistic and corporate creativities and promote social causes.

### What Do Corporate Partners Want?

Corporations could seek inspiration for business development and management through arts–business partnerships, as identified by AFTA, such as driving innovation, showing gratitude to employees, and cultivating a healthy work environment. However, collaborations between nonprofit arts organizations and corporations are dominated by co-promotion, marketing, and sponsorship,[26] driven by the prestige and branding effects associated with arts organizations as well as the tax benefits that come with supporting nonprofits.[27] Businesses also commission artworks from nonprofit arts organizations for corporate art collections and branding.[28]

Corporations may facilitate joint research and development with nonprofit arts organizations, through artist residency programs. These partnerships serve as incubators for socially relevant artistic experiments or profit-generating cultural products. Besides, socially responsible corporations have been actively engaging in venture capital investment of nonprofit arts organizations like museums to advance their social missions and support cultural heritage preservation while lowering risks in gaining financial returns.

## Partnership Types with Corporations

Sponsorship is the most common type of arts–business partnership, which is based on "exchanges between two entities"[29] and aims to bring mutual benefits to corporations and arts organizations. In return for financial, media, equipment, or venue support, corporations benefit from the brand value associated with arts organizations and the social impacts generated through sponsored programs. Most sponsorship packages thus require nonprofit arts organizations to commit to promoting sponsors via different channels, fundraising campaigns, and signature programs. Sponsorships may evolve into other types of arts–business partnerships like co-productions, co-programming, joint marketing, venture capital investment, and business arts incubators.[30] For example, Aeroplan and Tapestry New Opera transformed their financial support-oriented sponsorship into a programming-based partnership.

### CASE STUDY: THE EVOLVING PARTNERSHIP BETWEEN AEROPLAN AND TAPESTRY NEW OPERA

Originally the frequent flyer rewards provider for Air Canada, Aeroplan "reinvented itself as a diversified loyalty marketing company"[31] around mid-2005. For a long time, the company sponsored Tapestry New Opera, a nonprofit arts organization championing new contemporary opera works. Aeroplan provided financial support to Tapestry "in exchange for sponsor status, signage, tickets and hospitality."[32]

Their partnership also included many opportunities to collaborate on different types of projects. These projects provide useful examples for the types of activities nonprofit arts and their business partners might instigate. In 2005, Tapestry invited Aeroplan to plan its 25th anniversary celebration, which was also considered a good opportunity to rebrand Aeroplan. The small planning team decided to create a landmark artistic poster branding Aeroplan's new positioning in the airline industry, via the slogan selected by Aeroplan's marketing and design team and agreed on by Tapestry. Aeroplan representatives felt affinity for nonprofit arts organizations that see things un-conventionally, and Tapestry felt understood by a non-arts partner. Aeroplan naturally turned to Tapestry when planning its 2005 Aeroplan Days to boost the company's morale, through in-person meetings, telephone calls, and emails exchanges with Tapestry representatives. The event featured a presentation about arts and empathy by Tapestry's CEO. The creative Aeroplan-Tapestry partnership was also featured in a team-building event that engaged Aeroplan staff in the creation and performance of an opera. Aeroplan invited a small group of Tapestry artists to create a short work within 24 hours to resonate with a tragic incident in the company and provide arts therapy to employees.

The transformation of sponsorship between Aeroplan and Tapestry New Opera into an engaging partnership builds on finding common grounds (e.g. the appreciation of creativity) through effective communication among arts and business leaders.

The rising recognition of corporate social responsibilities brings corporations closer to nonprofit arts organizations. Many nonprofit arts organizations build social alliances with local businesses to develop local arts and cultural activities like after-school arts programs and cultural festivals for social changes and community development.[33]

## COMMUNITY PARTNERSHIPS

Community organizations dedicated to youth development, community service, advocacy, religious causes, and public health are major non-arts partners of nonprofit arts organizations outside of the private sector.[34] Though nonprofit arts organizations collaborate with public schools to develop arts education programs, their partnerships with libraries, social service organizations, community development groups, and religious congregations also bring arts education opportunities to different community groups. These partnerships also serve different social and civic agendas, such as preserving local cultural heritage and history, supporting community mental health, celebrating cultural diversity, and upgrading community spaces.

Partnering with non-arts civic organizations helps nonprofit arts organizations access additional financial resources. Government agencies, foundations, and corporations regard collaborative projects as preferable to solo ventures, as risks are shared among different entities. These projects are also more likely to be feasible and benefit a wider community.[35] Nonprofit arts organizations may actively partner with community organizations to advocate for the arts, through strategic alliances, awareness campaigns, and research.[36]

### What Do Community Organizations Want?

Community groups and members prioritize various civic and social agendas.[37] According to AFTA, they expect to improve community quality of life and cultivate cultural diversity and empathy through community-focused arts and cultural projects. In most cases, community partners facilitate the organization of arts activities, provide venues and funds, and supply volunteers. In exchange, they bring arts programs to underprivileged communities like the elderly, immigrants, incarcerated teens, and more. These arts programs are often held in unconventional spaces such as public housing complexes, senior care centers, and hospitals. Moreover, nonprofit arts organizations are invited into partnerships with public housing organizations, to provide affordable housing to the artist community (e.g. Artspace), or to boost cultural vibrancy in gentrified communities.

### Partnership Types with Community Organizations

The formation of arts-community partnerships requires a collaborative process and thus involves various formal and informal approaches to engage in conversations and build alliances with the community. Community leaders and influencers are critical to initiating and facilitating communication and interaction between nonprofit arts organizations and community organizations and members.

Yifan Xu

Committee meetings, informal networking, neighborhood surveying, and campaigns are often organized to hear the community's needs and feedback, and build community consensus and support. Governments and corporations are important financial supporters for community partnerships. Consequently, arts-community partnerships may evolve into complex ones like the community-wide arts education collaboration in Dallas, TX, which requires coordination among community organizations, nonprofit arts organizations, governments, and private donors.

## CASE STUDY: ARTS EDUCATION WITH COMMUNITY COORDINATION IN DALLAS

In 1987, three arts education advocates established a Young Audiences chapter in Dallas, offering arts education programs in schools.[38] In 1995, "Young Audiences of North Texas (YANT) and other local community-based providers"[39] addressed the equity concerns in arts education based on their audit of arts experience offerings in different Dallas school districts. Led by the City of Dallas Office of Cultural Affairs (CDOCA), ArtsPartners was launched as a public–private partnership between the CDOCA and YANT. Though ArtsPartners generally aimed to integrate arts learning into elementary schools, the Dallas Young Audiences chapter developed programs for a diverse population outside of formal educational settings.

Partnerships and the programs they create often snowball to create more programs serving a wider segment of the population. For example, the Young Audiences chapter was incorporated as a 501(c)(3) in 2004 as "Big Thought" to facilitate the program design, fundraising, governance, and financial management of its partners. Its donors expanded to local businesses, national and local foundations, and arts agencies. Big Thought initiated DALI in 2007 with the support from the Wallace Foundation, and for the first time led arts education development in Dallas. It invited elementary schools, out-of-school-time programs, and community centers for a community-wide arts education program and functioned mainly as "a broker between arts organizations and the school district" (p. 37). ArtsPartners has been an important partner in the community-wide arts education coordination and shows the way partnerships are rarely stagnant as they continue developing and reevaluating their collaboration.

Though nonprofit arts organizations could simply rent spaces to host community programs and present performances or exhibitions in local historical and cultural venues, libraries, and schools, other community partnerships require more interactions with various community partners. Murals are often commissioned when the partnership is led by community organizations with a close relationship to local arts, tourism, or economic development agencies.[40] Nonprofit arts organizations, however, lead partnerships that cultivate artistic development like artist residency programs. Common arts education-oriented, arts-community partnerships include after-school programs and summer camps. Arts organizations also program cultural events and festivals in partnership with local businesses, schools, arts councils, and social service organizations.

## INTERNATIONAL PARTNERSHIPS AND GLOBALIZATION

Though nonprofit arts organizations are mostly community oriented, symphony orchestras frequently exchange and collaborate with arts organizations and companies in other countries.[41] Art museums often rely on international touring of renowned artists and collections to offer quality artistic experiences to their audiences. Commissions and co-productions with performing arts groups from different cultures inspire innovative artistic experiments. Besides accessing resources offered by peers in other countries, nonprofit arts organizations also build international audiences and reputations by engaging in international artistic collaborations. Some international collaborations and cultural exchanges are coordinated and funded by cultural agencies, such as the U.S. Department of State and the British Council, making them diplomatic gestures involving formal agreements and government negotiations. Nonprofit arts organizations also partner with multinational corporations for financial support and with an international non-governmental organization (NGO) to preserve and promote arts in underprivileged communities.

## What Do International Partners Want?

Multinational enterprises often use arts to build brand characteristics, through co-planning business retreats and promotional events with nonprofit arts organizations.[42] Governments facilitate and fund international exchange and touring of artistic programs produced by nonprofit arts organizations to present an official cultural image abroad and promote intercultural dialogues. Private foundations, professional associations, and nonprofit arts organizations invest their expertise, networks, and financial resources into international collaborations for artists' professional development and the creation of new works. International NGOs like the United Nations Educational, Scientific and Cultural Organization coordinate cultural and professional exchange to preserve and promote diverse cultural expressions. The issue of fairness is often concerned by partners in international artistic collaborations, particularly between developed and developing countries.[43]

## Partnership Types with International Partners

Given the concerns of Visa application and international cultural relations, international collaborations with nonprofit arts organizations often involve the supervision of state agencies and hence are mostly formal.[44] Government agencies create programs for international cultural exchange to fulfill diplomatic agendas in targeted regions. International touring is the most common partnership nonprofit arts organizations build with their peers in foreign countries. Performing arts organizations frequently create new works through international commissions and co-productions. These international artistic tours and collaborations may involve professional associations and private foundations for financial and expertise support. Multinational corporations, however, provide sponsorships and marketing support for nonprofit arts organizations to design artistic programs that align with their development plans as well as social and branding agendas. The Guggenheim UBS

MAP Global Art Initiative provides an excellent example of a partnership between "a major global financial institution" and "a multi-site major museum."[45] The Swiss bank UBS has been actively supporting arts and culture, particularly contemporary art. The Solomon R. Guggenheim Foundation is dedicated to the collection, preservation, and research of contemporary art and "sought out the most advanced modern and contemporary arts" across borders.[46] UBS initiated the MAP Global Art Project with Guggenheim in 2012.

Mutual understanding was achieved from the very beginning of the partnership, as it was made clear to both partners that UBS targeted audiences in regions Guggenheim also aimed to develop connections in. The bank provided "financial support for new art acquisition"[47] by Guggenheim from under-represented regions in its contemporary art collection and "a research and educational program and international touring exhibitions."[48] UBS' local offices around the world provided marketing and operational support, contributing to a collaborative marketing strategy. In exchange, the bank expected to attract new clients and promote its business expansion and branding in regions with economic potential. It also fulfilled UBS' social responsibilities in promoting and educating art to a wider audience.

Through a joint venture, UBS and Guggenheim enjoyed high autonomy in planning the MAP project. The museum's sponsorship director came into the discussion of program details and places of exhibitions and events with a clear goal of creating win–win results for UBS and a steadfast position in advancing Guggenheim's artistic networking and collaboration agenda.

### INNOVATION IN THE ARTS – ENTREPRENEURSHIP

Arts entrepreneurship examines arts management processes and exercises that call on "an ongoing set of innovative choices and risks intended to recombine resources and pursue new opportunities to produce artistic, economic and social value."[49] Building nonprofit arts partnerships correspondingly requires the creativity of arts leaders and their willingness to take risks in seeking various collaboration opportunities.[50] Arts managers are encouraged to step out of their comfort zones and break stereotypical presumptions associated with their stakeholders' motivations in nonprofit arts partnerships, particularly corporations and international partners. It is a prerequisite for arts organizations to develop strategic and sustainable collaborations with appropriate stakeholders and navigate the complex partnership-building process.

## Opportunity Spotting and Risk-Taking

An arts entrepreneurial approach of building nonprofit arts partnerships and collaborations also relies on nonprofit arts leaders' skills in opportunity spotting as well as risk-taking and open minds. In preparation for the strategic partnerships to fulfill their artistic, economic, and social agendas, arts organizations should beware their socio-economic, political, artistic, and global contexts from which they could explore various collaboration opportunities with appropriately selected stakeholders. They should also assess their stakeholders' resources and expectations and their missions and assets to practice spotting additional opportunities and risks. As the needs and nature of collaboration evolve, the goals and formats of partnerships adjust based on the continuous assessment of the benefits and risks involved in different types of partnerships.[51] The responsibilities of each partner also need to be strategically assigned and adjusted to minimize and share risks, according to the ongoing evaluation of resources and expectations of nonprofit arts organizations and their partners.

## An Arts Entrepreneurial Process of Forging Strategic Nonprofit Arts Partnerships

Developing strategic nonprofit arts partnerships involves major decisions on selecting partners, as well as negotiating, building, and sustaining partner relationships.[52] Nonprofit arts leaders should ask themselves several important questions before reaching out to potential and preferred partners and entering formal partnership discussions (Figure 11.1). Particularly, nonprofit arts organizations can evaluate their organizational assets and capacities to decide whether a collaboration is necessary to fulfill their missions and sustain their operations. Stakeholder mapping is critical for arts organizations to spot collaboration opportunities by evaluating stakeholders'

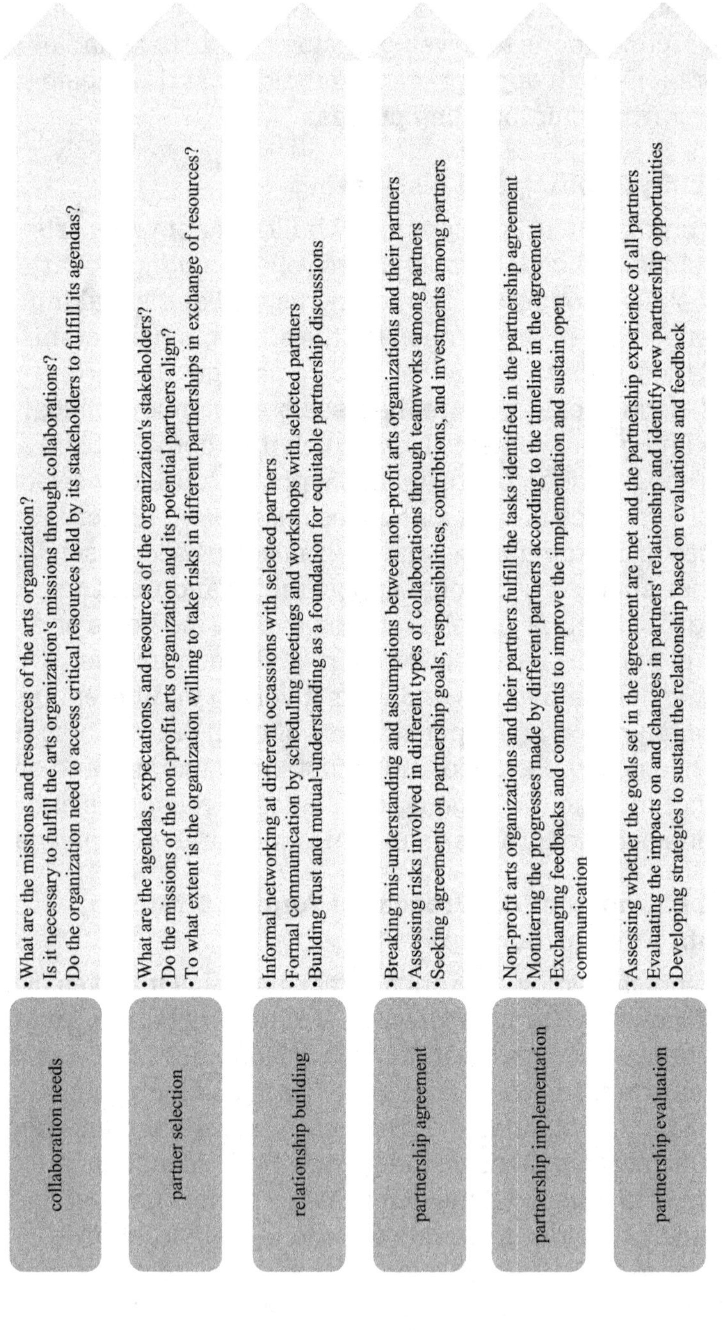

Yifan Xu

Figure 11.1 An arts entrepreneurship process of strategic nonprofit arts partnership building.

**collaboration needs**
- What are the missions and resources of the arts organization?
- Is it necessary to fulfill the arts organization's missions through collaborations?
- Do the organization need to access critical resources held by its stakeholders to fulfill its agendas?

**partner selection**
- What are the agendas, expectations, and resources of the organization's stakeholders?
- Do the missions of the non-profit arts organization and its potential partners align?
- To what extent is the organization willing to take risks in different partnerships in exchange of resources?

**relationship building**
- Informal networking at different occassions with selected partners
- Formal communication by scheduling meetings and workshops with selected partners
- Building trust and mutual-understanding as a foundation for equitable partnership discussions

**partnership agreement**
- Breaking mis-understanding and assumptions between non-profit arts organizations and their partners
- Assessing risks involved in different types of collaborations through teamworks among partners
- Seeking agreements on partnership goals, responsibilities, contributions, and investments among partners

**partnership implementation**
- Non-profit arts organizations and their partners fulfill the tasks identified in the partnership agreement
- Monitering the progresses made by different partners according to the timeline in the agreement
- Exchanging feedbacks and comments to improve the implementation and sustain open communication

**partnership evaluation**
- Assessing whether the goals set in the agreement are met and the partnership experience of all partners
- Evaluating the impacts on and changes in partners' relationship and identify new partnership opportunities
- Developing strategies to sustain the relationship based on evaluations and feedback

resources and agendas, while risk analysis helps to identify appropriate partners based on the assessment of each partner's capacities and expectations and that of potential risks and available resources in different partnerships. They also inform partnership feasibility evaluation.

The core of forging strategic nonprofit arts partnerships and collaborations is relationship building. It requires arts managers to communicate and negotiate with partners and create an operational plan specifying goals, responsibilities, timelines, etc. The final products of these partnership-building efforts are formal agreements on operational details. Nonprofit arts organizations need to follow through with assigned responsibilities and conduct timely feedback and evaluation to fulfill partnership goals. Ongoing and transparent communication contributes to the mutual understanding and trust among different partners and the quality of partnership projects[53] while sustaining partner relations and inspiring new collaboration ideas.[54]

## Final Thoughts

Nonprofit arts organizations collaborate and partner with their stakeholders to achieve different goals. Nonprofit arts partnership and collaboration require arts managers to be patient, creative, and open-minded in the process of finding the common ground with their preferred partners. This chapter provides a portfolio of the common expectations that major nonprofit arts stakeholders hold when building nonprofit arts partnerships with the purpose of providing a toolkit to guide nonprofit arts organization through the process of selecting partners and forging strategic partnerships with appropriate stakeholders.

These partnerships and collaborations take various forms, involve diverse groups, and may evolve in different contexts and over time. Nonprofit arts organizations are encouraged to strategically and sustainably collaborate with various partners to access financial resources, support artistic productions, and fulfill social responsibilities. An entrepreneurial mindset is as much needed to promptly and creatively address issues and opportunities in the partnership-building process as arts managers' understanding of nonprofit arts stakeholders and their partnership and collaboration mechanisms.

Nonprofit arts managers should also keep in mind that relationship building is always a discursive process that may or may not work for all parties involved. Consequently, communication skills and transparency are particularly important in successful and sustainable nonprofit arts partnerships and collaborations, in addition to the various questions and assessments nonprofit arts managers should ask themselves before, during, and after building partner relationships. Regardless of the case studies discussed in this chapter, arts administrators should always continue learning from peers and their own experiences in the daily practices of building nonprofit arts partnerships and collaborations.

## DISCUSSION QUESTIONS

1. Are there any unconventional partners of nonprofit arts organizations outside of the discussion of the five types of nonprofit arts partners?
2. What are the similarities and differences between common types of nonprofit arts partnership agreements?
3. What are the obstacles in arts–business partnerships? What communication strategies are effective for nonprofit arts organizations to build deeper partnerships with corporations?
4. How are arts partnerships and collaborations evaluated by governments, private sponsors, nonprofit arts organizations, and community organizations?
5. What are the goals, funding schemes, and criteria of government-sponsored programs for nonprofit arts organizations that encourage or require collaborations and partnerships?
6. How are the goals, funding schemes, and forms of international arts collaboration programs sponsored by governments differ from those initiated by nonprofit arts organizations?
7. What are different stakeholder mapping strategies used by nonprofit arts organizations?
8. What are the risks involved in nonprofit arts partnerships and collaborations? How are they assessed by nonprofit arts organizations?

Yifan Xu

9. What are the characteristics of long-term partnerships between nonprofit arts organizations and their various partners?

## FURTHER READING

American for the Arts' pARTnership Movement website (https://www.partnershipmovement.org/tools-resources#toolkits) offers toolkits, factsheets, research, and professional development resources for nonprofit arts organizations to cultivate effective arts–business communication. Arts managers can be inspired by the best practices of their peers and learn how to work with various stakeholders in a complex arts–business partnership, such as the Chamber of Commerce.

The blog post "5 Ways Arts Projects Can Improve Struggling Communities" (Borrup, 2009) offers deeper insights into how arts-community partnerships address five social and civic issues in the U.S., from promoting interactions and increasing civic participation, to engaging youth and promoting power. Tom Borrup articulated different cases of arts-community partnerships led by either nonprofit arts organizations, community civic organizations, or local governments.

Artplace (https://www.artplaceamerica.org/resources) is a government-led cross-sector creative placemaking partnership between nonprofit arts organizations and players from the community, commercial, nonprofit, and philanthropy sectors. It collected resources and lessons for stakeholders in arts and culture, local governments, and higher education, by investing in demonstration projects that promote equitable community planning and development through arts and cultural strategies.

## Notes

1 Walker, Christopher, "Arts and non-arts partnerships: Opportunities, challenges, and strategies," *The Urban Institute*, 2004, http://webarchive.urban.org/UploadedPDF/311043_Arts_Nonarts.pdf; Chong, Derrick, *Arts Management* (Routledge, 2009).

2 Freeman, R. Edward, "The politics of stakeholder theory: Some future directions," *Business Ethics Quarterly* 4, no. 4 (1994): 409–421.

3 Tschirhart, Mary, *Artful Leadership: Managing Stakeholder Problems in Nonprofit Arts Organizations* (Indiana University Press, 1996).

4 Byrnes, William, *Management and the Arts* (Routledge, 2014).

5 Backer, Thomas E, "Partnership as an art form: What works and what doesn't in nonprofit arts partnerships," *Human Interaction Research Institute*, 2002, https://www.csun.edu/sites/default/files/hiri_b25_0.pdf

6 McLaughlin, Thomas A, *Nonprofit Mergers and Alliances* (John Wiley & Sons, 2010).

7 Chong, *Arts Management*.

8 Mitchell, Ronald K., Bradley R. Agle and Donna J. Wood, "Toward a theory of stakeholder identification and salience: Defining the principle of who and what really counts," *Academy of Management Review* 22, no. 4 (1997): 853–886.

9 Ford, Robert C., William C. Peeper and Amy Gresock, "Friends to grow and foes to know: Using a stakeholder matrix to identify management strategies for convention and visitors bureaus," *Journal of Convention & Event Tourism* 10, no. 3 (2009): 166–184.

10 Walker, "Arts and non-arts partnerships."

11 Ellis, Adrian and Sonali Mishra, "Managing the creative–Engaging new audiences: A dialogue between for-profit and non-profit leaders in the arts and creative

sectors," *National Arts Strategies,* 2004, https://www.artstrategies.org/downloads/ManagingTheCreativeBackground.pdf

12  Office of Innovation and Improvement, "Urban arts partnership storystudio project," *United States Department of Education Office of Innovation and Improvement,* 2010, https://www2.ed.gov/programs/artsedmodel/2010/urbanartsnarr.pdf

13  Arthurs, Alberta, Frank Hodsoll and Steven Lavine, "For-profit and not-for-profit arts connections: Existing and potential," *The Journal of Arts Management, Law, and Society* 29, no. 2 (1999): 80–96.

14  Langeveld, Cees, Dóra Belme and Tessa Koppenberg. "Collaboration and integration in performing arts," *Enlagring Financial, Artistic and Social Value By Doing It Collectively: A Qualitative Study in the Netherlands,* 2014, https://www.academia.edu/10514652/COLLABORATION_AND_INTEGRATION_IN_PERFORMING_ARTS

15  Ostrower, Francie, "Cultural collaborations: Building partnerships for arts participation," *Urban Institute,* 2003, http://webarchive.urban.org/UploadedPDF/310616_CulturalCollaborations.pdf

16  Lam, Jessica Helena, *Collaborative Networks and Non-profit Art Organizations: The Case of Art City,* Master's Thesis, The University of Manitoba, 2008.

17  Chong, *Arts Management.*

18  Arthurs, Hodsoll and Lavine, "For-profit and not-for-profit arts connections."; Ellis and Mishra, "Managing the creative–Engaging new audiences."

19  Langeveld, Belme and Koppenberg. "Collaboration and integration in performing arts."

20  Lam, *Collaborative Networks and Non-profit Art Organizations: The Case of Art City.*

21  New York City Economic Development Corporation, "42nd Street development project," *NYCEDC.* https://edc.nyc/project/42nd-street-development-project

22  Arthurs, Hodsoll and Lavine, "For-profit and not-for-profit arts connections."

23  Lee, Ra Won, *Interorganizational Relationships and Mergers of Nonprofit Arts Organizations: Two Case Studies of Mergers of Nonprofit Arts Organizations,* PhD dissertation, The Ohio State University, 2016.

24  Weinstein, Larry, and John Cook, "The benefits of collaboration between for-profit businesses and nonprofit arts-or culture-oriented organizations," *SAM Advanced Management Journal* 76, no. 3 (2011): 31–42.

25  Lewandowska, Kamila, "It's not all about the profit: An analysis of changes in arts and business relations," *Economics and Business Review* 2, no. 1 (2016): 107–126.

26  Kim, HwiJung, *Making Creative Connections: A Study on the Relationship Evolution and Developing the Arts and Business Relationship Model in a Changing Cultural Policy,* PhD dissertation, The Ohio State University, 2009.

27  Alexander, Victoria D., "Art and the twenty-first century gift: Corporate philanthropy and government funding in the cultural sector," *Anthropological Forum* 24, no. 4 (2014): 364–380.

28  Lund, Ragnar, and Stephen A. Greyser, *Corporate Sponsorship in Culture: A Case of Partnership in Relationship Building and Collaborative Marketing by a Global Financial Institution and a Major Art Museum* (Harvard Business School, 2015).

29  Thompson, Beverley J., "Sponsorship as a bilateral relationship: The benefits of applying relationship marketing principles in the sponsorship exchange," *Asia Pacific Journal of Arts and Cultural Management* 3, no. 1 (2005): 189.

30  Kim, *Making Creative Connections.*

31  Preece, Stephen B., "Building an arts-business partnership: The case of Aeroplan and tapestry new opera," *International Journal of Arts Management* (2010): 49–58, 49.

32  Ibid.

33  Weinstein, "The design, implementation and management of social alliances for arts- and culture-oriented organizations."

34  Walker, "Arts and non-arts partnerships."

35  Ibid.

36  Bodilly, Susan J. and Catherine H. Augustine, *Revitalizing Arts Education through Community-Wide Coordination* (Rand Corporation, 2008).

Yifan Xu

37  Walker, "Arts and non-arts partnerships."
38  Bodilly and Augustine, *Revitalizing Arts Education through Community-Wide Coordination.*
39  Ibid., 37.
40  Walker, "Arts and non-arts partnerships."
41  Langeveld, Belme and Koppenberg. "Collaboration and integration in performing arts."; Ellis and Mishra, "Managing the creative–Engaging new audiences."
42  Preece, "Building an arts-business partnership."; Lund and Greyser, *Corporate Sponsorship in Culture.*
43  Graan, Mike de., "Beyond curiosity and desire: Towards fairer international cooperation in the arts," *Amsterdam: IETM, On the Move and Dutchculture,* 2018, https://www.ietm.org/en/system/files/publications/ietm_beyondcuriosityanddesire_2018.pdf
44  Ibid.
45  Lund and Greyser, *Corporate Sponsorship in Culture.*
46  Ibid., 11.
47  Ibid., 13.
48  Ibid.
49  Chang, Woong Jo, and Margaret Wyszomirski, "What is arts entrepreneurship? Tracking the development of its definition in scholarly journals." *Artivate* 4, no. 2 (2015): 11–31, 25.
50  Preece, "Building an arts-business partnership."
51  Walker, "Arts and non-arts partnerships."
52  Ostrower, Francie, "Cultural collaborations."
53  Graan, "Beyond curiosity and desire."
54  Preece, "Building an arts-business partnership."

# Human Resource Law in the Arts

Brea M. Heidelberg

## Chapter 12

Chapter 12 explores human resource law and human resource issues vital to the arts administrator. It begins by discussing employment classifications and then shifts into labor laws. The discussion here focuses primarily on the big two of occupational safety and health and family medical leave, particularly focusing on what every administrator should know. Next, we delve into occupational safety law (this is reviewed in Chapter 14, and the topic must be included here as from a human resources perspective as well). The discussion then moves to the execution of and working with unions and collective bargaining and finishes with Title VII of the Civil Rights Act that deals with anti-discrimination.

Anthony first met Brea Heidelberg several years ago at a conference for arts administration educators. He recalls being quite taken with her strong focus, clarity, and organization of a topic specifically linked to human resource issues in arts administration. Though many areas of human resource management work in essentially the same way, regardless of industry, Dr. Heidelberg made clear in her presentation that though the HR theories may be the same, in practice, the nonprofit arts are dealing with creativity and creative individuals, so the actual practice of HR is unique.

DOI: 10.4324/9781003207535-13

With a background in dance, Brea is both a practitioner and a researcher. She consults with organizations on issues related to HR, including the vitally important issues surrounding diversity, equity, inclusion, accessibility, and justice. She has served in leadership positions in many major organizations focused on developing and advancing arts administration in the United States. Because she holds master's degrees in both human resource development and arts policy and administration, and a Ph.D. in arts administration, education, and policy, she is exceptionally well-positioned to address issues related to HR in the nonprofit arts.

## HUMAN RESOURCE LAW IN THE ARTS

*A Contribution by Brea M. Heidelberg*

Many creative professionals work for a nonprofit cultural institution at some point in their careers. As nonprofit institutions continue to grow and evolve in response to issues like field-wide calls for social justice and a global pandemic, understanding the basics of employment law through the lens of nonprofit organizations is vital. Because nonprofit organizations are tax-exempt and regulated differently than for-profit companies, many mistakenly assume that compliance with employment laws is an option and not a requirement. This can be a costly error in judgment that could prevent your organization from meeting its mission, or even continuing to exist at all. Likewise, this lapse in judgment could harm employees and the community the nonprofit serves.

This chapter introduces federal laws that most often impact arts organizations, offering field-specific insights into how arts managers should incorporate consideration of these laws into their everyday practices. Since many arts organizations operate without a dedicated human resources professional on staff, it is vital that arts managers understand these laws and how to properly apply and adhere to them. Instead of a "hope nothing bad happens" approach, it is important to understand how to best treat and protect your employees as well as how to protect yourself and your organization from a negative action. This goal is complicated by the fact that employment law operates at the federal, state, and local levels in a number of complementary, discordant, and contradictory ways. This chapter focuses on federal law, but it is essential to review state and local laws in your area. Even if you are not an executive director or a manager, it is important to understand these laws as a member of the creative workforce. Knowing how to protect yourself (as an employee) and your organization (as a manager) is vital to creating and maintaining a functional and effective organization where artists and arts managers can thrive. That said, this chapter cannot replace the counsel of an employment lawyer, and all organizations should seek counsel to review their policies and procedures.

This chapter reviews employment classifications, equal opportunity laws, safety regulations, and collective bargaining rights. Each section will provide an overview of the laws most pertinent to the field of arts management followed by a discussion of how these laws may be integrated into standard practice within arts organizations.

**LEARNING OBJECTIVES**

After reading this chapter, you will be able to:

- Identify the most common employment classifications.
- Determine if a worker should be classified as an employee or an independent contractor.
- Identify key areas where discrimination against a protected class may occur in the workplace.
- Cite major areas of concern for workplace safety in cultural organizations.

**Employment Classifications**

When a new employee joins an organization, it is common to discuss the terms of employment so that both the employee and the employer agree on the stipulations attached to the position. These discussions often culminate with a written employment contract. Though verbal and implied arrangements (where the particulars are nonverbal and unwritten) are also possible ways to begin a period of employment, they may be difficult to uphold and can leave the employee and the employer vulnerable in a legal setting. It is always recommended to have any employment contract, regardless of employment classification, in writing with signatures of both the employee and an organizational representative. This document should clearly articulate the employment relationship including, but not limited to dates of employment, salary, work schedule, paid time off (PTO) and benefits eligibility, and stipulations about any reviews or probationary period. The more nuanced specifics of an employment contract are largely dependent upon the employment classification of the new hire. What follows is an overview of the most common types of employment classifications found in arts organizations and some preliminary guidance on how to determine what type of employment classification may best fit your organization.

### Full-time Employee

Full-time employees usually work 35 or more hours per week and are considered permanent staff. Employment contracts for full-time employees are almost always written because they include several elements, and it is important for both the employer and the employee that all of those elements are clearly articulated and agreed upon. Full-time employees are usually entitled to benefits including, insurance, PTO, and sick leave. When the organization has the financial capacity, additional benefits such as professional development, retirement contributions, and other workplace perks associated with your organization, discipline, or community may be included.

When hiring an executive-level employee, organizations may extend an executive contract. These types of working arrangements include all of the elements of a full-time employment contract, but they are likely to also highlight executive-level privileges, additional perks, and other incentives. These are often used to attract and retain high-level talent.

### Temporary Employee

Temporary employees or fixed-term employees are hired for a specific amount of time or to complete a specific task. These

Brea M. Heidelberg

employees may work full- or part-time. They are afforded all of the privileges and protections of an employee for a clearly defined period. These contracts are often used to fill a skill or worker gap in a time of need. These types of contracts are most often utilized when an existing employee suffers an injury that results in short-term incapacitation or for parental or caregiver leave.

### Part-Time Employee

Part-time employees usually work less than 35 hours per week. For many nonprofit organizations, it is common to see a workforce that is a mixture of full- and part-time or even a few full-time and majority of part-time employees. In many instances, part-time employees are granted the same protections as full-time employees but are usually not offered the same benefits such as insurance or PTO.

### Seasonal or Irregular Employment Agreements

Some organizations have a number of seasonal or casual employees who work for predetermined periods of time when the organization has or anticipates the need for increased capacity. Employers may utilize zero hour, casual, or seasonal contracts to articulate the details of employment. *Zero-hour* contracts stipulate that the employer will offer shifts as available but that they are under no obligation to offer other employee benefits. These contracts are most often seen in organizations that utilize intermittent labors or caregiving services. Casual and seasonal contracts are more common within cultural organizations, especially those with performance seasons or significant ebbs and flows in organizational activity. These contracts stipulate the work hours and guidelines for a specific time period and often afford employees some, but usually not all, benefits and privileges afforded to more permanent full- and part-time employees.

### Employee vs. Independent Contractor

The most important distinction facing many organizations is whether an individual is hired as an employee or as an independent contractor. This distinction is most often considered from two perspectives: cost and liability. From a cost perspective, independent contractors are less expensive than employees. When hiring an employee, organizations are responsible for withholding income, Social Security, Medicare, and unemployment taxes, a responsibility that does not exist when an organization hires independent contractors. The second major distinction involves an organization's vulnerability to legal recourse. An employer may be responsible for damages if an employee is negligent and causes harm. This responsibility, known as *vicarious liability*, does not apply to independent contractors. Though this may appear like a clear case for having more independent contractors than employees within an organization, organizations can quickly get into legal trouble with a blanket classification of all workers as independent contractors. Furthermore, there is a case to be made about the many benefits of employees, including their ability to contribute to institutional knowledge and their ability to invest in the long-term health and vibrancy of the organization. Employers found to have misclassified workers are subject to fines and penalties from both the state and the Internal Revenue Service. Employers who routinely misclassify workers also suffer in the court of public opinion, as workers learn to avoid exploitative workplaces. Additionally, the Department of Labor has made misclassification of workers a priority for enforcement officers. Worker misclassification both robs the government of tax revenue and prevents workers from receiving "important workplace protections" enjoyed by employees.[1] Of particular interest to creatives is that the distinction between employee and independent contractor also has implications for copyright retention and intellectual property rights.[2]

With such high stakes, it would be ideal if there was a clear-cut way to properly classify workers while also being mindful of the financial ramifications and long-term responsibilities of welcoming new employees. Unfortunately, that is not the case. The distinction between an employee and an independent contractor is defined by careful consideration of the nature of the relationship between the individual and the organization. To help guide employers, there are six factors commonly known as the *economic realities test*.[3] This test is an expansion of the *control test*, which focused on the relative amount of control an individual has over the nature of the work and the way the work is completed. The factors of the economic realities test are:

1. **Is the work an integral part of the employer's business?**

   Activities that would prevent the organization from operating wholly or in part are integral and individuals doing those activities should be considered employees. Individuals whose activities are a welcomed addition to the organization's operations, but are not vital to the organization's overall operation are likely to be classified as an independent contractor.

2. **Does the worker's managerial skill affect the worker's opportunity for profit or loss?**

   If a worker has the autonomy to make decisions about how and for whom they do their work, specifically in ways that affect their ability to make money, then they are likely to be classified as an independent contractor. Individuals who have limited autonomy about their work and how they accomplish it (e.g. their main choice about working in a different way to earn more money is working overtime) are likely to be properly categorized as employees.

3. **How does the worker's relative investment compare to the employer's investment?**

   Individuals who are making investments that primarily impact or benefit their own work, relationships, and business are likely to be categorized as independent contractors.

4. **Does the work performed require special skill and initiative?**

   Though it may seem that this question is about the relative skill set of an individual, it is actually an expansion of #2. If an individual is merely providing their skill or labor, no matter how technical or highly skilled, then they are likely to be categorized as an employee. However, if an individual is making decisions about the nature of the work (e.g. when, where, the cost of raw materials, or whether or not to juggle multiple jobs/contracts), then they are likely to be categorized as an independent contractor.

5. **Is the relationship between the worker and the employer permanent or indefinite?**

   Despite the mention of permanence in the question, this is more about the nature of the work than the relative time spent working with or for an organization. The more permanent the type of work, the more likely an individual is to be classified as an employee. This includes intermittent work that is the same type of work over an extended period of time. Conversely, independent contractors are more likely to take on a clearly defined project—even if it is for an extended period of time.

### 6. What is the nature and degree of the employer's control?[4]

This question is about the employer's control of the individual's work and their ability to take on additional work or engage with other organizations. If the organization has control over the aforementioned elements, then the individual working for them is likely to be classified as an employee.

Though it may seem daunting to sort through the elements of the economic realities test, it is essential to note that careful consideration of each element, coupled with a "common sense approach," should lead a "reasonable manager to know whether an individual is an employee or independent contractor."[5] Essentially, if the total consideration of all the economic realities indicates that the individual is largely dependent upon the organization they are connected with, then they should be classified as an employee.

Job analysis is one aspect of human resource management that can help managers gather and analyze information that will help answer the questions of the economic realities test. *Job analysis* is the process of determining what a specific position entails and the requirements for successfully executing the tasks associated with that position. There are many methods for conducting a job analysis, so even the most resource-strapped organizations have the ability to gather the necessary information to make a reasonable assessment of whether an individual should be classified as an employee or an independent contractor.[6]

It is important to note that this is not an exhaustive list of the types of employment seen throughout the workforce in the United States. As the workforce continues to shift and the relationship between employers and employees continues to change, organizations will continue to develop different types of employment to suit their needs. As these new and altered forms of employment emerge, it is important for cultural managers to keep themselves aware of the different types of employee/employer relationships and carefully consider the organization's staffing needs and what will best serve the organization's mission, structure, and work in both the short and long terms.

Brea M. Heidelberg

## CASE STUDY: INDEPENDENT CONTRACTOR OR EMPLOYEE?

A small theater company has been operating with an executive/artistic director, a number of volunteers, and independent contractors since its incorporation five years ago. In the latest board of directors recruitment cycle, they brought on an attorney who practices employment law. In their second board meeting, the new board member expressed concern over the organizational flow chart, particularly two independent contractor positions: a marketing contractor and a janitorial contractor. The board member is concerned that they may be misclassified and wants the executive director to investigate the matter.

The marketing contractor works solely with the theater company. They market for the entire season and run the social media accounts. The janitorial contractor has been with the theater for four years and counts the theater as one of many clients in the neighborhood. Some of his tasks are standard, but he also takes on larger projects when the theater needs it and he has room in his schedule.

Questions:

1. How would you determine if the marketing contractor is misclassified?
2. How would you determine if the janitorial contractor is misclassified?
3. What can the executive director do moving forward as they look to expand their organization's capacity but keep staffing costs low?

## Anti-discrimination

Nonprofit cultural institutions have been directly culpable for or indirect perpetrators of discriminatory behaviors that include creating barriers for individuals hoping to become cultural managers[7] and exclusion of certain audiences.[8] This behavior has been supported or condoned by funders[9] and arts service organizations.[10] Though anti-discrimination protections have existed since 1964, ignorance, confusion, diversity resistance,[11] and malicious intent have permeated the field. While uneven in understanding and action, the entire cultural ecosystem has begun to fully reckon with the work of dismantling oppressive structures, requiring renewed focus on not only anti-discrimination law, but practical application thereof.

At the federal level, there are a number of laws designed to prevent different forms of discrimination (Table 12.1).

Though all organizations should work to actively avoid discriminating against workers in the recruitment and selection, retention, promotion, and evaluation processes, there is often confusion about which federal laws nonprofit organizations must adhere to. This confusion primarily stems from the fact that these laws have associated employee thresholds. For example, Title VII of the Civil Rights Act of 1964, or Title VII (the most commonly referenced anti-discrimination legislation), only

**Table 12.1** Federal Regulation and Protections Afforded.

| Federal Law | Prohibits Discrimination Based On... |
| --- | --- |
| Title VII of the Civil Rights Act of 1964 | Race, color, religion, gender, or national origin |
| Age Discrimination in Employment Act of 1967 | Age (over 40), specifically related to employment |
| Equality Act (2010) | Gender, specifically related to pay |
| Older Workers Benefit Protection Act (1990) | Age (over 40), specifically related to benefits |
| Pregnancy Discrimination Act of 1978 | Pregnancy, childbirth, or related condition |
| Immigration Reform and Control Act of 1986 | Individuals who are not US citizens or nationals |
| Vocational Rehabilitation Act of 1973 | Disability |
| Genetic Information Nondiscrimination Act of 2008 | Genetic make-up |
| Americans with Disabilities Act of 1990 | Disability (with reasonable accommodation) |

Brea M. Heidelberg

applies to organizations or companies that employ 15 or more workers. Some organizations mistakenly assume that this is limited to for-profit businesses, but this law also applies to government and nonprofit organizations. Despite the fact that many cultural organizations operate with much fewer staff members, many cities and states have nondiscrimination laws that cover organizations not covered by the federal laws. Some state and local laws also include characteristics not addressed in federal law (e.g. gender expression, gender identity, and sexual orientation). In addition to federal, state, and local laws and mandates, a growing number of funders include anti-discrimination policies and proof of equity action as part of their funding requirements.

There are many areas where discrimination can creep or be purposefully inserted into the experience of working in an organization, starting with the recruitment, and selection processes. Ensuring that your organization's position descriptions, materials review processes, and interview protocols are all free from bias requires a thorough investigation and the willingness to dismantle longstanding practices.[12] There are two different forms of discrimination that may manifest in the recruitment and selection process: disparate (mis)treatment and disparate impact. *Disparate (mis)treatment* is inequitable treatment of a candidate based on how they self-identify or are identified by others. Disparate (mis)treatment is likely easier to recognize than *disparate impact*, which involves seemingly neutral policies that disproportionately negatively impact certain candidates. Despite the relative difficulty in identifying and dismantling discriminatory practices, it is the organization's responsibility to do so.

The process of conducting a job analysis, referenced in the employment classifications section, can help managers determine employee classification. It can also help determine recruitment and selection protocols that are based on the required knowledge, skills, abilities, and other attributes (KSAOs) and not conscious and unconscious biases by providing detailed information about the position and what is required for success in the role. It can also help managers struggling to create consistent interview protocols to develop interview questions that are focused on getting a true sense of each individual's strengths and weaknesses relative to the position they would like to hold.[13]

Under Title VII, once an individual is hired, they have the right to a harassment-free work environment. Though sexual harassment is the most commonly known form of workplace harassment, any harassment that targets any of the protected classes of Title VII can put an organization at risk for liability if reported cases are not handled appropriately. Creating mechanisms for employees to report incidents of harassment, discrimination, and bullying has become more common in cultural institutions.[14] What still needs more thoughtful consideration is the process of investigating claims, preventing retaliation, and holding wrongdoers accountable. In recent years, there have been a number of cases where longstanding executive and/or artistic directors[15] are finally being publicly held accountable for years—and sometimes decades—of allegedly condoning, turning a blind eye to, or outright perpetrating abusive and discriminatory behavior. Though this is a sign of progress, it also demonstrates the need for better accountability structures and organizations and boards willing to use them before the abuse goes on for decades. Organizations who are made aware of harassment or discriminatory behavior and take no action to stop or remedy that behavior may be found liable should an employee or former employee seek legal action.

Bias and discrimination can also permeate evaluation and promotion decisions. Again, disparate (mis)treatment and disparate impact are important to consider. If individuals from a protected class are consistently evaluated poorly or less favorably than their counterparts, or if the organization's leadership is largely homogenous, it is important to take a close look into evaluation structures and promotion decision-making processes to determine if there are discriminatory elements. Even without malicious intent, longstanding discrimination throughout the industry has permeated both formal and informal administrative practices. For many organizations, an organization-wide exploratory investigation to unearth

Brea M. Heidelberg

bias and discrimination in administrative practices is likely to also uncover many areas for administrative structuring and improvement. Organizations without standard procedures for recruitment, selection, evaluation, and promotion are more likely to engage in biased and discriminatory practices. Furthermore, stalled professionalization of the field has prevented the adoption of universal standards for operating practices.[16] Therefore, organizations with unexamined practices, as well as those who rely on one or a few senior staff members to create and maintain administrative procedures, may be particularly vulnerable to legal action.

## CASE STUDY: POSITION DESCRIPTIONS

The marketing director for your organization comes to you with a posting and ad for an opening in her department. She is requesting that applicants be "digital natives." In response to your questions, she describes these applicants as those who are comfortable with internet technology and compares them to someone who spoke a certain language from birth rather than learning it as a second language. She hopes to have someone who can take over the social media marketing for the organization, but that is not explicitly stated anywhere in the ad. She said that she had received some pushback for her job postings in the past, where she requested that applicants be "young and hip" and wanted to avoid further criticism—so she is asking for your help.

Questions:

1. What protected class might have a case against your organization based on the use of the term "digital natives?"
2. What federal law is this posting violating?
3. What is a better way for the hiring manager to ensure that she gets qualified applicants, instead of just younger ones?

## Occupational Safety and Health Act

The Occupational Safety and Health Act (OSHA) was enacted in 1970 in response to the increasing number of work-related accidents and deaths in the nation.[17] The mandate exists to provide workers with a workplace safe from hazards that cause or are likely to cause death or serious harm. In addition to the requirement to comply with federally mandated occupational safety and health standards, organizations must also keep an annual record of all work-related illnesses and injuries. Under this law, individual employees have the right to request an OSHA inspection, be informed of any exposure to health and safety hazards, and to have any violations posted publicly at their place of employment. As with many federal discrimination laws, OSHA has an employee threshold for some elements of the law. For example, OSHA requires record keeping for any work-related deaths, illnesses, or injuries for organizations with 11 or more employees. However, organizations with fewer than 11 employees should also strive to create and maintain as safe a workplace as possible.

Though many think of OSHA in the context of manufacturing and machinery, there are important implications in the arts. Some hazards are easier to identify and account for than others. Hazardous materials exposure for visual artists and designers working with toxic materials can be guided by warning labels included on the materials they are using.[18] Similarly, museum workers and set designers working with heavy machinery are also generally aware of the potential dangers and the required safety precautions. However, fewer people are aware of the potential of being crushed by a set piece or suffering an injury from a trap door, walking off the edge of a dimly lit stage, or experiencing skin trauma from pyrotechnics for cultural workers in theater and music touring.[19] Furthermore, the physical harm caused by repetitive movements, awkward postures, and experimentation with different elements of the body experienced by many musicians and dancers are even less well-known and often not accounted for in workplace safety and health planning. In order to obtain a full understanding of all the potential health and safety risks in your workplace, it is important to speak with each individual employee or regular contractor and to have an understanding of their primary, secondary, and tertiary work functions, but also the general way they go about doing that work. Once again, thorough job analysis data will help managers get a head start on this data-gathering process.

Cultural managers looking to be OSHA compliant and to demonstrate care for their employees should engage in a comprehensive assessment of the potential health and safety hazards present in all workspaces. Some managers think about the performance and rehearsal spaces, but forget to inspect their general offices; some managers forget that investigating rental spaces is important. A common mistake managers make is to direct health and safety discussions to specific subgroups among employees instead of ensuring that everyone on the premises is aware of any potential hazards and the organization's safety protocols. Simply mentioning these matters in an employee handbook is not enough and does not account for the way that most adults absorb and retain information.[20] A health and safety tour should be common practice for all new hires (contract or employee), and refreshers should be given at regular intervals. OSHA also requires employers to provide information about exposure and potential exposure to any hazardous chemicals in the workplace. It is important to note that many states also have *right-to-know laws* which require employers to provide employees with information about potential risks and side effects of any hazardous materials they may come into contact with. In some cases, the state laws are more stringent than the federal OSHA mandates. Therefore, as is the case with many other things discussed in this chapter, it is important to check your state and local laws.

### CASE STUDY: BACKSTAGE CHEMICALS

For a small dance company, it is always "all hands on deck" for load-ins and when a performance run ends and it is time for strike. There are a few fully trained stage crew and scenery design team members helping to organize and manage these events. However, most helping with taking downlights, cleaning the stage of debris, and resetting the wings are front-of-house staff and employees from the administrative offices. During one particular show, there were some chemicals used as an adhesive to craft an experimental set that can be toxic in large amounts. There were a few canisters of leftover chemicals stored in the immediate backstage area. All of the stage crew and scenery design team knew it was there behind a black curtain, but the marketing manager bumped into the stacked canisters while helping to take a set-piece backstage. The canisters fell and one was damaged, exposing the entire crew, and staff to the toxic chemicals. While the stage crew and scenery design team rushed into action, it was chaos for all the front-of-house and administrative staff, who did not know what to do.

1. What could have been done to prevent this particular accident from occurring?
2. What, generally, should the organization do if it is expected that all employees will assist with load-in and strike?
3. How should leftover hazardous materials be handled in the future?

**Final Thoughts**

This chapter is intended to be a starting point for creative workers and managers. While foundational knowledge of the laws that most often impact nonprofit cultural organizations is important, it does not take the place of larger vision-setting conversations about how to align an organization's mission with its human resources practices given the particular resource constraints of the specific organization. When compliance with local, state, and federal laws is integrated into the daily practices and lifeblood of an employer, a nonprofit organization can not only protect itself from legal action, it can also best serve its primary stakeholders and broader community.

Brea M. Heidelberg

## DISCUSSION QUESTIONS

1. What are the advantages of being an independent contractor vs. an employee working with a cultural organization?

2. Do you think the field relies too heavily upon independent contractors? Why or why not?

3. Search for some positions in the field. Do you notice position descriptions with biased or discriminatory language? If so, do any trends emerge?

4. Based on the position description for your current position (or a position you've held in the past), do you know what you need to do in order to receive a positive evaluation? Or a promotion?

5. Are you aware of the employment-focused equity issues in your artistic discipline or sub-field of arts and cultural organizations? If so, what are they? If not, how will you go about educating yourself?

6. Are you aware of the most common health and safety hazards for your artistic discipline or the organizations you'd like to work with?

7. In your working experience, have you been made aware of the potential hazards in your working environments? If so, how were you notified?

8. While workers over 40 are a protected class, workers under 40 are not. Do you think there is a case for younger workers to also be a protected class? Why or why not?

9. Do you think that organizations who rely on technology-based methods for recruitment and selection are less likely to be accused of disparate (mis)treatment or disparate impact? Why or why not?

10. How can you use the information in this chapter to guide your employment decisions moving forward?

### FURTHER READING

"Directive 2723: Reasonable Accommodations for Individuals with Disabilities." *National Endowment for the Arts.* April 17, 2016. https://www.arts.gov/sites/default/files/NEA-Reasonable-Accomodation-April-2019.pdf

This document, which went into effect in 2019, establishes the National Endowment for the Arts (NEA) policies on disability and accommodations for their employees. Here, the NEA defines key terms and outline procedures for establishing and maintaining accommodations. As the flagship arts organization at the federal level, the NEA's document can be informative for organizations working toward greater accessibility.

Kshatriya, Sunitha. "A Case Study of Job Analysis and Its Positive Impact on Behavioral Structured Interview," *International Journal of Research in Social Sciences 7*, no. 3 (March 2017): 643–667.

In this article, Kshatriya demonstrates the steps one can take to move from a job analysis to standardized interview questions for candidates for that job. Kshatriya starts by first identifying the KSAOs for a job posting, then expanding to Tasks, Context, and Counter-productive behavioral components. Having identified these key components from the job analysis, Kshatriya then applies an appraisal tool that helps to develop a Behavioral Description Interview tool that leads to standardized interview questions. Kshatriya's detailed process can serve as a model for organizations learning to conduct interviews in equitable job searches.

Prince, Samantha J. "The Shoe's about to Drop for the Platform Economy: Understanding the Current Worker Classification Landscape in Preparation for a Changed World." University of Memphis Law Review, Forthcoming, Available November 1, 2021 at https://ssrn.com/abstract=3942057

Prince is primarily concerned in this article with analyzing the efficacy of worker classification laws in light of the rise of app-based employment. As more and more people find precarious work on job-based apps, it has become apparent that previous employee classification laws—designed for more centralized service occupations—are not able to adequately spell out who is an employee and who is a contract worker, and, therefore, they are not up to the task of outlining important details involving workers' rights and companies' liabilities. Beyond its immediate use for understanding app-based employment, the article provides a broad overview of employment classification law that is helpful to have all in one place.

van Vulpen, Erik. "Job Analysis: A Practitioner's Guide." *Academy to Innovate HR.* September 9, 2020. https://www.aihr.com/blog/job-analysis/

van Vulpen provides an entry-level introduction to job analysis: what it is, how to do it, and why it's important. In addition to the useful overview, the centerpiece here is the five-step template organizations can adapt to their specific contexts in order to begin conducting job analyses.

https://www.osha.gov/

https://www.eeoc.gov/

The Occupational Safety and Health Administration (OSHA) and The United States Equal Employment Opportunity Commission (EEOC) websites are vital resources for understanding workplace safety and equitable work environments, respectively. In addition to defining each office's purview and functions, the websites offer a bevy of resources that help organizations better understand these sets of laws that protect workers' fundamental rights to safety and equity.

### Notes

1 David Weil, Administrator's Interpretation No. 2015-1 (The Application of the Fair Labor Standards Act's "Suffer or Permit" Standard in the Identification of Employees Who Are Misclassified as Independent Contractors) (pp. 1–15). Washington, DC: U.S. Department of Labor: 2015.

Brea M. Heidelberg

2  Thomas M. Murray, "Independent Contractor or Employee - Misplaced Reliance on Actual Control Has Disenfranchised Artistic Workers under the National Labor Relations Act," *Cardozo Arts & Entertainment Law Journal* 16, no. 1 (1998): 331–338.

3  Weil, "Suffer or Permit," 2015.

4  Ibid.

5  Julien M. Mundele, "Note - Not Everything That Glitters Is Gold, Misclassification of Employees: The Blurred Line between Independent Contractors and Employees under the Major Classification Tests," *Suffolk Journal of Trial & Appellate Advocacy* 20 (2015): 260.

6  Brea Heidelberg, "Strategic Staffing for Arts Organizations," in *The Routledge Companion to Arts Management*, ed. W. Byrnes and A. Brkić (New York: Routledge, 2020).

7  Antonio C. Cuyler, "An Exploratory Study of Demographic Diversity in the Arts Management Workforce," *Grantmakers in the Arts* 26, no. 3 (Fall 2015).

8  Morris Fred and Betty Farrell, "Diversifying the Arts Bringing in Race and Ethnic Perspectives," in *Entering Cultural Communities: Diversity and Change in the Nonprofit Arts*, ed. Diane Grams and Betty Farrell (Ithaca, NY: Rutgers University Press, 2008).

9  Helicon Collaborative, "Not Just Money: Equity Issues in Cultural Philanthropy," *Helicon Collaborative*, July 2017.

10 Brea M. Heidelberg, "Artful Avoidance: Initial Considerations for Measuring Diversity Resistance in Cultural Organizations," in *Diversity Resistance in Organizations*, ed. Kecia M. Thomas (New York: Routledge, 2020).

11 Ibid.

12 Brea M. Heidelberg, "The Professionalization of Arts Management in the United States: Are We There Yet?," *Cultural Management: Science & Education* 3, no. 1 (2019).

13 Stephen Taylor, *Resourcing and Talent Management*, 8th Ed. (New York: Kogan Page Limited, 2022), 63–88.

14 Anne-Marie Quigg, *Bullying in the Arts: Vocation, Exploitation and Abuse of Power* (New York: Routledge, 2016), 119–138.

15 For instance, see Sarah Bahr, "Leader of the Americans for the Arts Retires after Workplace Complaints," *New York Times*, May 27, 2021, https://www.nytimes.com/2021/05/27/arts/robert-lynch-afta-retires.html; Bridgette M. Redman, "Purple Rose Artistic Director Resigns Following Allegations," One Stage Blog, November 6, 2021, https://www.onstageblog.com/editorials/2021/11/6/purple-rose-artistic-director-resigns-following-allegations; and Peter Marks, "In a Stunning Turn, Ari Roth Resigns from Mosaic Theater, the D.C. Company He Created," *Washington Post*, November 18, 2020, https://www.washingtonpost.com/entertainment/theater_dance/ari-roth-resigns-mosaic-theater/2020/11/18/0bc10492-28f0-11eb-8fa2-06e7cbb145c0_story.html

16 Brea M. Heidelberg, "The Professionalization of Arts Management in the United States: Are We There Yet?," *Cultural Management: Science & Education* 3, no. 1 (2019).

17 United States Department of Labor, "OSHA at 30: Three Decades of Progress in Occupational Safety and Health," 2021, https://www.osha.gov/aboutosha/30-years#:~:text=OSHA%20was%20created%20because%20of,and%20deaths%20in%20the%20workplace

18 Hinkamp D., Morton J., Krasnow D.H., Wilmerding M.V., Dawson W.J., Stewart M.G., Sims H.S., Reed J.P., Duvall K., McCann M. "Occupational health and the performing arts: An introduction," *Journal of Occupational and Environmental Medicine*. 2017 Sep; 59(9): 843–858. doi: 10.1097/JOM.0000000000001052. PMID: 28692606.

19 Ibid.

20 Roger W. Morrell and Katharina V. Echt. "Presenting Information to Older Adults," *Journal of Museum Education* 26, no. 1 (2001): 10–12.

# Agents and Agencies in the Arts

Julia Atkins

# Chapter 13

Chapter 13 looks at agents and the agency relationship. It begins where most think of agents, as the seller's representative. The discussion considers who seller agents are, how they represent their clients, and where they are in order to contact them. The chapter then shifts to explore the lesser-understood notion of the buyer's agent from similar vantage points. Next, the reader can consider the legal agreements agents use and how they are developed, how agreements are negotiated with and by agents, the limitations of agency, and self-representation.

The agency relationship is unique to professionals in the arts and creative fields. Though few professionals in other fields (with some notable exceptions, such as major league sports) have an agent representing them in business dealings, the complex structure of artistic endeavors often makes it a vitally important ingredient. Agents represent their clients by having industry connections and a well-practiced approach to ensuring that details are clarified and that everyone understands how each will provide their artistic service. Often, artists, unlike agents, are not skilled at the details of legalese regarding contracts and their stipulations. It is why agents are so heavily used in the arts. The work is substantial, and to do it effectively, the agent must be skilled at negotiation and ensuring nothing is left to chance.

DOI: 10.4324/9781003207535-14

It is a topic rarely addressed as a full course, but nonetheless important for every arts administrator to understand because they will eventually be working with an agent (even if that agent is only a child's stage mother) to plan how the client and organization will interact.

For the topic of agents and agency, we again looked to Julia Atkins. Because she has the background of a professional musician and is a professional arts administrator in music, she has had an opportunity to see first-hand how agents and organizations interact and brings that knowledge to her discussion here.

## AGENTS AND AGENCIES IN THE ARTS

*A Contribution by Julia Atkins*

As every industry develops and grows, specialized skills become a requirement for participants. In the case of the arts, this means artists must continue to strengthen their talents in creating art and are also required to know about complex business issues that may go beyond their expertise. As in all industries, when the level of expertise required becomes vital, others with those expert skills step in to *represent* those whose areas of expertise may be more closely aligned with the nature of the industry. This form of representation is referred to as an *agency relationship*, otherwise known as the *principal–agent relationship* within the entertainment industry.[1] Many professional artists rely on an agent to find them jobs and represent them in their careers. This chapter explores what agency is in this context, the types of agents, and the many challenges of an agency relationship. It will then discuss agency in the arts, finding an agent as an artist, and how to become an agent.

---

**LEARNING OBJECTIVES**

By the conclusion of this chapter, you should be able to:

1. Describe the theory of agency and the types of agents
2. Explain the challenges of an agency relationship
3. Describe how agency is involved in the arts
4. Explain how to find an agent in the arts
5. Describe how to become an agent in the arts

---

## About Agency and Types of Agents

In an agency relationship between two parties, one person, the agent, works to represent the other, the principal.[2] In this relationship, the agent is subject to the principal's control and instruction. However, principals having delegated decision-making to their agent with the assumption that all decisions will be made with the principal's best interest in mind bring the principal to what the agent does on their behalf in the form of a written agency agreement.[3] This relationship is both consensual and fiduciary.[4]

In general, there are five different types of agents: (1) general agent, (2) special agent, (3) agency coupled with an interest, (4) subagent, and (5) servant.[5] A general agent is someone who has the authority to carry out a broad range of transactions on behalf of the principal, including being able to act in any way required by the principal's business.[6] A general agent is therefore typically considered a business agent. It requires the principal to lay out the limitations exactly as they deem fit; otherwise, the general agent has full authority to make decisions as they see fit.

Though a general agent has authority in multiple areas on the principal's behalf, a special agent can only make decisions on the principal's behalf in specifically designated instances or sets of transactions.[7] An example of this would be a real estate agent hired by the principal to find land to purchase. The real estate agent can help find the land to purchase and even help negotiate a price but cannot necessarily sign the contract at closing. Similarly, this would be an agent who can find the artist a venue or an organization to perform with but cannot necessarily sign the contract. The agent could help negotiate the contract terms, but the artist would hold the final decision.

Agency coupled with an interest is an agent who has a property interest in a business and whose reimbursement is dependent on the business.[8] This scenario is commonly found in the literary field, where an author's agent agrees to sell the published work in return for a certain percentage of all works sold. In the arts, this would be similar to an agent selling a composition in return for a certain percentage of what is sold, although the artistic property may be a creative endeavor instead of a tangible product. The agent has an interest in the artistic property and therefore makes money when the principal makes money. As a result, the agent works to benefit the principal as much as possible to ensure a high return for them both.

A subagent assists the main agent in executing contracted responsibilities.[9] This is common in insurance companies. For example, an insurance agency may have a main agent who runs the firm but will hire subagents who also carry out the duties of the insurance agency. A subagent is an agent of both the general agent and the principal. Additionally, both the principal and general agent are liable for the work of the subagent. Though this is common in places like insurance agencies, it is less common to find in the arts.

The final type of agent is a servant. This term is not widely used today but is still considered an agency. According to the Lumen learning module on the *Introduction to Agency and the Types of Agency*, "Until the early nineteenth century, a servant was an employee whose work was subject to an employer's control." According to The Restatement of Agency, a servant is "an agent employed by a master [employer] to perform service in his affairs whose physical conduct in the performance of the service is controlled or is subject to the right to control by the master."[10]

### Challenges with Agency

Artists and arts organizations have used formal and informal agencies for centuries, but it does not mean that it comes challenge free. Disagreements and disputes often occur between principals and agents, especially surrounding finances. Agency theory, therefore, "aims to explain and resolve disputes between principals and their agents."[11] The theory originated in 1973 with Stephen Ross and Barry Mitnick from organizational theory and economic agency theory.[12] As previously stated, the purpose of an agent is to make decisions in the principal's best interest. Agency theory, therefore, acknowledges that differences in opinions, interests, and priorities do occur.[13]

In the context of business and finance, agency theory typically categorizes financial disputes into two key areas: a difference in goals or a difference in risk aversion.[14] A difference in goals is

Julia Atkins

clear-cut. The agent and principal have different goals in mind regarding finances. A difference in risk aversion is related to how much the agent and principal are willing to risk in terms of finances.[15] How much loss or gain both parties are willing to accept can differ, causing a dispute. The principal often takes on greater risk in agency relationships than the agent does.

These disputes can usually be resolved by reducing agency loss.[16] Agency loss in the business world is the amount that the principal contends was lost due to the agent acting contrary to the principal's interests.[17] In the arts, agency loss is defined as the difference between the best possible outcome for the principal and the actual actions of the agent. Rather than a quantifiable amount, it is a loss of satisfactory representation (agency) in a manner due to dissimilar goals and motives. The outcome produced by the agent does not match the desire of the principal.[18] Resolving loss is accomplished by the agent offering incentives to corporate managers to maximize the profits of their principals (business) or modifying appearances, venues, or options to rectify the loss with a creative client.[19] Additionally, "resolving disputes may also require changing the system of rewards to align priorities, improving the flow of information, or both."

## Agency in the Arts

At its core, agency in the arts is the same as other industries: it involves a working relationship between the agent and the principal where the agent works on the principal's behalf. There are several different types of agents within the arts. One of the most common is a "talent agent," where the agent works to find opportunities for a particular artist. Other agencies include talent buyers, licensing agents, artist agents, promoters, festival organizers, and venue managers.

***Talent Agents*** for individual artists are responsible for finding and securing jobs for the artists they represent.[20] They are the people who help market their clients and negotiate contracts with organizations and corporations in which their clients will perform. Other common terms are "booking agents," "touring agents," or "music agents." Though an artist can find employment on their own, and most artists start that way, it is far easier to have the help of an agent. Additionally, having an agent and agency representing you helps solidify your reputation as a solo artist in the entertainment industry.

Talent agents are the chief steward of a client's career path, helping with career development, branding, public relations, and networking, especially for up-and-coming artists.[21] Talent agents typically work on commission and earn anywhere from 10% to 20% of gross earnings.[22] For a high-profile client, the role of the talent agent is comprised of fielding interest in their client while curating their client's public image. Additionally, it could involve planning national or world tours, scheduling radio, television, or other media appearances, and securing advertising deals or sponsorships.[23] It could also involve securing high-profile roles on Broadway or other major regional theatre productions. Regardless, the more well-known and respected the artist is, the more successful the talent agent is at continuing to curate the artist's public image, allowing continual work.

In addition to scheduling, agents also negotiate deals for their clients and oversee travel logistics and hospitality for artists on the road. A *good* agent is sincerely invested in their client's career no matter what.[24] They pitch their client for the roles they know they are right for, schedule auditions, and advocate on the artist's behalf in negotiating employment. These responsibilities result in the agent developing close relationships with talent buyers (also called "bookers"), promoters, festival organizers, and venue managers.[25]

**Talent Buyers** or "bookers" are responsible for identifying and booking the right talent for a particular venue or event.[26] Depending on the size of the event, they may also be responsible for managing a show's budget, assessing whether a show will sell, and determining an appropriate promotional campaign to help sell tickets.[27] The buyer position varies depending on where the talent buyer works. For instance, a talent buyer who works for a venue will be primarily responsible for hiring talent to perform at their venue, whereas a talent buyer who works for a production company will be responsible for hiring the talent and finding the venue for the performance.[28]

Generally, **Licensing Agents** service copyrighted material.[29] They perform specific duties depending on the agency they work for and can be called "licensing representatives," "licensing sales representatives," or "licensing reps."[30] Distinct types of licensing agencies control different copyrights and licenses. Organizations such as the American Society of Composers, Authors and Publishers (ASCAP), Broadcast Music, Inc., and The Society of European Stage Authors and Composers control performance licenses; record companies control their master rights; and music publishers can control mechanical and synchronization rights.[31] Licensing agents with performance license agencies work with arts organizations, amusement parks, nightclubs, radio stations, and social media. In contrast, licensing agents for record companies, music publishers, music libraries, or copyright administration companies tend to work with television, film, and advertising companies who are looking to use certain songs for their craft.[32] Licensing agents all work around the rights for using copyrighted entertainment, including recording and distributing copyrighted entertainment and using copyrighted entertainment for visual media such as film.[33]

## CASE STUDY: ASCAP AS AGENCY

In 2018, the ASCAP filed 11 separate copyright infringement actions against several bars and restaurants nationwide. These establishments were playing copyrighted music with no license.[34] ASCAP is a licensing agency that ensures songwriters, composers, and music publishers receive their share of profits from the music they produce. In fact, 88% of licensing fees received by ASCAP by venues and organizations go straight back to the songwriters, composers, and music publishers they represent,[35] as this is how many of these people earn their living. Therefore, ASCAP serves as a primary agency that works on the principal's behalf. In this instance, the principals are songwriters, composers, and music publishers. ASCAP's goal is to ensure businesses comply with the rules and regulations of copyrighted music so that their principals (the creatives) receive payment for their work. Any business can play music legally by obtaining a license, typically through agencies like ASCAP. The bars and restaurants that received the copyright infringement action were notified multiple times by ASCAP licensing agents, and ASCAP received no response. The establishments continued to play the music unlawfully and unlicensed, resulting in lawsuits. All venues must have a license to have live or recorded music playing in their venue to avoid copyright infringement and ensure that creatives receive the necessary funding they rightfully deserve.

**Artist Agent** is a term used most commonly in visual arts and represents an agent who works on behalf of an artist to represent, promote, and sell their work.[36] Artist agents represent the business of the visual artist and will most typically help pursue sales, licensing deals, publicity, and commissions for the artist. Artist agents can also be private art dealers, art consultants, and even art galleries.[37] Like other agents in the arts, artist agents have connections that help sell their client's artwork and build their reputation in the field. Artist agents help provide time for the artist to continue to create instead of focusing on the business side of the art.[38]

**Promoters** independently plan, market, and sometimes produce live concerts, productions, tours, festivals, and special events.[39] Though it sounds like a function of marketing, a promoter in this sense works as an agent to gather talent for events. A promoter can also be called a "concert promoter" or "tour promoter." For many promoters in for-profit models, the job comes down to budgeting: determining expenses and projecting potential revenue for maximum return.[40] Though this description sounds similar to an arts manager in a nonprofit organization, a promoter always seeks the highest return on investment. This mission is critical because promoters work in the for-profit industry, and making money is essential. Therefore, promoters make decisions based on the highest potential return. Success for a promoter lies entirely on their marketing ability, good negotiating skills, and their capacity to bring out an audience.[41]

**Festival Organizers** are responsible for the logistical planning, organization, and execution of art and entertainment festivals.[42] This can include visual arts, theatre, music, and more. Examples include Coachella Valley Music and Arts Festival, Lollapalooza, and even New Orleans' Mardi Gras. Festival organizers are sometimes called "festival directors" or "festival producers" as they work closely with talent buyers and concert producers to book artists for their festivals. For many festival organizers, the job is very detail-oriented in planning and executing the festival they manage.

## CASE STUDY: HOW LACK OF PLANNING BY FESTIVAL ORGANIZERS CAN CAUSE CROWD CRUSH

On November 5, 2021, the Astroworld Festival in Houston, TX. had approximately 50,000 people in attendance.[43] The event featured various artists with rapper Travis Scott performing near the end of the night. When Travis Scott took the stage at around 9 PM, a crowd began to surge forward toward the stage. The surge created a crowd crush that left 11 people dead and several more injured. Festival staff and medical personnel were overwhelmed, and many were left confused as to how the crowd crush even began.

Crowd management personnel claim that a crowd crush can easily occur at festivals in standing room only situations. They additionally claim that a crowd crush builds up over time and is not something that "just happens." Of course, investigators talked to event organizers and witnesses to determine the cause of the crowd surge. They looked into how the venue was laid out, whether the venue had enough exit points, and what prevented people from escaping. All these logistics come from crowd management training and festival planning mechanisms.

The logistics, of course, land on the festival organizers. However, Travis Scott's agent also comes into play. At the publication of this book, over 300 lawsuits had been filed, with many of them targeting Travis Scott.[44] Nonetheless, Scott has requested to be dismissed from several of them and claims that he was not the sole reason for the crowd crush. To the agent representing Scott, this now ushers in the question of whether Scott's publicity may have contributed to this horrific event, and what decisions must be made in the future representation of Scott.

How did Scott's reputation and publicity play a role in this event, if at all? Does the agent choose to publicly acknowledge Scott's role in the festival's events? How will the agent continue protecting and promoting Scott's image moving forward? Will Scott become uninsurable? How might this affect his success? Is it worth it for the agent to continue representing this artist after this event? These are the types of questions an agent would have to decide, understanding that some choices could result in life or death.

*Venue Managers* are what their name entails: they manage venues. Venues include concert halls, theaters, nightclubs, and even bars that provide live entertainment.[45] The primary role of a venue manager is to supervise the day-to-day operations of the venue which involves administrative, logistical, and creative duties. They also communicate with performers before and after the show. Their responsibilities involve working closely with talent agents, tour managers, talent buyers, and concert promotion companies.[46]

### When to Look for an Agent and How to Find One

For many up-and-coming artists, finding an agent can be tricky. It is a bit of a Catch-22 – the up-and-coming artist needs work to build a portfolio, but most reputable agents and agencies like to see a client have experience before taking them on. Many artists just starting do not necessarily need an agent representing them to find work. Instead, artists use online resources and networking to find performing opportunities. Many of today's greatest artists that now have agents representing them started out on their own. However, artists looking to land high-profile jobs will eventually need an agent or agency to represent them.

Backstage,[47] a platform for casting tools and opportunities for actors and performers, has a good list of questions to determine if an artist is ready for an agent or not. If an artist can answer "yes" to most of the questions below, then they are ready to start looking for an agent:

- Has the artist trained with qualified teachers? Is their potential agent likely to recognize their teachers' name(s)?
- Is the artist ready to commit to acting, performing, or dancing? Can they focus on going out for auditions, and is their life in order?
- Do they already have headshots, a social media presence, a website, or a showreel?
- Are they in the union? Being a union member helps the agent submit an artist to far more roles/performance opportunities than otherwise.
- Does the artist have any industry connections? Do they know anyone already established and willing to vouch for them?

Unions publicize different agencies for different artists. Therefore, the first thing an artist must do is determine what kind of agency they want. For example, some agencies only specialize in commercials, whereas others specialize in Broadway. Additionally, some agents in the music industry have a genre-specific focus (pop, country, classical, and more), and some specialize in a certain type of performance like soloing for a symphony orchestra versus singer/songwriter employment. This genre-specific practice is also common in dance, where some agents specialize in ballet, whereas others specialize in backup dancing for pop stars. Finally, talent agents know the right people in the field and tend to have personal relationships with them, providing a clearer path to opportunities for their clients. Therefore, doing research is a crucial first step in finding an agent.

To engage an agent, an artist must submit a portfolio of their work. The portfolio could include a resume, headshot, a cover letter, or even recordings of performances. Like any other job, a meeting with an agent should be treated as a job interview. Therefore, an artist must dress professionally and represent themselves at their best. The purpose of the interview is to give the agent a chance to know if the artist can make it as a performer and if they feel comfortable representing the artist.[48] It is also a time to determine if the artist can work with that particular agent. Both parties must determine if they can work together before moving forward.

As with any job, it sometimes requires multiple interviews with different agents to find the right match. The process requires patience, as finding the right agent takes time.[49] Additionally, rejection by an agency is common, especially for beginning artists. Many famed artists of today were rejected by agencies at first, including Kevin Costner, Angelina Jolie, and Brad Pitt.[50] However, rejections are an opportunity to learn from mistakes and move on to find someone else. There is a litany of reasons why an agent rejects an artist.[51] The process requires persistence and determination, trusting that the right relationship will come along.

## How to Become an Agent

Many agents have worked as artists and chose to move into a career in management.[52] Some agents have never been performers but enjoy supporting a performer's career or see agency as a path to earning a living. Regardless of the circumstances, becoming an agent is certainly a valid career choice. Many universities offer degrees, such as a music business degree, that help prepare people for a career with an agency.

Though a degree is helpful in pursuing this career, any aspiring agent must have a certain skill set to make it. The most vital skill is strong communication.[53] Not only does the agent communicate with their clients, but they also must negotiate and promote clients to others. Other professional skills include:

- Knowledge of venues and the field of choice (acting, singing, dancing, instrumental music, and more)
- Marketing and promotion
- Contracts and negotiation
- Making and maintaining professional connections
- Written and verbal communication
- Organization
- Multitasking

Becoming an agent is not easy. The career path of an agent is often deemed a "mailroom career," meaning that many agents work their way up the corporate ladder through hard work and determination.[54] Not every agent's career necessarily starts in a mailroom, but many began either as an intern at an agency or in a lower-level position, like an assistant. Like many other careers, one has to start at the bottom and learn through experience to make it to a more established role.

Competition for jobs is high for agents, especially in the entertainment industry. Therefore, developing a personal brand and networking is key to building a career as an agent.[55] This allows the aspiring agent to make connections and find their niche that sets them apart from the rest of the crowd. It will also help with climbing the corporate ladder. As with any other career, aspiring agents must be dedicated and willing to work hard.[56]

## Final Thoughts

This chapter provided an overview of agencies and agents, especially as they pertain to the arts and entertainment industry. By this point, you should appreciate what agency is, the different types of agents, and certain challenges that can arise with agency relationships. Additionally, knowing the different types of agents within the arts and gaining some insight into how to find and become an agent should provide an understanding of agency in the arts. Agencies are experts at promoting artists and dealing with the business of the craft. They aim to help their clients build their careers and perfect their craft. Hiring an agent is a great step in pursuing the dream of becoming a performer or visual artist.

## DISCUSSION QUESTIONS

1. Though this chapter discusses challenges surrounding finances regarding agency, can you think of any other challenges with agency not discussed in the chapter?
2. If you were an artist looking for an agent, what would be one indicator that would help you find an agent?
3. Look online, can you find agencies local to your area?
4. What questions would you ask an agent in the interview process?
5. If you could choose to be any agent in the arts, what would you choose to be and why?

## Notes

1 Swainston-Harrison, Atholl. "Managing Artists in the Classical Sector: Definitions and Challenges." *The Classical Music Industry*. Routledge, 2018. 55–66.

2 "Agency Theory," Investopedia, last modified September 4, 2021, https://www. investopedia.com/terms/a/agencytheory.asp.

3 "Agency Relationships: An Overview," accessed November 15, 2021, https://www. shsu.edu/klett/agency%20et%20al.htm.

4 "Agency Relationships: An Overview," accessed November 15, 2021, https://www. shsu.edu/klett/agency%20et%20al.htm.

5 "Introduction to Agency and the Types of Agency," Business Law, Lumen, accessed November 15, 2021, https://courses.lumenlearning.com/masterybusinesslaw/ chapter/introduction-to-agency-and-the-types-of-agents/.

6 "Introduction to Agency and the Types of Agency," Business Law, Lumen, accessed November 15, 2021, https://courses.lumenlearning.com/masterybusinesslaw/ chapter/introduction-to-agency-and-the-types-of-agents/.

7 "Introduction to Agency and the Types of Agency," Business Law, Lumen, accessed November 15, 2021, https://courses.lumenlearning.com/masterybusinesslaw/ chapter/introduction-to-agency-and-the-types-of-agents/.

8 "Introduction to Agency and the Types of Agency," Business Law, Lumen, accessed November 15, 2021, https://courses.lumenlearning.com/masterybusinesslaw/ chapter/introduction-to-agency-and-the-types-of-agents/.

9 "Introduction to Agency and the Types of Agency," Business Law, Lumen, accessed November 15, 2021, https://courses.lumenlearning.com/masterybusinesslaw/ chapter/introduction-to-agency-and-the-types-of-agents/.

10 "Introduction to Agency and the Types of Agency," Business Law, Lumen, accessed November 15, 2021, https://courses.lumenlearning.com/masterybusinesslaw/ chapter/introduction-to-agency-and-the-types-of-agents/.

11 "Agency Theory," Investopedia, last modified September 4, 2021, https://www. investopedia.com/terms/a/agencytheory.asp.

12 Barry M. Mitnick, "Origin of Theory of Agency," accessed on November 18, 2021, https://sites.pitt.edu/~mitnick/agencytheory/agencytheoryoriginrev11806r.htm.

13 "Agency Theory," Investopedia, last modified September 4, 2021, https://www. investopedia.com/terms/a/agencytheory.asp.

14 "Agency Theory," Investopedia, last modified September 4, 2021, https://www. investopedia.com/terms/a/agencytheory.asp.

15 "Risk," Investopedia, last modified October 6, 2020, https://www.investopedia.com/ terms/r/risk.asp.

16 "Agency Theory," Investopedia, last modified September 4, 2021, https://www. investopedia.com/terms/a/agencytheory.asp.

17 "Agency Theory," Investopedia.

18 Payne, G. Tyge, and Oleg V. Petrenko. "Agency theory in business and management research." *Oxford Research Encyclopedia of Business and Management*. 2019.

19 Agency Theory," Investopedia, last modified September 4, 2021, This link does not work.

20 "Career Communities: Music Agent," Berklee, accessed on November 15, 2021, https://www.berklee.edu/careers/roles/agent.

21 "What Is a Hollywood Talent Agent? How to Launch a Career as an Agent in the Entertainment Industry," Masterclass, last modified on September 3, 2021, https:// www.masterclass.com/articles/what-is-a-hollywood-talent-agent-how-to-launch-a-career-as-an-agent-in-the-entertainment-industry#what-is-a-talent-agent.

22 "What Is a Hollywood Talent Agent? How to Launch a Career as an Agent in the Entertainment Industry," Masterclass, last modified on September 3, 2021, https:// www.masterclass.com/articles/what-is-a-hollywood-talent-agent-how-to-launch-a-career-as-an-agent-in-the-entertainment-industry#what-is-a-talent-agent.

23 "Career Communities: Music Agent," Berklee, accessed on November 15, 2021, https://www.berklee.edu/careers/roles/agent.

24 https://www.backstage.com/magazine/article/get-acting-agent-5144/

25 "Career Communities: Music Agent," Berklee, accessed on November 15, 2021, https://www.berklee.edu/careers/roles/agent.

26 "Career Communities: Talent Buyer," Berklee, accessed on November 15, 2021, https://www.berklee.edu/careers/roles/talent-buyer.

27 "Career Communities: Talent Buyer," Berklee, accessed on November 15, 2021, https://www.berklee.edu/careers/roles/talent-buyer.

28 "Career Communities: Talent Buyer," Berklee, accessed on November 15, 2021, https://www.berklee.edu/careers/roles/talent-buyer.

29 "Career Communities: Licensing Representative," Berklee, accessed on November 15, 2021, https://www.berklee.edu/careers/roles/licensing-representative.

30 "Career Communities: Licensing Representative," Berklee, accessed on November 15, 2021, https://www.berklee.edu/careers/roles/licensing-representative.

31 "Career Communities: Licensing Representative," Berklee, accessed on November 15, 2021, https://www.berklee.edu/careers/roles/licensing-representative.

32 "Career Communities: Licensing Representative," Berklee, accessed on November 15, 2021, https://www.berklee.edu/careers/roles/licensing-representative.

33 "Career Communities: Licensing Representative," Berklee, accessed on November 15, 2021, https://www.berklee.edu/careers/roles/licensing-representative.

34 "Venues Refuse to Pay Songwriters While Profiting from Their Music," ASCAP, last modified on February 14, 2018, https://www.ascap.com/press/2018/02/02-14-infringement-filing.

35 "Venues Refuse to Pay Songwriters While Profiting from Their Music," ASCAP, last modified on February 14, 2018, https://www.ascap.com/press/2018/02/02-14-infringement-filing.

36 "A Guide to Artist Agents," Agora Gallery, last modified on April 26, 2016, https://www.agora-gallery.com/advice/blog/2016/04/26/guide-artist-agents/.

37 "A Guide to Artist Agents," Agora Gallery, last modified on April 26, 2016, https://www.agora-gallery.com/advice/blog/2016/04/26/guide-artist-agents/.

38 "A Guide to Artist Agents," Agora Gallery, last modified on April 26, 2016, https://www.agora-gallery.com/advice/blog/2016/04/26/guide-artist-agents/.

39 "Career Communities: Concert Promoter," Berklee, accessed on November 15, 2021, https://www.berklee.edu/careers/roles/concert-promoter.

40 "Career Communities: Concert Promoter," Berklee, accessed on November 15, 2021, https://www.berklee.edu/careers/roles/concert-promoter.

41 "Career Communities: Concert Promoter," Berklee, accessed on November 15, 2021, https://www.berklee.edu/careers/roles/concert-promoter.

42 "Career Communities: Festival Director," Berklee, accessed on November 15, 2021, https://www.berklee.edu/careers/roles/festival-director.

43 Ray Sanchez, "Beyond Your Control: The Recipe for a Deadly Crowd Crush," CNN, last modified on November 7, 2021, https://www.cnn.com/2021/11/06/us/what-is-a-crowd-surge/index.html.

44 Jon Blisten, "Astroworld Victims Died of 'Compression Asphyxia,' Medical Examiners Determine," Rolling Stone, accessed on January 21, 2021. https://www.rollingstone.com/music/music-news/astroworld-victims-cause-of-death-1272930/

45 "Career Communities: Venue Manager," Berklee, accessed on November 15, 2021, https://www.berklee.edu/careers/roles/venue-manager.

46 "Career Communities: Venue Manager," Berklee, accessed on November 15, 2021, https://www.berklee.edu/careers/roles/venue-manager.

47 "Backstage," accessed on November 15, 2021, www.backstage.com.

48 "How to Get a Talent Agent," Project Casting, last modified on September 29, 2021, https://www.projectcasting.com/tips-and-advice/how-to-get-a-talent-agent/.

49 "How to Find the Best Talent Agent for You," Casting Agencies Directory, accessed on November 15, 2021, https://www.castingagenciesdirectory.com/acting-modeling/how-to-find-the-best-talent-agent-for-you.

50 "How to Get a Talent Agent," Project Casting, last modified on September 29, 2021, https://www.projectcasting.com/tips-and-advice/how-to-get-a-talent-agent/.

51 "How to Get a Talent Agent," Project Casting, last modified on September 29, 2021, https://www.projectcasting.com/tips-and-advice/how-to-get-a-talent-agent/.

52 "Career Communities: Music Agent," Berklee, accessed on November 15, 2021, https://www.berklee.edu/careers/roles/agent.

53 "Career Communities: Music Agent," Berklee, accessed on November 15, 2021, https://www.berklee.edu/careers/roles/agent.

54 "Career Communities: Music Agent," Berklee, accessed on November 15, 2021, https://www.berklee.edu/careers/roles/agent.

55 "How to Become a Talent Agent," Indeed.com, last modified on March 15, 2021, https://www.indeed.com/career-advice/finding-a-job/how-to-become-talent-agent.

56 McHugh, Kenna, "How to Become a Successful Talent Agent," ToughNickel, last modified on April 30, 2021, https://toughnickel.com/industries/I_want_to_be_Ari_Gold_How_to_Become_a_Talent_Agent.

# OSHA, ADA, and Other Government Mandates

Elise Lael Kieffer

## Chapter 14

As a closing chapter, we wanted to address common challenges often far removed from the larger policy issues that artists and administrators must deal with regularly – but remain vital to maintaining compliance with Federal-level regulation. Most arts administrators have learned to navigate their local health and safety regulations, typically through a relationship with the local fire chief. However, there are also nuances to dealing with rules and regulations established by national law in the United States. Dealing with national laws at the regional level seemed to be the best approach. Though we focus on how these types of mandates operate in the United States, their counterparts in other countries operate in a similar fashion.

Because we wanted to present this information in a way that would be accessible for arts administrators in small local arts organizations, we again turned to Dr. Elise Kieffer. Because Dr. Kieffer can address issues like these from the lens of a regional arts administrator and academic who studies regional arts, she offers the discussion a more practical approach than we might find from other academic writers. We felt this approach was

DOI: 10.4324/9781003207535-15

essential for a chapter that would otherwise likely be dry to read. So instead, we have an informative, useful, and interesting approach to the topic.

In Chapter 14, the exploration is focused on governmental mandates, laws, rules, and regulations. In contrast, policies and procedures within the organization are also covered. The discussion then centers on the Occupational Safety and Health Administration (OSHA), how the administration works, how one must follow OSHA mandates, and how penalties can be assessed if OSHA rules are not followed. Finally, the chapter concludes with a lengthy discussion of the physical requirements of the Americans with Disabilities Act, who must comply, and how one can do so.

## OSHA, ADA, AND OTHER GOVERNMENT MANDATES

*A Contribution by Elise Lael Kieffer*

In the United States, arts organizations of all sizes and disciplines are subjected to the same governmental regulations as any other type of business or organization.[1,2] The various forms of arts organizations mean that OSHA and Americans with Disabilities Act (ADA) requirements affect each organization differently. From a high-tech production with live fire spectacles, to Spiderman flying and repelling across a Broadway stage, to band directors subjected to loud music, to small, rural arts organizations trying to convert old buildings into educational facilities. Every group must conform to common standards and face similar penalties for noncompliance.

---

**LEARNING OBJECTIVES**

By the end of the chapter, readers will have the ability to:

- Describe governmental mandates, laws, rules and regulations that affect arts organizations.
- Distinguish between governmental and organizational policies.
- Highlight the importance of OSHA mandates and penalties for failing to meet those standards.
- Instruct an arts organization about how to apply basic requirements of the Americans with Disabilities Act.

---

Elise Lael Kieffer

## OCCUPATIONAL SAFETY AND HEALTH ADMINISTRATION

The United States Congress passed the "Occupational Safety Act" in 1970, creating the OSHA.[3] At its inception, OSHA was established to ensure both healthy and safe working conditions for the US American workers. OSHA sets and enforces standards and also provides training, outreach, education, and assistance for companies and governments. According to its published materials regarding its governance:

> OSHA is housed within the United States Department of Labor and its primary administrator is the Assistant Secretary of Labor for Occupational Safety and Health. OSHA's administrator answers to the Secretary of Labor, who is a member of the cabinet of the President of the United States.[4]

---

**General OSHA Guidelines** (The source documents for the below guidelines are readily available from OSHA Compliance Assistance).[5]

In a general work setting, OSHA guidelines relate to the following:

1. **Hazard Communication Standard**. This aims to ensure that both employers and employees are informed and knowledgeable about potentially hazardous chemicals present in their workspace. This knowledge must necessarily include how to work safely with those chemicals and what to do in case of accidental exposure.[6]

2. **Emergency Action Plan Standard**. The emergency plan dictates employer and employee behavior in the event of a fire or other workplace emergency. Perhaps you recall fire drills when you were in grade school. This is the workplace equivalent. Employers communicate this action plan and employees should be sufficiently fluent in the plan to execute it when an emergency arise.[7]

3. **Fire Safety**. As with the above standard, it is recommended that all workplaces have a plan specifically for fire prevention.[8]

---

4. **Exit Routes**. OSHA requires specific planning and training with regard to exit routes and strategies in the event of an emergency.[9]
5. **Walking/Working Surfaces**. One of the leading causes of workplace injury and death is falling. This includes falls from heights and working surfaces. OSHA provides specific guidance on how to prevent accidents and injuries from falling.[10]
6. **Medical and First Aid**. Medical and first aid supplies must be provided by employers and available to employees. The available supplies should be appropriate for the unique hazards of the particular workplace.[11]

These guidelines are general workplace requirements. The distinction between "required" and "recommended" varies by state, type, and size of the organization. For those intricacies, specific OSHA guidelines can be accessed based on state and industry of operation.

## OSHA APPLIED TO THE ARTS

### Hearing Loss

There are myriad applications of OSHA guidelines to arts organizations. Some are the same that would affect any office, anywhere in the United States. These relate to ergonomics, clean air and water, and other environmental factors. However, as organizations producing unique products, there are times when the arts organization must be distinctly vigilant to maintain adherence to OSHA standards.

As one example, from the world of concert music, Holland (a music education researcher) examined the long-term risk of hearing loss for band directors in university settings.[12] Noise-induced hearing loss research previously focused largely on industrial and nonmusical applications. Holland applied the OSHA standard to concert bands. Using the OSHA standard as the baseline, Holland explored the routine exposure of conductors to determine if universities were meeting the

Elise Lael Kieffer

guidelines. The study concluded that, while there does exist a risk of hearing loss in a concert band setting (specifically related to position within the ensemble), the sound exposure experienced within a concert band setting is within the established limits allowed by OSHA policies.

The risk of hearing loss while working as a band director is mitigated by a variety of sound engineering technologies that insulate the room and absorb sound. An arts organization needs to be aware of these risk factors and vigilant about meeting OSHA standards. Holland's study encouraged that the responsible arts administrator should strive to go above minimum standards when assuring the health, safety, and well-being of their performers.

## Special Effects

Another example that is uncommon in standard office settings but that might occur in an arts setting is special effects such as fire, fog, smoke, mist, haze, or other environmental disruptors. Rossol (an experienced artist, chemist, and industrial hygienist) looked at how different special effects influence air quality and singer's voices.[13] In her estimation, the standards crafted by OSHA were outdated and unhelpful. She cited that even many OSHA guidelines are voluntary recommendations they provide for employers. Even OSHA documents suggest that organizations should set more conservative limits than their own recommendations. As in the case of the concert band study, merely meeting OSHA standards does not always fully assure adequate protection of arts workers. Rossol concluded that OSHA standards are not the same as "best-practice" standards.

Though the arts manager must comply with OSHA regulations, doing so might not always, in itself, protect the manager or the organization from backlash. Likewise, those standards might not provide the protection ethically required for the artists within the organization.[14]

## Mandates from Arts Organizations

As one example of an organizationally sponsored endorsement of OSHA best practices, in 2017 (and updated in 2019) the National Art Education Association updated their standards for safety in physical spaces of art education.[15] These standards apply to schools, cultural institutions and organizations, as well as community-based art education programs. The motivation behind their publication was not only to advise safety protocols for administration, educators, and students. They further promoted the importance of training young artists in best-practice safety standards. Their aim was to teach safety as an integral part of students' approach to all arts activities because "safety and creativity are not mutually exclusive."[16]

**OSHA Noncompliance.** The penalties for failing to comply with OSHA standards are shown in Figure 14.1. If a small or young arts organization faced one of these penalties it could be financially catastrophic. In addition to these federally imposed fines, employers open themselves and their organizations up to lawsuits based on their failure to meet OSHA standards. Penalties for OSHA violations begin at $13,653 for the first serious violation. Failure to remedy the hazard results in an additional $13,653 fine. Willful or repeated violations result in fines of $136,532 per violation. Clearly, it is costly to breach OSHA standards and guidelines and prudent to preemptively meet or exceed their required standards.

It is further worth noting that, while these financial penalties are steep, the infractions for which they are imposed might not be life-threatening or otherwise incredibly grievous.[17] An infraction might be minor to the employer and employee, but if it is a true violation of OSHA policy, the punishment is the same.

### CASE STUDY: *SPIDERMAN: TURN OFF THE DARK*

In 2010, during rehearsals and previews for an upcoming new Broadway musical, *Spiderman:*

*Turn off the Dark*, the production was cited with three serious violations.[18] The citations include risks of falling during some of Spiderman's web-slinging stunts and being struck by moving objects. The nature of the show, including a superhero that swings from the top of skyscrapers, was inherently dangerous and required specific planning, preparation, and mitigation efforts. Unfortunately, the production faced repeated difficulties with the required technology and especially acrobatic components of the

Elise Lael Kieffer

show. These challenges and subsequent citations caused *Spiderman: Turn off the Dark* to become the longest running show still in preview. (This is not an accolade sought by Broadway producers.)

OSHA has no theatre-industry-specific standards. Its observations and penalties of the *Spiderman* production primarily utilized OSHA's general work standards – those applied to other industries. The New York Department of Labor (NYDOL) inspected the *Spiderman* workplace before any injuries occurred, nevertheless, injuries did occur, resulting in OSHA's involvement.

NYDOL referred OSHA to the production after the lead actor fell from a suspended height and an actress received a concussion during a flying sequence. The OSHA investigation cited that the actors in those routines were at great risk due to "improperly adjusted or unsecured safety harnesses."[19] The production was also cited for a failure to provide adequate fall protection.[20]

Both the NYDOL and OSHA imposed financial penalties and increased safety requirements to prevent further accidents.[21] These actions did not prevent all future mishaps, however. Even with the potential of further inspection and with a history of numerous citations, additional incidents occurred, injuring both cast and crew employees.

All arts organizations should take heed from the lessons available through *Spiderman*. OSHA citations and ensuing delays resulted in the most expensive Broadway production in history.[22] Although it ultimately ran for two and a half years, it closed at a huge financial loss and usually lucrative national tours were canceled.

## AMERICANS WITH DISABILITIES ACT

President George H. W. Bush signed the ADA into law on July 26, 1990. The ADA is legislation prohibiting discrimination against people with legally defined disabilities, it seeks to guarantee that civil rights are not infringed upon based on a person's disabilities. In theory, the ADA also ensures that people with disabilities have the same opportunities as fully able-bodied people to "participate in the mainstream of American life – to enjoy employment opportunities, to purchase goods and services, and to participate in state and local government programs and services."[23] This legislation took its model from the 1964 Civil Rights Act, which prohibits "discrimination on the basis of race, color, religion, sex, or national origin." "The ADA is an 'equal opportunity law for people with disabilities'."[24]

Though the ADA does not individually name all impairments covered under the law, in order to receive ADA protection, an individual must live with a disability, described as a "physical or mental impairment that substantially limits one or more major life activities, a person who has a history or record of such an impairment, or a person who is perceived by others as having such an impairment."[25] ADA compliance is required for all organizations that "fit one or more of the following criteria: All local, county, state, and Federal government agencies. Any business that relies on the general public or for their benefit. Privately run companies that currently have 15 or more employees."[26]

Additionally, there is some variation in the level of required compliance based on whether the construction of a building is new or existing. All new construction must be ADA compliant, while some older buildings may be able to receive exceptions.

### ADA Compliance

When ADA was first passed into law, standards included physical infrastructures such as wheelchair ramps, preferred accessible parking, handicap accessible restrooms, elevators, and other features that would benefit individuals with physical mobility.[27] Other common applications of ADA included audible crossing signals and braille text on signs.

With the growth and ubiquity of the internet, an entirely new field of necessary compliance has emerged and it is one of which arts organizations should take note. ADA accessible web design ensures that users with visual and sensory impairments are able to navigate the rich information sources available online.[28] The socially responsible and ADA-compliant arts organization needs to be aware of these standards, in addition to the physical compliance required by ADA.

Elise Lael Kieffer

Edwards (an attorney in New York City specializing in issues of access and equity) drew attention to ADA loopholes that Broadway has frequently used to avoid fully complying with ADA standards.[29] She concluded that many theatres fall short of realizing the inclusive spirit of the ADA by having a lack of accessible: (1) entrances, (2) restrooms, and/or (3) seating arrangements. In Edwards' estimation, Broadway has taken advantage of the "undue burden" and "reasonable accommodation" exemptions and verbiage in the ADA to avoid true, ethical compliance. This text aims to encourage the arts business leader to strive for a higher standard in accessibility observance.

## General ADA Guidelines

The following areas of focus are especially important for the arts organization. The below list was initially proposed by *Access Advocates* to facilitate ADA compliance in public library settings. With that inspiration, they are here adapted for standard performing arts organizations. As with the previous OSHA guidelines, the full set of requirements for compliance can be found directly through ADA resources. Below is a list of recommendations:

1. Parking – It is necessary to dedicate a van accessible parking space for individuals with disabilities. General requirements dictate that the space be 8 feet wide and have an accompanying aisle also 8 feet wide. The space should be paved, level, and well-marked. Depending on the size of the parking lot, more than one space might be necessary or recommended.

2. Signage – It is important that sins are readable from the street. This requires that large signs should be large and clear enough for someone with a vision impairment to read. When considering signage, colors, contrast, height of posted sign, and clarity are all factors. Consider the importance of posting signs to indicate wheelchair accessible entrances and walkways, elevators, restrooms, and any other handicapped dedicated spaces.

3. Entrance – Those in wheelchairs, or using mobility assisting devices, should have a smooth, level surface on which to navigate their entrance into the building. ADA recommendations suggest that doors be at least 36 inches wide and easily openable by someone with a disability. It is also important to consider the height of thresholds and the width of paths between obstacles.

4. Elevators – If your building has more than one level, it will be important to include a handicapped-accessible elevator.

5. Floors – Floors should not be bumpy and should be clear of obstacles.

6. Box Office – If box offices or information desks are behind counters or windows, an individual in a wheelchair should be able to look into that window and see the attendant. This might mean lowering the whole counter or dedicating one section to those for whom it is preferred.

7. Restrooms – As with entrance doors, these should be accessible by a clear path and easily opened by someone with a disability. Dedicated stalls should be 5 feet by 5 feet to provide for movement in a wheelchair and sidebars should be included in the dedicated stall.

The above recommendations primarily serve patrons, but accommodations should also be made for employees with disabilities. Requirements for employees might include computer terminals, break rooms, backstage spaces, and more. Additionally, above are only recommendations and many other possible accommodations might be necessary or preferred for any given space. Responsible arts managers should take specific stock of their facilities and determine what compliance is required in their space by ADA.

### ADA Noncompliance Penalties

Under Federal law, the first violation of ADA guidelines can result in fines of up to $75,000.[30] Arts organizations are susceptible to fines of up to $150,000 for additional violations.

Elise Lael Kieffer

Beyond those hefty penalties, state and local governments can impose additional fines and might subsequently require businesses or organizations to meet even higher accessibility standards than those required by the ADA. It is also permissible for states and/or local governments to levy additional fines or require businesses to conform to a higher standard of accessibility than required by the ADA. Risking such financial penalties, it is prudent to invest in assuring ADA compliance. The vigilant arts manager avoids these fines by being fully adherent to ADA standards.

## ADA IN MUSEUMS

With the 1990 passage of the ADA, public spaces and buildings became legally required to be physically accessible. Now, with the 30th anniversary of the ADA's passage, art institutions should dig deeper, going "beyond the material" to investigate how our programmatic offerings can support the goals of access and inclusion.[31]

The arts administrator bears the responsibility for inclusion of those of all abilities into the creative space. The original requirements of the ADA focused largely on physical infrastructure that would aid those with physical disabilities. Many arts organizations skirted those requirements by finding loopholes within the law.[32] This created an inequitable environment for access to the arts for those with physical disabilities. Similarly, those with other disabilities were not universally accommodated.

Though Sandstrom (a museum educator specializing in issues of equity and access) acknowledged the groundbreaking nature of the ADA, and the sweeping improvements it facilitated for people with disabilities, the most remarkable feature of the act was that it placed the responsibility of accessibility on businesses and institutions, rather than on those with disabilities. "In other words: it is up to society to better provide for everyone, not up to individuals with disabilities to make room for themselves in the world."[33]

In the museum discipline, ADA compliance first began with modifications to physical infrastructures, such as adding ramps and renovating restrooms. However, museums have further embraced the ADA with modifications such as "low-sensory days" and improved interpretation offerings.

The International Council on Museums modified its definition of a museum in 2019. The new definition stated that museums should be "participatory and transparent, and work in active partnership with and for diverse communities to collect, preserve, research, interpret, exhibit and enhance understandings of the world, aiming to contribute to human dignity and social justice, global equality and planetary wellbeing."[34]

Gfeller's study concluded that people with disabilities were less likely to participate in performance groups than their able-bodied peers.[35] In 1994, Nwa concluded that only 60% of students with diagnosed disabilities were part of or participated in extracurricular activities, including but not limited to band, orchestra, and choir. One of Nwa's findings was that these students failed to participate due to a perceived lack of support from their educators.

By pursuing integration with the community, sustainability within the community, authenticity in representation, and connection at an individual level, accessibility becomes possible not only for those with disabilities, but for all patrons. This active inclusion then benefits those who are able-bodied and disabled alike.

## CASE STUDY: NEW YORK ART GALLERIES

ADA was passed into law in 1990. At that time, due to the newness of the technology, no website mandates were included in the bill. Due to the ensuing emergence of the internet as a dominant communication and accessibility tool, new standards were added to the law in 2010. The updated law required the rules to making internet providers ensure accessibility to online offerings.[36]

In 2019, more than 75 art galleries in New York City faced legal action due to the noncompliance of their websites under the ADA. The lawsuits alleged that for those who were blind or visually impaired, the galleries did not provide accessible websites or reasonable accommodations.[37] An ADA-compliant website requires specific coding that enables the text to be read by screen-reading software, facilitating an audio translation for the user.[38] This problem persists. As recently as January 2022, an additional 50 art galleries were cited in a lawsuit alleging ADA noncompliance.[39]

This requirement poses a potentially more challenging mandate for fine arts organizations. Arts organizations include more variable content on their websites than many other industries. This creates the need for a greater level of care for arts organizations.[40]

## Final Thoughts

In addition to the Federal standards prescribed in the OSHA and ADA legislation, it is imperative that the arts manager review local and state ordinances in their own locales. As illustrated in the *Spiderman* case, infractions resulted in fines from both OSHA and the state of New York. In some cases, state and local requirements are in line with OSHA and ADA requirements but without complete alignment, the arts manager must be certain to meet the standards prescribed by all governing bodies. Being in compliance with Federal OSHA standards will not protect an organization if they are in defiance of a local standard that meets a higher level of conformity.

The final conclusion readers should take from this chapter is the social responsibility under which we operate, beyond legal mandates and requirements. To safeguard the legal and fiscal health of the organization, the arts manager needs to be aware of and in line with Federal, state, and local standards. However, more than those obligations, arts leaders have the imperative to ensure their standards meet best practices for equity, inclusion, and safety because it is the socially conscious thing to do. As presented in the ADA case of museums, sometimes the requirements of the law are not sufficient to meet the spirit of the law. Strive for the latter.

## DISCUSSION QUESTIONS

1. Do you think OSHA and ADA compliance is uniquely important for arts organizations? Why or why not?

2. Discuss the benefits and challenges of compliance, beyond the potential penalties imposed.

3. Beyond legal compliance, discuss the social responsibility driving compliance with OSHA and ADA regulations.

4. What do you think of the "undue burden" exemption allowed to organizations under the ADA?

5. Who are the beneficiaries of compliance with Federal standards such as ADA and OSHA?

## FURTHER READING

ADA Design Standards (2010). 2010 ADA Standards for Accessible Design. https://www.ada.gov/regs2010/2010ADAStandards/2010ADAstandards. htm#pgfId-1009819

The 2010 Standards set minimum requirements for facilities to be readily accessible to and usable by individuals with disabilities. It is important that each arts administrator review the standards independently, to ensure that their unique organization is appropriately compliant.

Day, L. B. (2013). Turn off the danger: The lack of adequate safety incentives in the theatre industry. *New York University Law Review (1950), 88*(4), 1308–1347.

Day presents the legal and financial ramifications for noncompliance with OSHA and state mandates. Additionally, the article goes further into the subject by introducing the influence of Unions in the conversation about safety and access.

*Introduction to Modern Atmospheric Effects*, 5th Edition (2015). New York, NY: Plasa North America.

This is available for purchase from ESTA or USITT and is a must-read for anyone working with atmospheric special effects.

Kinsella, E. "More Than 75 New York Galleries Are Slammed with Lawsuits for Allegedly Violating the Americans with Disabilities Act." *Artnet News. Art World*, January 30, 2019. https://news.artnet.com/art-world/dozens-of-new-yorkgalleries-slammed-with-lawsuits-for-ada-compliance-on-websites-1450276.

Kirk, R. (2018). Theatre safety and what we can learn from the construction industry. Retrieved July 21, 2021 from https://www.propared.com/blog/theatresafety-and-what-we-can-learn-from-the-construction-industry/

This is an easy read and there are other resources on their site. Propared, is a company that works to improve operations for arts organizations.

OSHA Guidelines (n.d.) OSHA Compliance Assistance Quick Start. https://www. osha.gov/complianceassistance/quickstarts/general-industry

This webpage is a good starting point when determining your specific work setting's OSHA needs and standards. It enables the user to identify major OSHA general industry requirements and guidance materials that may apply to your workplace. The steps lead you to suggestions for how to comply.

## Notes

1  "About OSHA." Occupational Safety and Health Administration. Accessed October 28, 2021 https://www.osha.gov/aboutosha

2  "2010 ADA Standards for Accessible Design." Americans with Disabilities Act. Accessed July 20, 2021 https://www.ada.gov/regs2010/2010ADAStandards/2010ADAstandards.htm

3  "About OSHA." Occupational Safety and Health Administration. Accessed October 28, 2021 https://www.osha.gov/aboutosha

4  Ibid.

5  "Compliance Assistance." OSHA Requirements That Apply to Most General Industry Employers. Accessed July 20, 2021 https://www.osha.gov/complianceassistance/quickstarts/general-industry

6  Ibid.

7  Ibid.

8  Ibid.

9  Ibid.

10  Ibid.

11  Ibid.

12  Holland III, Nicholas V. "Sound Pressure Levels Measured in a University Concert Band: A Risk of Noise-Induced Hearing Loss?" *Update: Applications of Research in Music Education* 27, no. 1 (2008): 3–8.

13  Rossol, Monona. "Theatrical Fog, Smoke, and Haze Effects." *Journal of Singing* 77, no. 5 (2021): 645–652.

14  Gorrell, Jerry. "STOP in the Name of Safety." Stage Directions (West Sacramento, Calif.) 17, no. 5 (2004): 39–40.

15  "NAEA Position Statement on Physical Safety in the Art Classroom." National Art Education Association. National Art Education Association, May 16, 2019. https://www.arteducators.org/advocacy-policy/articles/527-naea-position-statement-on-physical -safety-in-the-art-classroom.

16  Ibid.

17  Sapper, Art. "Advantages of Knowing the Law: Top Misconceptions about OSHA Enforcement." *Professional Safety* 65, no. 12 (2020): 28–31.

18  "OSHA Slaps Spider-Man, Taymor Spins Out." *Stage Directions* (West Sacramento, Calif.) 24, no. 4 (2011): 4–.

19  *Spidey Falls and OSHA Calls. Safety Compliance Letter.* Aspen Publishers, Inc, 2011.

20  Kevin Flynn. "'Spider-Man' Is Cited Again For Violations: Metropolitan Desk." *The New York Times.* 2011, Late Edition (East Coast) edition.

21  *Spidey Falls and OSHA Calls. Safety Compliance Letter.* Aspen Publishers, Inc, 2011.

22  "False Starts! Cast Injuries! New Storylines! Retracing *Spider-Man*'s Journey to Broadway." Broadway Buzz. Accessed November 11, 2021 https://www.broadway.com/buzz/156763/false-starts-cast-injuries-new-storylines- retracing -spider-mans-journey-to-broadway/

23  "2010 ADA Standards for Accessible Design." Americans with Disabilities Act. Accessed July 20, 2021 https://www.ada.gov/regs2010/2010ADAStandards/2010ADAstandards.htm

24  Ibid.

25  "ADA: Americans with Disabilities Act of 1990." Pub. L. No. 101-336, § 12102, 104 Stat. 328. Accessed October 28, 2021 https://www.ada.gov/pubs/adastatute08.htm

26  Ibid.

27  "2010 ADA Standards for Accessible Design." Americans with
    Disabilities Act. Accessed July 20, 2021 https://www.ada.gov/
    regs2010/2010ADAStandards/2010ADAstandards.htm

28  Falstad, Hank. "12 Basic Requirements for ADA Compliance at the Library -." Access
    Advocates, April 2, 2014. http://accessadvocates.com/ada-compliance-library/.

29  Edwards, Naomi. "Unburdening Broadway: Spotlight on the Americans with
    Disabilities Act." *Journal of Law and Policy* 27, no. 1 (2018): 94–.

30  "2010 ADA Standards for Accessible Design." Americans with
    Disabilities Act. Accessed July 20, 2021 https://www.ada.gov/
    regs2010/2010ADAStandards/2010ADAstandards.htm

31  Sandstrom, Natalie. "Museums and the ADA at 30". *VoCA Journal*, 2020. Accessed
    July 20, 2021 https://journal.voca.network/museums-and-ada-at-30/.

32  Edwards, Naomi. "Unburdening Broadway: Spotlight on the Americans with
    Disabilities Act." *Journal of Law and Policy* 27, no. 1 (2018): 94–.

33  Ibid.

34  Sharon Heal. "The Policy Column." Museums Association. *Museums Journal*,
    August 13, 2020. https://www.museumsassociation.org/museums-journal/
    comment/02092019-policy-column

35  Salvador, Karen. "Inclusion of People with Special Needs in Choral Settings:
    A Review of Applicable Research and Professional Literature." *Update :
    Applications of Research inMusic Education* 31, no. 2 (2013): 37–44. https://doi.
    org/10.1177/8755123312473760.

36  "The Americans with Disabilities Act (ADA): Application to the Internet."
    EveryCRSReport.com. *Congressional Research Service,* March 28, 2012.https://
    www.everycrsreport.com/reports/R40462.html.

37  Kinsella, Eileen. "More than 75 New York Galleries Are Slammed with Lawsuits for
    Allegedly Violating the Americans with Disabilities Act." Artnet News. Art World,
    January 30, 2019.https://news.artnet.com/art-world/dozens-of-new-york-galleries-
    slammed-with-lawsuits-for-ada-compliance-on-websites-1450276.

38  Ibid.

39  Kinsella, Eileen. "A New Wave of Lawsuits Accuses 50 Art Galleries
    of Allegedly Violating the Americans With Disabilities Act." Artnet
    News. Art World, January 22, 2022. https://news.artnet.com/
    news-pro/a-wave-of-new-lawsuits-has-hit-art-galleries-2063662

40  Ibid.

Elise Lael Kieffer

# Index

Two Rivers Art Gallery 22
Tynes-Miller, Robin 34, 45–46, 55

UBS 233–234
United Scenic Artists (USA) 153–154
United States Census 203
United States Department of Labor 282
Universal Studios 156
University of Alabama 99
University of Alaska Southeast 202
unrelated business income tax 39
Urban Arts Partnership 222–223
U.S. Bill of Rights 141
U.S. Department of State 232

values 77
vaudeville 8
venue manager 267, 272
vicarious liability 248
Virginia Museum of Arts 99

vision 18, 62–63, 77
Volunteer Lawyers for the Arts 39
volunteers, board member 67–68

walking surfaces 282
Wallace Foundation 100, 231
war on poverty 208
Webber, Andrew Lloyd 139
western European fine art 204
West Side Story 140
Whiteman, Paul 154
Women of Color in the Arts 85
Wooster Group, The 34
working conditions 172
works for hire 130

young audiences 231

zero-hour contracts 247
ZOPA 166

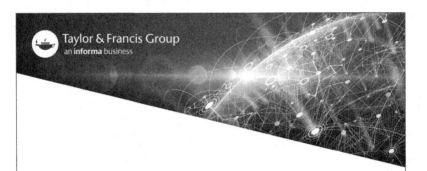

Printed in the United States
by Baker & Taylor Publisher Services